Jasper

DAR DRAPER

PRESS
ON
PUBLISHERS

3386 Merchant Lane
Davidson, NC 28036

Cover design by Marcello Aquino
triple7creative.com

Dedicated to Family...
Mine and Yours
and to our Dear Father
Who loves so well.
This book is for You.

And to Andrew...
Thank you for being
exactly who you are—
my wonderful husband.
I love you and our story...

CONTENTS

Invitation Into the Story

Within the heart of every child
No matter what your age,
Abides a hope to live a tale
Worth writing on a page.

A tale of courage and of love,
Of battles bravely won—
Oh that this story we should live
Be read of everyone!

Within the pages of this book
You hold within your hand,
Is one such treasured tale to tell
That started in the sand...

From gritty earth, a princess comes
Who dreams of love so deep.
She wanders through her way each day
Alive, but fast asleep.

Till one appointed moment breaks
This curse of life she lives;
An invitation calls her home
And hope this calling gives.

This call is made by one such *me*,
And Jasper is my name;
I keep the treasure chest of all
That's needed for her gain.

Oh will she come? Will she depart
The ruts her life has laid?
Can she now trust and yield her heart?
To journey, she was made.

Into this story, I invite
All young and old to come.
Receive reward from treasured truth
And see what you'll become...

1

Asleep in the Wastelands

The land smoldered under a blanket of busyness that never ceased. From the air it looked like threads of smoke, weaving a dark, textured fabric that hovered over this great landmass, allowing no light to penetrate its cover. Underneath, to the groundlings that occupied this place, all was normal. They were at home in the Wastelands.

At the center of the Wastelands was the largest city of the region: the City of Excess. It was a spectacle for sure. Its buildings not only scraped the sky, they seemed to pierce and penetrate the ceiling of it from the perspective below. The buildings themselves were a marvel as well, for they were made of "stuff." All kinds of stuff. Whatever materials the inhabitants could gather to possess, they would use to create buildings and structures to display the conquests of their labor. *Stuff* was the great game of the Wastelands, particularly in the City of Excess where the grand presentation of stuff was the highest art form that existed.

Around this central city was a wall—of *stuff.* Those who lived within these walls were quite proud to have made it inside. They were the envy of all who dwelled in the Wastelands and the surrounding regions, for *their* stuff was thought to be more beautiful and artistic. They displayed more possessions than any other city, and the additions and renovations were continually being made. The city was never complete. The work never

9

stopped. The citizens of Excess worked hard to accumulate so they could contribute to the skyline of their great city and to their own castles. Whenever they acquired something new, they would mount it to their houses, thinking it would make them look bigger and better. Neighbors would then fixate on each other's new belongings and be driven to buy their own, and post for all to see. This determination was never spoken of, but it drove the residents of Excess nonetheless. Theirs was an internal drive with an external driver as well. They were led by their mayor, Striver, who made sure the fame of their city would be known to all.

Mayor Striver's voice was well recognized as it blared through the city's intercom system each day. Periodically, his declarations boomed, "Do More! Get More! And LIVE more!" This was the formula by which they lived. Everyone wanted more. Theirs was a noble calling, they believed, as what could be wrong with *more*? The Mayor's message was relayed in a variety of ways over the airways—in rhyme, in commercials—sometimes subtly and sometimes not. "You need more STUFF!" Mayor Striver would often close his addresses with this line. Everyone would scramble at his proclamation, wanting to be good citizens and do their part to build Excess, maintaining its status as the most impressive city in the Wasteland's region. "More! More! More! More!" Every heart in Excess seemed synced to this beat, as Mayor Striver led his band of followers day in and day out in their pursuit of success through "MORE."

Right outside of the city limits, up against the walls of Excess were homes that encircled the town. They were not grand enough to be inside the city, but had hopes of one day being annexed and included as an official part of Excess. They too could hear the constant call of Mayor Striver and were motivated by him as well.

In one of these little hovels, there dwelled a girl named Sandy, who appeared to be no more than average in every way. She was of average height, average stature, and felt somewhat below average in appearance, especially in comparison to the city dwellers of Excess who seemed to have so much more to work with to enhance their looks. Sandy had sandy-colored hair that was straight and as limp as her spirit. Her eyes were a grayish-blue, encircled by dark shadows produced by the exhaustion of living so close to Excess. She dressed plainly, mostly in gray, desiring just to blend in and not draw attention to herself, at least not until she was able to make a name for herself and stand out in a way that would make her a proud citizen of Excess. That was her dream, or so she thought—to live *inside* the walls of Excess, and no longer be marked as a mere outsider of the great city. Sandy may have blended into the outer landscape of the city, but inwardly her heart was being tuned to the sound of Mayor Striver's daily charge. She desired a life of "more, more, more," for what she currently had was not nearly good enough.

Within this gray girl's average outer appearance however, there was wonder, fast asleep. Sandy was a dreamer, and she had a sleeping dream within her. It all started when she was a little girl. She found an old book in the attic and made her mother read it to her. It was a treasury of stories about princesses rescued by handsome princes, hideous villains captured, and endings of happy ever-afters. Sandy was enthralled by these tales, and pondered them more often than she would ever disclose. Even though she was older now, she would still grab that book, most often before bedtime, and give her guarded heart the relief of relaxing in this fantasy of fiction. Her family and friends would laugh if they knew of her frequent escapes to imaginary worlds, and she found no need to tell them. She loved the story—the same one told in a variety of ways—the story of the prince, rescuing the girl who was really a princess, or became one at least. This is what she daydreamed her life would be. She dreamed of being a princess, pursued and dearly loved, and beautiful to her prince who would be devoted to her for always. And this one night, outside the City of Excess in her humble home, Sandy fell asleep with the book of fairy tales on her chest and began to dream a dream that would awake her wonder forever...

*****

There was light. The air seemed made of light. A golden glow radiated in every direction, and its source was unknown. It carried within it sounds and fragrances never experienced anywhere else. Pure love and loveliness were the essence of this world Sandy had entered. "Where am I?" she wondered as she wandered through the waves of peace that permeated her entire being. Beauty surrounded her. Though the air was golden, colors burst forth in a vibrancy she had never seen before—new colors! How could this be? Indescribable landscapes were under her feet and painted around her, though this was no canvas. She examined textures with her feet and hands. The ground was covered with a plush softness that cushioned her every step. Its hue of green captivated her stare and triggered a rest within her. As she knelt to further inspect this ground covering with her hands, music met her touch. The land resounded with a sweet melody to match each movement she made. Sandy's soul was tickled in perplexed wonderment. Where was she? Her usual skepticism could not refrain her. It had no place here.

She proceeded in awe and delight, examining every sight. Gentle, majestic creatures roamed through the grandest of vibrant gardens, flourishing with unclassified plant life. The swirl of their fresh fragrances relaxed Sandy as she inhaled their soothing scents. Beyond the gardens she saw shimmering structures that reflected the encompassing light they bathed in, creating a warm glow that grabbed Sandy's focus and further welcomed her in. Every surrounding sight was a marvel, perfectly placed in this wondrous paradise. Where was she? No description in any fairy tale she ever read could compete with this.

Sandy saw people—beautiful, radiant, pure-hearted people. Their skin was ageless, and they seemed to brim with loving kindness and joy. Who were they, and why was she among them? They began to nod and bow slightly when they saw her, and knowing smiles covered each of their faces. They parted, making a path for her that she knew she was to take. Where was she headed? The unearthly music intensified into a crowning crescendo, causing a surge of anticipation to rise within her. She walked on, down the path, surrounded by an overwhelming sense of acceptance and even admiration that she had never known in her life. She turned to study the knowing faces along her path. What mystery she met in them, yet something was familiar.

When she turned her attention to the path ahead, a form broke through the light before her. He was there. Her eyes locked instantly into the gaze of the most glorious man she had ever seen. His face was almost transparent and glowed. She could not move her eyes from him. His eyes blazed with a pure passion that melted her heart. She felt almost liquid in his presence. He reached out to grip her, helping her to stand, for she was faint with love—love. There was a connection of love with this man she had never known in her life. Her entire being was drawn to know more of him. She stared unwaveringly at his lovely countenance, drinking in the love and life his eyes emitted. After an unknown lapse of time, the edge of his mouth turned up with a loving, knowing smile as he lowly whispered, "Come, Princess. Let's go see your father, the King…"

✳✳✳✳✳

The loud blare of the city intercom startled Sandy from her sleep. Her fairy tale fell from her chest as she jolted up straight in bed, but the dream lingered in her heart. "GO! GO! GO! DO!

13

DO! DO! GET! GET! GET! And LIVE!!" The familiar voice of Mayor Striver rang in her room, but she was still coming to reality after this beautiful dream. For a moment, she felt like a princess. For a moment, it seemed, she knew true love. It was so real. She had felt it. Her heart was still beating fast in its residue of wonder. She didn't want to move. She wanted to go back—back into this dream that may have been the sweetest peace she had ever known.

The familiar creaking of steps in the hallway further aroused Sandy from her slumbering state. Sandy's mom was headed her way with the daily load of dirty laundry she had gathered to wash. The two of them lived alone. Her mother was a burdened lady, overwhelmed by the tasks of living so near the City of Excess. It was hard to be a single mother and keep up with so many things, always trying to improve life for her and her daughter. Her brow was always furrowed with worry, and peace was a foreigner to her soul.

As she approached Sandy's door, she peered in then paused to adjust her basket and summon her daughter, "Time to get up, Sandy! Why are you just sitting there? There's _work_ to do." There's work to do. There was always work to do. And usually Sandy was doing it by now—but that dream had her lingering in peace.

"There's mail for you." Sandy's mom grabbed a small bundle she had shoved in the side of the dirty laundry and tossed it on Sandy's desk by the door. She then firmly took hold of her load, breathed in deeply and proceeded down the hallway, as if she were convincing herself to press through into this day.

Sandy wanted to replay the dream over and over in her mind and not lose one bit of its effect, but it was already beginning to fade. She grabbed the journal by her bed, to record just a glimmer so that she could hold on to something of it. She wrote, "I dreamed I could be loved—deeply—by a prince whose eyes burned with pure passion...and I was a princess, the daughter of a king." That's all she wrote. That was enough. Those words would take her back to the scene and her great sense of peace and joy. Sandy closed her pen in her journal. Perhaps she would process this more later. But now it was back to the real world.

As her feet hit the floor, the gravity of her world quickly brought Sandy to reality. She was heavy in this place. Many thought living life on the outskirts of Excess would be a dream life—never a need, with stuff all around. People who came to visit were enamored with the shopping and the buildings of *stuff*. They found the design of it all intriguing. But for those who lived there or close by, the pressure was suffocating. There was the constant need to achieve and acquire, a never-ending drive to make a *name* for yourself—and she had a name like "Sandy," a plain, earthy name.

She did not like her name. Sandy once asked her mom why she chose it. The story was sweet enough. Her mother had visited the Shores, and met and fell in love with her father. And when she had his child, she named her "Sandy," to remind her always of those beaches where she met the greatest love of her life. Sandy's dad was not around anymore. His was a fading love, and he left her and her mother when Sandy was very young. Sandy's mom raised her alone...until her stepdad came along, but he was not the great love of her mom's life, and that love didn't last long either. Sandy wondered if her name brought sadness or disappointment to her mom. Did it even make her angry? Her mother certainly was not a happy woman. She was dutiful at best, working hard to make it through the disappointments of life, trying to gain as much as she could for herself and her little family.

Now Sandy was behind. She grabbed the bundle of mail and headed to the bathroom to splash some water on her face and hopefully revive herself out of this useless contemplative state. She discarded the catalogs and magazines and ads her mother had handed off to her. "Thanks, Mom!" she sarcastically said as she tossed them in the trashcan next to the sink. One piece of mail remained. At first she thought it might be an ad as well, for it was a postcard. Just when she was about to toss it with the rest of the paper intruders, her attention was grabbed. The postcard was a picture of the shore, a beautiful beach with a curved foam line of surf and the ocean stretching beyond it. A postcard. With interest she flipped it over to see her name and address, handwritten. It was for her personally, and the only words inscribed were,

"You are invited, Princess...Wake up and come..."

What? Sandy dropped the card in the sink, then quickly picked it up, not wanting it to get wet, but hesitant to hold it. *What in the world!* She read it again, flipped it over to stare at the picture, then again flipped back to the words:

"You are invited, Princess...Wake up and come..."

Was she going crazy? *The stamp!* Her eyes scanned the short distance from the words to the stamp. There was one, but she had never seen one like it before. It was a gilded insignia in the shape of a shield. It looked to be a family crest, bearing a crown on a roaring lion. It was regal and intricate, yet masculine and official. She felt honored for a moment, but then quickly brushed that sense away. *Wake up and come?* Now she felt offense rise within her. *Who is telling me to wake up? And come where? Who sent this?*

Sandy searched the face of the card for any other information. On the side, in fine print, the card was marked,

"Shores of the Lowlands, at Mid-Morning Low Tide."

And that was all—a picture, a place, her name, and a message:

"...Princess...Wake up and come..."

"Princess." Was someone mocking her dream? How could anyone know? That's all she ever desired to be. But she lived in the Wastelands, virtually walled into the City of Excess. Exit from this place was never easy. It was hard to even escape for vacation. The maintenance of all her "things" and her family's belongings required much energy and time. She did not feel like a princess at all. She functioned more as a slave. It was a cruel joke to be sent this card—an invitation to which she did not even know how to respond.

Sandy marched back to her room, shoved the unwanted solicitation into her journal, and headed down to the kitchen to fuel herself for the day. There was much to do. "Go! Go! Go! Do! Do! Do! Get! Get! Get! And LIVE!" This was the cadence of her life, far from sandy beaches and dreams of royal identity—and love. She must carry on in the real world, her world, until it was time to dream again.

[handwritten annotations] Wt is our wasteland - busyness always trying to be get more, be more, be the best. Achieve more, be better. And if we dont we are envy of those who have. Society itself pushes us even so.

Sandy was a dreamer, the dreams start @ a young age. then the dreams die because of all she had to deal w/ around her.

Wt dream you had that die

2

At Work in the City of Excess

With one final slurp from her mug of usual morning sustenance, Sandy resolved to head into the day with no more thoughts of that postcard nor of the dream that threatened her focus. She grabbed her purse and called out a quick goodbye to her mother, then hurried down her front three steps to land on the sidewalk where normality seemed restored. People were quickly moving up and down the streets, on their way to work. Most worked in the city, and this majority flowed towards the train station. Sandy slipped into the pack of committed citizens, who proceeded towards their means of "more" just as commissioned by Mayor Striver. His voice on the intercom seemed especially loud today—or oddly jolly, or desperate. Sandy couldn't tell. But something was different. She didn't usually analyze like this and was puzzled at herself for making note of his tone at all. What a strange morning it had been. Sandy dismissed her thoughts with a practical one. *Now to step in line and get to work!* It was time to head into the heart of Excess, the city she loved and longed to be knit into.

Her train was right on time. Relief washed over Sandy as she stepped inside and the doors closed, hemming her into her means of escape from "the outside." She sighed as she settled into a window seat. Now she could relax and prepare mentally for her day of serving some of the biggest names in Excess. Sandy was a waitress—for now—at "BIG'S," one of the most popular lunch spots in Excess. She saw it only as a means to an end. Many famous and influential people ate at BIG'S. It was owned by Mayor Striver's son-in-law, Mr. Big. This restaurant was known for its extra-large portions and over-sized furniture and décor. Everything about the place was *big* and Sandy hoped to make a connection with one of the *big names* that frequented the place. She desperately wanted to live downtown and make a big name for *herself.* She didn't feel particularly talented at anything, but had lots of drive to be successful. She knew she could work hard, and thought working for the mayor might be an excellent fit for a diligent girl like herself. Yes, a job in city government appealed to her, and what better way to be exposed to the "right" people than to serve them at their favorite restaurant? This was her plan, and she used this ride in as time to focus on how she might present herself to the advantageous customers she may serve.

A call from without interrupted her planning. "Wake up, Princess..."

What? Sandy straightened her back in instant response to this voice that alerted her senses. She pivoted her head, looking for the source of these words she had clearly heard. *Is this another joke?* she wondered.

"Princess..." The blood drained from her face as she heard that word echo again. She searched the car. Nothing. Every face on the train appeared innocent of this assault on her. They all looked strangely familiar—like her mother and her. They looked asleep. Their eyes were open, and yet they seemed fast asleep...

Sandy shook her head. *What kind of thinking is this?* She had never thought like this before. "What is wrong with me?" she muttered under her breath, turning her gaze to the street outside. Something peculiar caught her eyes: a plumed purple hat that looked to be of another era. This velveteen beret sat on the head of an even more peculiar looking man who stared straight back at her, locking eyes. His face was weathered but warm, and his gaze was friendly and inviting. Eye contact like this was never made in this city. He smiled slightly and mouthed something to her. It looked like he spoke the word "princess" then kindly nodded and turned into the crowd. Sandy's heart stopped then started again with fierce pounding. "What is happening?" she said aloud. No one even turned to acknowledge her trembling cry.

The train halted. It was her stop. Sandy lingered for just a moment. *Of course. It's my imagination. Too many fairy tales,* Sandy determined. Relieved by this reasoning, she sprang to her feet and stepped off the train into the hordes of people in the big city. She felt a surge of energy now. To reinforce it, she darted to a drink stand and downed her additional daily cup of "liquid adrenaline," kick-starting the next phase of her morning: work.

As Sandy entered the back door of BIG'S, all the familiar scents of the kitchen hit her nostrils as a wake-up call to work. Yesterday's grease, bleach and detergent mixed with the smells of simmering soups and baking bread for today, all reminded her of the constant preparation necessary to feed the people of this city. There was a continual appetite to be fed, so the kitchen cycled from prep through clean up all the time. Sandy clocked into her turn in the cycle and checked her appearance in the mirror. "Still the same. No crown here," she mumbled. Yet she lifted her chin and straightened her shoulders to assume the posture of one worthy of attention in this town.

"HELLOOOO!"

Sandy jumped and gasped as a sudden face appeared in the mirror directly next to hers. It was Sandy's co-worker and closest friend, Pride. "Stop doing that, Pride! You know I hate being startled by you!"

Pride laughed, "Oh, I am STARTLING, aren't I?" He then whisked in front of her and plopped onto the counter. "I like the

FIRST part of that word for sure—STAR!" That is what Pride truly longed to be—a star. He would tell practically everyone he met or waited on, "I'm really an actor. I'm just working here at BIG'S until I make my 'big break!'"

He was an actor for sure, always acting like someone or something he wasn't—"trying on" different characters, as he would say. Pride was amusing to Sandy, but also exhausting to have as such a close friend. He was arrogant and full of himself, but he usually made Sandy feel good about herself too. He helped her to justify herself when others seemed to doubt her. Other times he would trip her up as he darted about. He had even caused her to fall on her face while working in the kitchen, acting like he knew how to do everything best. Pride was known to mouth off, having little to no restraint in the things he talked about. He was boastful and opinionated, and Sandy's reputation was tarnished at times due to their close association. Sometimes she wondered if her job was in jeopardy, as she often got caught up in Pride's antics and opinions. But Pride would assure her that Mr. Big could not run this restaurant without them, and that they had to stick together. Despite all the trouble Pride caused her, he was her closest friend, and she could not think what it would mean to separate herself from him.

Through the back door came another co-worker—Restless. He wasn't a server, like Sandy and Pride, but worked about every job in the back. He was unsettled and moody. He was not a close friend, but had been part of the BIG'S family since before Sandy was hired, so she gave him respect and was friendly to him. As Restless clocked in and began his routine of prepping the kitchen for the day, the three of them chatted about their lives.

"I had the craziest dream last night," Pride announced.

"Yeah, what was that?" Restless asked out of reluctant courtesy as he unhooked two large hanging pots and clanked them on the stovetop below.

"I dreamed I was climbing this very tall mountain, and it was cold, and I only had shorts on and I was FREEZING!" Pride loved telling about his dreams and was very demonstrative as he did so. "And I just knew I could climb this mountain, but I kept slipping and falling and then I slid all the way to the bottom and disappeared! Like 'POOF!' Gone! Isn't that wild? What do you think that means?"

"It means you shouldn't wear shorts when mountain climbing in winter," retorted Restless sarcastically. Pride threw back his head and exhaled a quick huff, displeased with Restless's dismissive response.

"I had a weird dream too." The words came out of Sandy's mouth before she had a chance to stop them.

"You *did?*" Pride's turned his attention on her. "Well, I thought you said you *never* dream, Sandy! What was it?" With Pride prodding, she could never drop it, so Sandy intended to give the abbreviated version of her dream.

"Well, I was in this beautiful place and everything was pretty much perfect, and at the end this guy comes up and calls me 'Princess.' That's all."

"Princess?!? Wow! That dream is *much* better than mine! Sounds heavenly! What did the guy look like? Was he a PRINCE?" Thankfully, before Sandy could answer Pride, Mr. Big burst through the back door. Everything about Mr. Big was big, just like his restaurant. He was taller and bigger than everyone who worked there. He had an extra large head and big features to go with it—big eyes, a big nose, big ears, and a very large mouth. His voice was big too, and everyone snapped into position when they heard his booming orders.

On entering, the orders commenced. "Today is a BIG day at BIG'S, everyone! My father-in-law, the Mayor, is coming in today with my wife and some very special guests. Now, I want everything to be PERFECT! Perfect food, perfect presentation, and

PERFECT SERVICE! Is that understood?" Mr. Big stared at Restless, then Pride, and then at Sandy. He paused on Sandy and stated, "And I want *you* to wait on them, Sandy."

"What?!?" Pride could not contain his outrage, then composed himself, masking his anguish. Pride smiled falsely and said, "But Mr. Big, I've worked here MUCH longer than Sandy, and don't you want the Mayor to have the most *EXPERIENCED* server of your fine establishment?"

Mr. Big stared back for a moment, looked Pride up and down, narrowed his eyes and told him straightly, "I said Sandy." Then he turned and proceeded directly into his office.

The mood of the kitchen was immediately altered. Pride spun on his heels with a "humph" and busied himself with shining silverware.

"I'm sorry." Sandy reached for Pride's hand as she tried to make amends for an offense she had not committed.

Pride jerked his hand away and turned his back to Sandy. She figured he was now going to give her the silent treatment he was known to administer when he got in his moods. Instead, he shot her a murderous look and seethed, "Looks like you're getting things your way, PRINCESS!"

Sandy stared at Pride's back in stunned silence. Not only had she unintentionally shared her dream, it was now being used to mock her by the person she called her best friend. Her heart dropped. Pride could be mean, but she was seeing a new facet of him in these present circumstances. Quietly she turned and passed Pride, ignoring his mutterings. True friendship was surely hard to find in a city of people looking out for themselves first. What did she expect?

Restless mustered up some compassion and called her over to his side of the kitchen. "Hey, will you help me get the bread out?"

"Sure." Sandy was glad for the escape from the server's prep station.

"So, anything else? In your dream?" Sandy was surprised at the interest Restless was taking in her and her dream, but she was glad for the distraction of talking to someone other than Pride.

"Well, yeah. There was more to my dream. But then this other thing happened." Sandy didn't mean to share this either, but she found herself spilling her other private mystery. "I got this postcard in the mail inviting me to the Shores of the Lowlands. There was no name, but it was addressed to me and just told me to come, at mid-morning, low tide."

Restless was intrigued. "So, are you going to go?" he asked, as if she should.

"I—I don't know. No. I wasn't planning on it." Sandy shrugged.

"Why not?" Restless prodded. Have you ever been to the Shores?" Sandy had never known him to be so interested in something.

"Well, when I was little..." she began.

"You should go," said Restless. "Everyone needs to get away once in a while. Excess isn't all it's cracked up to be, you know." Sandy sensed an unsatisfied search in Restless' advice. Before she could answer him, Mr. Big started out of his office barking loud orders. Morning prep was in full swing and all hands were on deck to make sure this ship sailed in the smoothest of waters. Mr. Big had demanded perfection, and his crew was being driven to make it happen. Besides, the connections that could be made were motivation enough to have each staffer striving to make their best impression possible. It was all for one, and all looking out for number one. This was the accepted meaning and purpose of life in Excess.

Sandy had felt the sting of Pride's way with her, but instead of being defeated by it, she allowed it to fuel her determination. She secretly felt victorious in being chosen to wait on the honored guests, and would make the most of this opportunity. Sandy took a look in the mirror by the swinging kitchen doors leading to the dining room. She lifted her chin and inspected her face one last time before heading into this opportune day. "Let's make it happen, girl," Sandy told the face in the glass. Then both faces turned to the double doors. Sandy pushed through into her great hope for change.

Soon the lunch crowd streamed in. The first table was seated in Pride's section. They were regular customers, Sick and Tired, a married couple that looked older than they actually were, and who displayed varying looks of forlorn exhaustion in each of their faces. Pride was less than thrilled to be waiting on them.

"Can you seat us away from the drafty door?" Sick, the wife, wheezed. "Last time we sat over there I caught the cold of death itself! Barely have recovered!"

Pride pounced on this request, "Why, certainly! We will be happy to accommodate you!" Pride moved them right over to Sandy's section and shot her a sneer.

Sandy greeted Sick and Tired with a friendly smile, fake as it may have been, and took their drink orders, all the time standing back, hoping their conditions were not contagious. Sick and Tired always took more time than reasonable in making a decision of any kind, and while they were asking Sandy about each and every drink BIG'S offered in search of one they had not grown bored of, the restaurant began to fill up.

Pride flattered and flirted with the hostess to assure he got all the pleasant and well-to-do customers for himself, while Sandy got the more undesirable regulars seated in her care. There was the table where Unsatisfied, Dissatisfied and Never-Good-Enough came in for their monthly lunch date. They were very wealthy, prominent, older women in Excess, but complained like no customers Sandy had ever tended. Compare and Critic, two older gentlemen, were also seated in her section—twice. They didn't like their first table and demanded to be moved to a more desirable location. Pride took great pleasure in catching their complaint and offering them the table that had been reserved for Mayor Striver's party. This completely unnerved Sandy, for she knew Mr. Big would not be happy about the switch. The only table left in her section was by the kitchen door, where Mr. Big would never seat his honored guests. She was flushed with a mixture of panic and disgust that Pride would hurt her so. But now she had to play the actress and master her role as the best waitress in Excess. This was her chance. She caught sight of Mayor Striver with his company of guests through the glass windows that spanned the front of the restaurant. The Mayor was making his entrance into BIG'S. It was show time.

Mayor Striver's appearance did not quite match his booming bass voice. He was a short man, rather slight in stature, except for his belly that popped out below his chest in the exact shape of child's playground ball. It was where he stored his "excess" he would joke as he patted his belly. "What kind of Mayor of EXCESS would I be if I didn't STORE STORE STORE...MORE MORE MORE!!" The citizens would laugh with him and then "eat up" as encouraged by the Mayor.

Today the Mayor's lunch dates were his daughters. Ms. Vain Conceit, or "Vanity" as she was called, was married to Mr. Big, and Ms. Selfish Ambition was single, but hoping not to be for long. His daughters were decked out in the latest fashion, and over-adorned in costume jewelry and accessories. Vanity was tall and slender, and might be perceived as pretty from afar, except that her lifted look of arrogance caused most to feel intimidated and look away. Despite all her efforts to look good, Vanity was hard to look at, let alone befriend. Her air of superiority isolated her, and her only companion seemed to be her sister. Selfish Ambition was shorter and thicker in stature, and more powerful and pushy in personality. She often paved the way in social settings for the family, always capitalizing on the family name. She loved that she bore the Striver name, though she hoped to soon hyphenate that name with "Success." Upon arrival, the three Strivers awaited with great expectancy the entrance of Ms. Ambition's date, Mr. Success.

Mr. Big entered through the kitchen doors right on cue as the Mayor approached the hostess stand. "Ah! Mayor! My favorite father-in-law!" Mr. Big proclaimed his greeting loud enough for every patron to hear. "I'm so pleased you could join us today! And YOU, lovely ladies! So honored to have *you* as well, my dearest wife and her striking sister!" Mr. Big sang his insincere greetings, and sealed them with kisses and winks.

"That's enough, Big," Vain Conceit sneered. "Just make sure everything goes perfectly in here today. Father has been trying to meet with Mr. Success for some time and it is of utmost importance that you and your people don't mess anything up for him!"

As Conceit warned Big, the Mayor scanned the dining room. "Where is our table, son? Didn't I ask for our regular table?"

Now Big zeroed in on the table, seeing Compare and Critic sitting there, and red flooded his face. "Just a moment." Mr. Big darted into the dining room and snatched Sandy's elbow. With gritted teeth he asked in a low tone, *"Why* are those people at the Mayor's table??"

"They...they..." she caught Pride glaring at her from the booth beside them as she spoke, "It was an accident. I'm sorry." Sandy was not made to sustain this kind of pressure. She was beginning to crumble inside.

Mr. Big continued in his tight-jawed whisper, "You find them a table and I will deal with you later." He let her go and flew through the kitchen doors at the back. Sandy sheepishly approached the party that glared at her in strong and silent discontent, when, to her relief, the fourth member of their party arrived and distracted them from their reproach of her.

"Mr. Success! How good of you to join us at my son-in-law's establishment," bellowed Mayor Striver in false cheer. His daughters followed his example and fawned over their guest with exaggerated adulations. Mr. Success was not hard to look at. In fact, people gaped at him wherever he went. He was the perfect height of tall and was lean, muscular and fit in every way. Charm oozed from his every pore. His smile was broad and beguiling, a flawless grin that was hard to resist. Everyone in Excess knew of him and wanted to be associated with him one way or another. And much of the greatness and grandeur of the city could be accredited to his myriad of business dealings. Sandy too wanted everything an association with Mr. Success could bring. She watched his every move, and could not believe he was right in front of her, to be served—by her!

"Enough! Enough already!" gloated Mr. Success as that magnetic smile spread across his smooth chiseled face. "It is *my* honor to dine with *you*, fine Mayor and these most *gorgeous girls* of yours. How young are you? Your faces are as fresh as babies! Yet I was told to meet the Mayor's *grown* daughters!"

The party howled at the hilarity of his compliments yet consumed them as choice morsels. "Please, Mr. Success, let us sit and sup together! BIG'S is the *best* spot in town to bond over a bowl of...well, *anything* you could be hungry for!" Ms. Ambition grabbed the arm of Mr. Success while Ms. Conceit gave Sandy a high nod to lead them on.

Sandy took them to the only table left—the least desirable one near the kitchen. The party tried to ignore this unsavory location. Mr. Success lost his huge smile for a moment, cleared his throat, and then sat without a word. All sat with him, in a second of awkward silence. "We're thrilled to have each of you with us today!" Sandy rallied what remained of her enthusiasm for this moment. "I'm Sandy, and it is my pleasure to serve you. What may I get you to drink?" They quickly gave their orders without even looking at her, and proceeded to spread their smiles out once again for each other, while their lilting voices rose and fell in a cascade of empty compliments.

Sandy was deflated. They didn't seem to notice her at all. This was her chance. How could she make the most of it? As she backed away from the table considering her next approach of them, she caught a glimpse of something bright outside the window, and along with it, she heard the words that were haunting her this day: "Princess...Come!" The bright spot outside was a purple hat—the same one she had seen on the street earlier when she was on the train. She could see no face this time, just the hat, moving slightly above the crowd of people passing by. Then there was a break in the crowd, and for one second, that kind face looked directly into hers with a knowing, confident look, and disappeared again. Sandy froze in bewilderment. Again, she was being called...

"Waitress!" Ms. Unsatisfied's voice rang out. "This meat is too well-done! I said medium!"

"And my tea is too weak. It was certainly not steeped long enough," grumbled Ms. Dissatisfied as she pushed her saucer away, dropping her gloved hands in her lap while straightening her posture in protest.

"And our table wobbles—and the salt shaker is dirty, not to mention the floor under my feet is sticky," Ms. Never-Good-Enough complained, pointing and waving her jewel-dripped hands. "What are you going to do about it?"

"I will take care of it," Sandy quietly promised. She started for the kitchen with this list of drinks and complaints balanced in her head, trying not to drop one from her memory, yet distracted still by the man in the purple hat and that voice...

"Miss!" Tired called out from her first table. "We need our check. And we need it now. My wife is not feeling well."

"I'll be right with you," promised Sandy, snapping to.

"Ma'am! Ma'am!!"Compare chimed in with his plea. "I changed my mind on my order. I want what the woman at *that* table is having..." Compare pointed to Sick's food.

"Are you sure about that, good man? I think that made me

30

SICK! I feel awful," Sick cried dramatically back across the dining room.

"Well, *our* food was just not prepared right! It didn't even *look* right. Where's the owner? I want to talk to the owner," Critic demanded.

Sandy was being crushed under the bombardment of critiques and complaints. "Are you sure I can't help you?" pleaded Sandy, knowing how upset Mr. Big was already.

Critic raised his voice and stood up, "If you can't get me the owner I will walk out of this establishment and never set foot in it again!" Now the whole restaurant hushed and turned its attention to Sandy and her table. Her face flushed with humiliation. Success would never look favorably on her now. How could she redeem the situation? Her circumstances were unraveling quickly.

In the midst of swirling thoughts and emotions, a voice reached for her again. "Princess, wake up! And come..."

A wave of regality swept over her, then vanished. She had no time for this. She must pacify these customers and cater to their demands. But she felt paralyzed by her inability—and this call.

Pride rose up. "I'll fetch him, sir." He offered to "help" before slipping immediately through the doors to the kitchen. There was no way of telling what Pride would say or how he would spin the situation, but in a moment Mr. Big was at Critic's table. Sandy took the opportunity to disappear into the kitchen, barely remembering what had been asked of her. She gathered the drinks ordered by Mayor Striver's table and delivered them to the table where the three ladies were gathered for their luncheon. In a daze now, their objections didn't even register. She took their food and immediately gave it to Sick and Tired's table, and gave Tired's bill to Mr. Success, who was yet to have one sip of a drink.

"Uh, Miss?" Success questioned as he offered the bill back to Sandy amidst the aghast and apologetic whispers of Ambition, Striver, and Vanity surrounding him.

All of the other tables called out their complaints as well, but

Sandy could hear nothing except for the one resounding phrase that rang relentlessly through her head: "You are invited, Princess. Wake up and come..."

All the more frazzled, Sandy started to clear all of her tables, removing the drinks she had just placed before ladies, and gathering the plates set before Sick and Tired only moments earlier.

"What kind of server is this?" Critic questioned loudly. Sandy turned towards his voice in reaction to this judgment of her, and when she did, her tray collided with Pride's and all of their dishes crashed to the floor. Their eyes met for only a second before Sandy internally collapsed. She could take no more.

Sandy was desperate for escape. She spun without a word, pounded through the doors of the kitchen, and approached Restless. "Will you take me there? To the Shores? You said everyone needs to get away sometime. Will you drive me there?"

Restless cracked a half smile and jerked his head back in a quick nod. "Sure. This weekend. Let's go."

Sandy only nodded to thank him and confirm their plan. She took off her apron, hung it on the hook by the office and, without another word, proceeded through the back door and out into the alleyway. A strange and instant relief comforted her. If anyone came after her, she was unaware. She was sure she would be fired whether she had stayed to finish her shift or not, but that is not what drove her out of those doors. The plain, gray girl from the Wastelands had been called to a place beyond this one. She did not understand this call, but was moved to answer it, or at least hear it, and she found a way out in an unlikely friend. Soon Sandy would join Restless in pursuit of some answers, but for now she headed for the train to join the sleeping on her return home.

3

A Ride to the Lowlands

No alarm was needed the morning set for departure. Before the break of dawn, Sandy was up. She had arranged to meet Restless outside her house by the gate early that morning. The trip to the Lowlands was several hours, and she could not leave soon enough. Sandy grabbed an oversized bag from the top shelf of her closet. This would be just a day trip, but she wanted to be prepared. Prepared for what, she did not know.

A twinge of anxiety shot through her body as she considered what to pack. *What am I doing? Who do I think I'm meeting?* Sandy sat back down on her bed, leaning her troubled head into her hands. "Am I crazy?" she asked herself in a desperate whisper. "'Girl from Wastelands Disappears, Following Voices in Her Head...' Sounds like tomorrow's headline!" Sandy's tone turned slightly sarcastic as she questioned her plans for the day. She remained still for just a moment more before reaching for the journal on her nightstand. The postcard, the invitation, was real. It stuck up above the edges of the closed journal, revealing just the slightest image of those shores. Sandy took a minute to review the card, front and back, verifying its authenticity one last time. Yes, it was a real piece of paper, confirming the reason for this trip. At least she had one piece of evidence.

Sandy decided to stick with her plan, crazy as it was, and threw the journal with the postcard in it, in the bottom of the bag.

Without much thought, she packed various other items one might need for a day at the beach, including a nice change of clothes. She laughed at herself again. *I mean, what if my prince is there? He might want to take me to the castle for dinner!* With that she zipped her bag and finished getting herself ready. It was almost time to meet Restless outside.

Sandy proceeded down the stairs carefully, not wanting to wake her mother, for it was the one morning she slept in. Besides, she had no desire of explaining this mysterious trip to her. She quickly scrawled a note on the memo pad in the kitchen: *Be back tonight. Out for the day with a friend. Sandy.* The two of them did not gush with affection for one another. They loved each other as mothers and daughters do, but did not show much emotion. This courtesy was all that was needed. Sandy grabbed an energy drink from the fridge and headed out the door.

Just as she approached the gate, Restless pulled up. Perfect timing. He had a red convertible, an older car, ideal for just such an excursion. There was a nip in the morning air, but soon the sun would be up and the warmth would justify the convertible top being down. Restless was already anticipating this. "Jump in. Throw your stuff in the back." He was a man of few words and short sentences. Sandy wondered if he had already used up his allotment for the day.

She did as instructed, saying simply, "Thank you," and jumped in the car.

Sandy drank her breakfast and watched as the sun rose over the skyline of the structures ahead. They drove through the suburbs of Excess, passing through layers of shops, businesses, homes, and restaurants, one after another. The buildings remained gray with the sun at their back. Sandy turned for a moment to see what the great City of Excess looked like in the sunrise. She was awestruck by the effect the horizon's light had on the cityscape. A pink and amber glow colored its metallic buildings, filling Sandy with a peculiar wonder.

Impressed as she was, she turned back around and searched for a break in the buildings ahead. As much as she thought she was made for the city and its crowds of people and *stuff*, today she wanted space—open space—and a clear view. Whether anyone would meet her at the Shores or not, Sandy could look forward to a change of landscape, and that settled her mind a bit more in her constant assessment of this trip.

The road soon wove past the towns and rounded a gradual bend that led them to scenery unfamiliar to Sandy. Natural forms sporadically began to line their way: trees and other green plant life. Their shapes intrigued Sandy, but their fast travel prohibited any close observation of them.

"So this is country living." Restless finally built up more words to share for the day.

"I guess so. Wow. I haven't been anywhere like this— anywhere without buildings all around me, in a long time." Sandy inhaled after this reflection. She felt her tension ease and she leaned back into her seat, letting the rural air fill her lungs as she relaxed, breathing it deeply. What was so relaxing about this air? Perhaps it was the quietness of it. There was only the hum of the car filling her ears—no orders being yelled by Mr. Big, or from the city intercom for that matter. Where she lived, there was always an order being broadcasted in one form or another, insisting how residents of Excess should live and build and add *more* to their world. Not here. Here there was no intercom, no boss, no Striver—just open country. There was no structure to "stick" anything to, and even her own thoughts felt free to roam where they would.

Restless perked up with the change in the atmosphere and engaged Sandy in conversation. "I've thought of moving, you know. Quitting BIG'S and finding my spot in the world—out here somewhere maybe."

"Really?" Sandy asked, surprised.

"Yeah, I mean, do you ever feel that you're getting nowhere in that city? Like you're just part of some kind of—machine?" He didn't take time to listen for an answer. Restless squinted his face in slight disgust and allowed his inner turmoil to tumble out in word-form to Sandy. "I mean, we walk around like robots, clocking in and out, in and out, serving some sort of *master* we don't even know. You know?"

Sandy wasn't sure if she should reply now or not—or if she knew how. She had always been focused on the prize. She knew what she wanted. She wanted MORE. She wanted success and everything that came with it. More possessions for her family, a better place to live, the respect and the admiration of others—this is what she was striving for, and the City of Excess was the promised land of all of that and more! What other place in her world could offer her the success she hoped for?

Sandy turned to Restless, then stopped to study his expression. There was something appealing, even attractive about him. She had never taken notice of him like this before. His spirit that wanted *more* in an opposite way of the city dwellers had her seeing something new in him that drew her into his thoughts.

"I mean, what if we just never went back, Sandy?" Now he had gone too far.

"What? What in the world are you talking about? I was *made* for the city! I *will* be successful one day! I know I'm meant to be someone, and someone *big!* Everyone will know who I am in Excess. I'm just getting away for one day, then I am going back!" Sandy was astonished at her own response. Where did all of that energy come from?

"Ok, Ok! I was just throwing that out there for conversation's sake! You don't have to prove anything to me, Sandy. I know who you are." Did he? Did Restless understand her—maybe better than herself? Maybe he did.

"I'm so sorry. I don't even know what in the world that was. Just been thinking a lot—about a lot of things. You just pushed some kind of button in me I guess, Restless."

Restless smiled and laughed as he turned to look her in the eyes for a second. "Aw, it's nothing. I often have a crazy affect on city girls who have been in there too long!" Then he focused on the road ahead, ran one hand through his hair before he firmly gripped the wheel and turned mute again, leaving Sandy alone in her thoughts.

What was that button he pressed? What was this die-hard allegiance to city life and all it promised? And what was this loosening she felt in the tension she lived under as she drove further away from her place in the Wastelands? She opened her mouth and drank in yet another full portion of this nourishing air. She had no answers to any of these questions, but she had this day, and the company of someone she had more in common with than she had previously realized. Sandy and Restless were on their way to the Shores. She was unsure of his mission for the day, but somehow knew hers would be discovered upon arrival. She had been summoned, and she was responding. Sandy was making her pilgrimage back to where her life had started, and little did she know it was about to start all over again.

4

Arrival at the Shores

*T*he red car swept along the rest of its dusty path all the way to its destination. It was not quite mid-morning when Restless and Sandy entered their new and unknown domain for the day. Sandy felt cautious as she gazed about, not knowing exactly what she was looking for, or who was looking for her.

"Got any place in particular you want me to drop you?" Restless was ready to explore on his own, so it was time for Sandy to decide where she would set foot first at these shores.

She spotted a café across from a beach access. "Right here is fine. I have a little time to kill before low tide…" She felt silly even saying this. "Right here is great."

Restless pulled over into the shoulder on the beach side and lifted Sandy's bag up for her from the back seat. He lowered his sunglasses and gave Sandy a look that any big brother might give. "Take care. I hope this is a good day for you. I'll meet you back right here, by sunset." Restless nodded towards the shabby café, gripped his wheel again and drove off.

Sandy stood in stillness, watching the red car that carried her here disappear into the puff of smoke and sand behind it. There went her only tie to real life in the Wastelands. Now she was here, in a foreign place with no tangible direction as to what to do next. Was she wrong in letting Restless drop her off here? Should she have asked him to bring her at all?

Sandy was awakened from the trance the car's smoke trail had left her in by the great sound of crashing. It was the sea. She could see it in the distance, beyond the dunes, and it tugged on every part of her. Sandy felt herself drawn to the wooden stairs of the access, but forced herself to stop. "No, it's not low tide yet. I need to get ready," she instructed herself, then stiffened her back and crossed the street, aiming for the door of the simple café.

Cool air and scents of refreshment greeted Sandy as she made her way inside. This café was modest and quaint, and surprisingly inviting. Everything about it stood out in contrast to the restaurant Sandy clocked into day in and day out in Excess. At the entrance, she was welcomed by a sitting area, complete with a worn couch, an old stuffed chair, and a simple low table for plates and saucers. Sandy surveyed cozy tables for two with mismatched chairs throughout the room. To her left was a quilt-cushioned window seat that made up half of a makeshift booth with the best view of the house. A long wooden table filled the center of the room, and a narrow counter at the back bordered by round, metal stools completed the interior furnishings of this haven overlooking the sea.

"Well, hello!" Sandy's study of the café was interrupted by the friendly greeting a woman who appeared from a door at the back. "Welcome! Looks like you are the last of our breakfast crowd. Or are you the first of our lunch customers? No matter, my dear. We are happy to have you." Sandy was looking directly into the most sincerely warm and welcoming face she had ever noticed. It was the face of a woman approaching retirement age, yet still possessed a sparkle and vibrancy in her manner that removed all marks of time. She was lovely. Her long white hair was tied up in a loose bun; wispy strands that had broken free in the fast yet pleasant pace of the morning breakfast rush encircled her face. Her eyes were blue—bright blue and clear, with nothing hidden behind them. And her smile remained steadfast, even as Sandy stood there and stared.

"What is it, my dear? Will you have a seat? We are just tidying up from the breakfast crowd, but my husband and I would love to wait on you. Pick a spot—any spot in the cottage. Just make yourself at home. I'm Kindness, and I'll be right back to tell you about everything that is special for you here."

Kindness? Did she say her name was Kindness? What an odd name, Sandy thought. She had never known someone with that name, and had certainly never been waited on by such a woman. Sandy watched as Kindness busied herself behind the counter and called through the window to what must have been the kitchen. Another warm, smiling face appeared through this window, and Sandy caught sight of his hand waving an additional welcome as well. That face soon disappeared, then popped through the door next to it, appearing in full as an older gentleman who proceeded towards Sandy at the window seat she had chosen.

"Good morning, dear. We are so glad you came to see us today! It's just a perfect day for it."

Sandy was caught off guard by this comment. It was almost as if they knew she was coming. "Well, thank you?" she replied in a questioning tone.

Kindness laughed softly. "Don't let my husband puzzle you. He believes each day is a perfect day—"

"—and each person who comes is just the perfect one for us to meet!" Her husband completed her sentence with a tone of acceptance that settled Sandy in the sweetest of ways. "I'm Contentment, and we are happy to have you as our guest in this moment."

Who talks like this? Who even thinks like this? Sandy pondered silently, but responded with, "Thank you. I...I love your place. It's so..."

"Comfortable, I hope. That's what we wanted to create. A little refuge of comfort with a view of the Great Sea..." Kindness looked out of the window behind Sandy with a knowing smile. Sandy wondered what she knew of those waters, but before she could

41

speculate too much, Contentment continued in his wife's sentiments.

"We see our cottage as a prime place to fill up or refuel for whatever journey lies ahead! And we get to be the ones to provide just the right sustenance required. So what'll you have, my dear?" Contentment was so confident in his offer. Sandy loved his merry way, yet was still unsure what they served or what she needed.

"I…I don't even know if I'm hungry," Sandy confessed, though she was confused as to what real hunger was.

"Well, what have you eaten today?" asked Kindness.

"I…well, I drank something from home, hours ago, before sunrise. That's all I've had, I guess." Sandy reflected on the fact that she mostly drank her nutrition. She filled herself with one liquid after another, always eating on the go some portable portion of energy to keep her going. She rarely sat down to eat anything of real substance. She was loyal to the mandates of Excess and its leader, after all, always on the "go, go, go!"

"Well, then you are in the right place today!" Contentment knew what had to be done. "Kindness and I will select the perfect dishes for you. I know a hungry one when I see one, and *you* need a good dose from the kitchen of Kindness and Contentment today. It will settle that appetite of yours and give you all you need for what is next."

These two sweet servants retreated excitedly into the kitchen. When they had disappeared from view, Sandy took a deep breath and let out an audible sigh. She scanned the dining room, picturing what it might be like, full of folks feasting on the delights of Kindness and Contentment. She imagined the varying pitches of laughter, mixed with sounds of scraping plates and encouraging conversation. What memories of joy blended with peace she could sense in this place. It was silent now. The atmosphere itself was preparing her in some way, but for what?

Before she could find her answer, a tray was set before her.

On it was a basket of steaming breads, a colorful ceramic plate of flavored butters and jellies, and a matching mug of hot drink that smelled spicy and sweet. "This is just to start. Eat up! You will leave this place satisfied if Contentment has anything to do with it." Kindness turned with a wink and disappeared to prepare their next edible creation for Sandy.

Sandy stared for a moment at the tray. What was this feeling that rose within her? A tear came to her eye as she breathed in the dance of aromas under her nose. *Kindness* was serving her and it moved her, softening something inside. She lifted the short butter knife with one hand as she chose a piece of hot bread with the other. This bread was denser and more moist than the bread at BIG'S. It was homemade for sure, and her mouth watered in anticipation. She had not held a knife in quite sometime, at least not one to use for her own dining. Funny how she lived a life serving others food, but rarely did she ever feed herself. She spread one butter, then tried another on the far side of the slice. The first bite did not disappoint, nor the second, third, or the rest of the basket. Sandy ate the whole small loaf, and sipped the hot, spicy, sweet mixture between all the bites. She was hungrier than she realized. It was good to really eat again.

As soon as she was finished with this appetizer, Kindness and Contentment entered the dining room, each with two trays. They approached Sandy, who giggled in delight, never having been served like this in her life. "Now, we know you cannot possibly eat all of this," Kindness admitted as they rested their trays on the table's edge, opposite Sandy, "but we wanted to prepare everything you might like."

"Yes. Just pick what you want and eat until you are satisfied," Contentment added. Sandy was overwhelmed. It looked like every breakfast food imaginable had been prepared, and several lunch entrees as well. There were eggs, soufflés, crepes, and quiches—samples of hearty soups, medleys of fresh salads, and petite sandwiches of all kinds. Each portion was a perfect size for sampling, and had been created with exquisite skill, just for her.

"You eat what you like, and we'll be back to check on you. Enjoy yourself, dear. Sometimes you need a feast set before you to remind you of all that is truly good." Kindness's words and way were a mystery to Sandy. Sandy did not doubt that her words made sense; she just did not understand them. But her appetite, now aroused, *did* understand the invitation of the food in front of her. She dug in, savoring bites from each dish, and ate until she was satisfied indeed. She was full, and in more ways than she knew. Sandy sighed again, this time in much relief.

The door to the kitchen flew open, "Well? Have you had enough?" Contentment beamed as he reentered with his wife to check on their guest.

"I most certainly have. I...I can't even explain what this has meant to me...Getting to enjoy real food...I have never experienced anything.like this."Then Sandy remembered—*the bill.* All this must cost a great deal. She hoped she had enough in her account. "How much? How much does all of this cost?"

Kindness slid into the chair beside her and Contentment followed, sitting across from her on a bench. "Dear, sometimes you just have to receive. This is one of those times."

What did she mean "receive"? Did she mean "free"? "I don't get it. I...I don't understand what you mean. I'm not very familiar with that word." Sandy was slightly skeptical now.

"We know," said Kindness. "It's Ok. You are from the City, aren't you? The City of Excess?"

"Yes," replied Sandy. "How did you know?"

"I knew it when you walked into the cottage. The people from Excess all have a certain hunger that we are now experts at recognizing. To tell you the truth, we used to live in Excess ourselves," Kindness admitted. Sandy could not believe it. She had never run into anyone like these two in the city.

"Wow...I would never have known that," Sandy acknowledged.

"We've changed a lot. I barely smiled when I lived and worked in the big city. Can you believe that? I could never get enough, and it affected everything about my manner, even my looks," Contentment said.

"Yes. His hair may not have been as gray then, but his skin was. The drive had him on the verge of exhaustion. He was sick and tired all of the time, and nothing would make him better." Kindness shook her head sadly, remembering her love's poor state.

"Well, how did you escape?" Sandy used this word without even thinking, yet it seemed to fit in the context of the story.

"I got an invitation—to come here. I can't really explain it, and it might not make sense if I did, but I received an invitation to come. So I did, and I was completely changed, never to return the same again."

Sandy's heart stopped. *An invitation? Like the one she had received? What kind of invitation did he mean? And "completely changed?" "Never to return the same again..." What did that mean?* She didn't even want to know. This was too much. She enjoyed and even appreciated the kindness shown her, but if her coming here was some sort of trick—a plot to change her—no.

Pride's face flashed in front of her. Even though they had parted on bad terms, she wondered what he would say about all of this. "Get out of there, Sandy! No one needs to change you! You have a big life waiting for you in Excess! You are *young*, not an old worn out man who is too *weak* for success. Get out of there!" Pride's voice rang loud in her head.

"Are you Ok, dear?" Kindness reached for Sandy's hand, and she came to.

"Yes. Yes I am, though I need to go. I have to meet someone at low tide. Is it almost time?"

Contentment looked past Sandy who remained with her back to the window overlooking the sea. "Yes. Yes, it is. You have a few moments if you need them. We will remove all of this and let you just sit and digest it all."

Sandy said not a word as they cleared the remains of this extravagant gift. She was torn between her admiration of these two beautiful people who served her such goodness, and her long-standing relationship with Pride who had molded so many of her opinions. Kindness and Contentment took the dishes to the kitchen, giving Sandy one final moment alone. She reached into the bottom of her bag and opened her journal where the card marked it and read again, "I dreamed I could be loved... deeply...by a prince whose eyes burned with pure passion...and I was a princess...the daughter of a king..." This was the record of the dream etched in her heart, written the morning this whole journey began. She reviewed the postcard as well, "You are invited, Princess....Wake up and come!"

With a full belly and hesitant curiosity, Sandy decided to get up and go. She felt stronger in a sense, and encouraged in a way, but still was unsure. She had come this far, and it was now low tide. It was time to cross over to the other side and step into the sand she was named after. Perhaps she would find contentment herself this day, or at least resolve to this mystery that had her distracted from her ambitions in Excess. She hoped for both.

Kindness and Contentment left their final impressions for the visit as they waved from their post at the door of the Cottage Café. Sandy waved back, then turned and crossed the paved street. She climbed the steps of the beach access and continued along the splintered wooden planks. Soon she descended the steps, removed her shoes, and placed one bare foot in the sand. It was mid-morning, low tide, and Sandy had arrived at the Shores.

5

The Call of the Sea

I was waiting.

It had been years since Sandy had experienced this soft grainy ground between her toes, and I watched as she took her first step. Sandy returned to her childhood instantly in expression as joy washed over her, from her sandy feet up. She belonged here. I looked on from a distance as Sandy gazed in amazement at the ocean, rejoicing over the laugh and dance of the sea. Its spray tickled her skin and the salty winds carried a mysterious healing in them. I could tell Sandy's soul was opening in a way that surprised her. For the first time in many years, maybe even in her life, she looked...awake.

Sandy stared wide-eyed in wonderment as waves rose and crashed unceasingly. She scanned the waters, finding no end to them beyond her, to her right or left. It was pulled back from the beach, being low tide, but still it continued in its rolling rhythm, beckoning to this girl on its shores.

I watched her response as the shoreline called her. Sandy made her way to the water's edge, but dared not step in. She would get quite close, then spring back as if she thought the surf might grab her. Her resistance revealed a belief she belonged to the sand—to the earth—yet she clearly longed for the sea, but could not commit to enter its element.

My Sandy had made it here, to the Shores of the Lowlands at mid-morning low tide. And here I looked on with eager anticipation while an undefined debate in her heart ensued as she faced

47

the great waters. The expanse of it captivated her focus and lulled her into a dreamy daze until it was time. She heard a familiar voice directly behind her, now welcoming her.

"Princess, you came!" Sandy gasped and turned. It could not be her imagination this time. It was *me*.

"Hello, Princess."

Sandy began to melt, feeling weak in the knees. I reached, of course, to her aid. "I'm...I'm...I'm..."

"I know. You are Sandy," I gently interrupted. "I know you well."

"You...you...you're beautiful," she stammered, her eyes searching my face as I hoped they would.

"As are you, lovely one. At last, we finally meet!"

"But I don't know you...I mean, I want to, but I..." Sandy shook her head, with fear now masking her face.

"I know. But I know *you*. And you must understand that is of far greater importance for now."

Sandy breathed her deepest breath that day and held it, as if this air would hold her together. "I'm very, very confused," she began. "Who are you? Are you the one who sent me the card? Is it your voice I keep hearing? Why did you call me here so far away from home? What am I doing here?"

Sandy had backed a few steps away, trying to regain her own ground. She held a concerted look on her face while I studied it. (I didn't have to study it. I just wanted to.) Finally I gave her the first answer she had requested. "I am Jasper, and yes, I invited you here."

"Jasper..." Sandy repeated my name as if it was one she was recalling from a distant memory. "I feel as if I should know you." For just a moment she let her guard down and drew closer in heart.

"You *should* know me, dear one, and you *shall*, if you *will*."

My words puzzled her and she looked down, trying to capture her thoughts to make sense of this moment. "I am not here to confuse you, my love...I am here to invite you...to come!"

"But I came. I'm here. Now wait a minute—who are you? I mean I know you said your name is Jasper, and I mean no disrespect, but *who are* you? And why do you call me all of these *words* like 'love' and 'dear one' and...'Princess.'"

She paused before she added "Princess."

"That is the one you are particularly fond of, is it not... 'Princess'?"

Sandy stared at me with a mixture of hurt and unbelief. "Why do you call me that? Do you know..."

"Yes, I know." What she did not know was that hurting her would never begin to be part of my plan. In fact, it was quite the opposite. Now I just had to get her to see herself as I did, and as she actually was. After a pause, I softly responded, "Sandy, I know the dream of your heart. And I know that Kingdom you dreamed of. And Sandy, it is *real.*"

Disbelief was the only expression on her face now, but that would never halt my pursuit of delivering this necessary truth. "Sandy, you *are* a princess, and your father is the King. And there is a Prince coming for you that loves you fiercely. And I am Jasper, your helper who will see you are united in his Kingdom of Love.

Sandy could not speak. She turned away to the right of the surf, looking down at her feet. Now shame crept up her face, and I watched as a salty tear fell from her eye and hit the sand between her toes. I looked and longed to reach for her, but could not, as I am a gentleman and know when I must be reached for first.

After minutes of pondering in silence, Sandy lowly stated, "I could never be a princess. I'm just a plain, simple girl who will try with everything I have to do something great." She paused again then added, "I can't accept that a position like this could just be

49

handed to me. It makes no sense at all."

Sandy and I both turned to the sea and stared in silence. The longer we stood, the more conflicted she was. Practical reason challenged my promises to her. In her struggle to accept my truth, she dug her toes into the sinking sand. Doubt flooded her heart and questions crashed in her mind like the waves we watched. Yet my presence compelled her.

Finally, she turned to me and lifted her eyes to me with a whispered request, "Tell me more about this Kingdom."

"Let's have a seat."

And so we sat together in the sand, a short distance from the water's edge, and for the next perfect span of time, I described for the Princess many details of the Kingdom.

"This Kingdom is like none you could imagine on earth. It is not like your world, nor of this world. It is a Kingdom of opposites in many ways—a Kingdom where the little can be great—where the unknown are well-known—where the discarded find honor —where the poor inherit everything."

Sandy said nothing, but listened intently while she stared over the sea, trying to take in these vast thoughts and sights together. For hours I explained the majestic intricacies and simplistic marvels of this Kingdom—the perfect *rightness* of it—and the essence of the peace and joy that are benefits to citizens of it.

I then added this final notion for her to consider. "Those who reside in the Kingdom freely receive...and freely give. They serve others in the name of the King and meet the greatest needs of men. Because they have been lavished with so much true wealth, they overflow with generosity," I explained. Though Sandy had experienced this kind of receiving just a few hours earlier at the Cottage Café, she could not comprehend the inclination to give at this time. Her world was wired for attaining and possessing, not giving away. She informed me of her puzzlement with a doubtful look, to which I answered, "There's so much splendid mystery to

50

be discovered in the Kingdom, dear love, but it cannot be known all at once. You will find it out one step at a time."

She stopped me after this. "So how do you become a citizen of this Kingdom? And how do you get there? How would I find it if I wanted to go?"

"Sandy..."My voice summoned her eyes to mine, and she stared with an innocent desire to truly know what she could not yet fathom. "This Kingdom costs everything you have. In fact, you must give up your very life for it."

The shock of my statement altered the soft expression of my Princess's face. A shade of horrified disgust now fell instead. "Give up my life? You mean die?" She got up and distanced herself from me and this mystery I was revealing.

I rose and approached to comfort her. "Only a death to life again—a new life. A royal life. The kind of pure life that joy and peace can dwell in. Sandy, the Kingdom is not *only* a place to be found, it is a Kingdom that is placed *within* you, that grows in your pursuit of it until you arrive to dwell in it forever!"

My words confounded her. I understood. She was made of earth, and would have to be transformed to understand this new world she was intended for. We looked out over the sea again. "Sandy, this call to the Kingdom, to live where you were made to live and have the Kingdom life within you, is like the call of the sea. The deep of it calls to the deep in you—the part of you made to understand the mysteries of the deep. You cannot see what is out there, but there is a longing within you to dive into it and discover...is there not?" She nodded slightly without a word, and continued to stare out.

"My dearest one, I could not tell you that it is easy from where you stand to consider giving yourself to the sea...to launch out into it and get in over your head, not knowing what is out there. I happen to know you have fear, having never faced the waves that will envelop you. But I must tell you that the sea before you...it is

51

made of love—perfect love. And as you step into it, all fear will dissolve and you will find the treasure your heart has been made for. The journey to the Kingdom begins with you stepping into this ocean of the King's love. Will you step in?"

She actually paused, as if she considered saying yes, then shook her head with a jerk as though she were bringing herself to her natural senses. "Wait—I can't swim well. And I can't breathe under water! And you said I must give up my life for this Kingdom. Are you trying to *kill* me?" Fear had completely taken her hostage now.

"Precious Sandy, I would not ask you to give up anything without the promise of everything in return—nor would your father, nor would your Prince. We know what you truly desire, and we know that you long to be saturated in this ocean of love. Whatever the cost, whatever he requires is worth the trade."

She stared again, then turned suddenly, heading away from the surf, erupting in sobs. "I can't! I can't! I can't go! I will crumble in those waves! I will be washed away! I will lose my footing! I can't swim out there! I've never known love like that before!" She sobbed and she sobbed.

That was it. She feared the loss of what was familiar, as empty and weak as it was. She wasn't ready, but I am patient.

"Dear child, will you sit with me again?" I extended my hand and she consented by taking it and sitting close. We sat for quite some time, and said not a thing. After a while passed, some children ran onto the shore, and played before us in the surf. We both watched. She studied them intently.

"You know," I said, "The Kingdom—it belongs to them, and to those who are like them."

She cocked her head with a questioning expression, "You mean...kids?"

"Indeed," I replied as I exhaled with a smile and looked on. "Just watch them. They are amazing! Oh, the King delights in them

52

so. They hold on to so little. They carry no care. They enjoy the moment. They so easily believe, and they are full of *hope!*"

"Hope..." Sandy repeated, then watched them all the more carefully as they squealed and frolicked in the surf, so full of life and delight of the sea.

"Yes, the Kingdom is theirs! They get it. And we can learn oh so much from them—well, *you* can! And I can help you." This additional mystery was too much for Sandy to process. She didn't want to recall her own childhood, and was happy to have made it past that stage of life. What would the life of any child have to offer her?

My would-be princess got up and dusted the sand from her pants with nervous energy. She began to find reasons to escape me.

"Well, where has this day gone? It is nearly sunset! I'd better get ready to catch my ride. It really was nice to meet you, Jasper," she said, but would not look me in the eye.

"Stop," I said.

She did. Her gaze locked on my own. I needed this moment before her departure to deliver a parcel of utmost importance. "Sandy, I understand your response today." I paused for her to consider my admission.

"You do?" My Princess was real again, not hiding behind excuses for exit.

"Yes, I do. But you see that sea?" We both looked again. "It IS made of love, and there is a lot of it. So when you are ready, I want you to return. Until then, I want you to have this..." I took from my pocket a small glass vial, bound by a golden rope. I took off its corked top and walked towards the ocean. I bent down to let the rising surf fill it, then sealed the opening once again. On the vial was inscribed one word:

"<u>Hope</u>," Sandy read as she received my gift. I helped to place it around her neck. The vial settled at her heart, and a peace came over my beloved Princess.

She held her hand over her heart, shutting her eyes. I knew she felt the warmth of his love, just that little bit of it, enclosed in the vial.

"...And hope does not disappoint us," I whispered. She nodded knowingly, though unknowing. Soon she would know far more.

The screech of tires and three quick honks of a car horn interrupted this final moment of decision for Sandy. Restless had arrived for her. She lingered just a moment longer, hand still on her chest, and then opened her eyes directly into mine. "I'm sorry." She dropped her look. "I must go." Then my Sandy looked up into my face and stared one last time. Tears lined her eyes as she asked again with a greater intensity, "Who *are* you?"

"I'm Jasper," I whispered back, "and we will never give up in our pursuit of you." Her head fell back down and she turned without another word, departing slowly as the sun began to set. I watched as she lifted her heavy foot from the sand back to the wood of the beach access steps. It was a step away from her dream and this Kingdom she was made to be part of. But I had left her with hope—and hope would appoint her back to me and her dream again.

6

Going Back

With a slam of the heavy red door, Sandy's steel carriage was thrust into motion, whisking her away from this perplexing encounter with a force beyond her capacity to comprehend. She sank in her seat, under its lingering impact on her heart. Love. She had been entreated by love itself, yet she could not consent to answer its call.

What is wrong with me? This thought blared in her head, but her lips remained tight. Sandy turned to her door window, seeking some distraction for her mind from its condemning thoughts. She glanced over the parading landscape of the Lowlands, then dismissed each sight as quickly as it passed. The beauty of this region could not comfort her now, not after she had rejected its Great Sea.

Sandy felt doomed. A deeper loneliness now settled into her heart—a loneliness that could only be known by being offered the exact companionship she desired, and then purposefully refusing it. It was a loneliness perpetuated by fear—a fear of never having what you know you need. Sandy was paralyzed in this moment. The farther they drove, the greater grip fear had on her heart.

While fear held her heart, a battle of doubt commenced in her mind. *What if that was it? What if I will never have a chance at love? Why could I not step in? What am I scared of? Can I learn to swim? Who cares if I'm swept away? Would that be better than life now as it is?* Crazy questions.

55

So many times we are inviting people to come to a higher place, But fear, fear of the unknown makes us give up. But why? No!

Restless joined in. "So, did you get what you came for? Find what you were looking for?"

Sandy paused uncomfortably. "I'm not sure what to say. I don't know."

Restless shifted in his seat, unsatisfied with that answer. "Well, did someone show up? You were invited by someone to come, right?"

Another lengthy pause preceded Sandy's answer, "Yes. He showed up. And that's all I can say." Her head turned completely away from him and she leaned her forehead on the cold window glass.

"Fine." Restless shook his head in brief frustration, but conceded to her obvious wish for solitude. He stepped on the gas and committed to consider only his own inner turbulence for the rest of the ride home.

Sandy had her own unease to process. Her head was swirling with the words and images—like the face of Jasper. Jasper. Even that name produced conflict within her. She was drawn to him and yet repulsed by him at the same time, as though two hearts beat within her chest. Part of her longed for every promise Jasper made, and she felt a willingness to yield to him. But the stronger side slammed her heart's door on any invitation that would take her away from her world, her home, and her ways.

As she sat in silence next to Restless, she experienced the last of the salty air washing through her hair. Soon the air changed. It thickened with the darkness that settled into the evening sky. The smog of the Wastelands was more pungent than ever, reaching her nostrils even before the region was in sight. It seeped into her heart. She felt its weight, and with it, a greater sadness. A tear rolled down her cheek as she rejected her own dream, denying in full belief that she was or could ever be, a princess.

Restless turned the corner and Sandy hastily brushed this watery sign of weakness away, and stiffened her body upright. In the distance she heard the boom of the city intercom, "Go! Go! Go! Do! Do! Do! Get! Get! Get! And PARTY!" It was now the second night of the weekend, and all the residents of the city indulged themselves after a week of hard work. Whether they had the energy or not, they drank potions that would revive them and fuel the expected behavior of a weekend night in the City of Excess.

Restless ventured to speak again. "So, which party are you going to tonight? Want me to drop you off somewhere?" he offered. "I'm going to Club Compromise. Have you been?"

"No," Sandy answered. "I've heard of it though."

"Yeah, it's kind of the new hot spot. Just about anything goes there. They have the latest flavors of potions there, and when you try them, you'll do almost anything. It's wild."

Sandy would normally be curious, especially in her restless state. Part of her desired to take the easy escape of a potion and change of environment. But she was too ill of heart and just wanted to take a shower and wash the sand from her feet. She wanted to rinse any sign of that sandy encounter from her entire being. She wished she could erase it from her mind.

"No, just take me home," she answered.

"Suit yourself!" Restless relented, then squealed down the last stretch of highway leading to the Wastelands.

When she arrived home, Sandy mumbled a "thank you" to her daytrip companion. He sped off without a reply, eager to seek his next destination and escape his own identity for a few hours. It was exhausting being Restless all the time.

Sandy opened the gate to her small yard and approached her house. She saw lights inside and knew her mom must be home. "Great," she muttered under her breath. Explaining where she had been all day was *not* what she felt like doing, and she knew the questions would come.

There were voices inside. She heard their mellow tones as she stepped onto the porch. Sandy opened the door gingerly, wishing to make it inside unheard. No such luck.

"Sandy? Is that you?" Her mother's voice was higher than usual, with a dash of fear.

"Yes. It's me," Sandy replied, empty of feeling or energy to say much more.

"Come here, Sandy. Disappointment is here. She wants to visit with you." Her mother's best friend, Disappointment, came by often. Sandy tried to avoid her, for she was not a very pleasant woman. She lived in the past and always told the same old stories of all the unfair things that happened in her life. This would get Sandy's mother thinking of her disappointments as well, and together they were miserable company. Tonight, Sandy was drawn to their table. She actually wanted to sit with them and have company in her own misery.

"So where are you coming in from?" Mother asked.

"The Lowlands. I took a day trip to the Lowlands," Sandy answered as she searched for a snack.

Her mother was shocked at Sandy's admission. "You mean... by the Shores?"

Sandy nodded in honesty.

"Whatever made you go there?" Her mother was visibly taken aback.

"A friend was going, so I went along. It was nothing great," shrugged Sandy as she busied herself in the kitchen, preparing a warm drink to soothe her.

"Nothing great indeed!" Disappointment chimed in from the table. "Why, the last time I went to the Shores, there was a *hurricane* watch the entire time. The weather was so dark and dreadful with no sun at all! We were all in a tizzy wondering if we should evacuate or stay—and then it never even hit. Such a dreadful vacation *that* was!"

58

[handwritten marginalia: "Disappointment has a way of keeping us in our hurt...even when try to be positive & bring us back. / bring hope into my Disappointment / Hope drives Disappointment away / when hope is in it brings the light"]

"Nothing so exciting happened today," Sandy responded as she sat. "Just waves, crashing over and over again."

"I miss the beach..." Her mother's tone cracked the negative atmosphere with a ray of light. "I had good memories there."

"Don't be silly, friend! The greatest disappointment of your *life* started there!" Disappointment was quick to correct the mood of the moment.

"True, but at least I got something wonderful out of it. My princess, Sandy."

Sandy sat stunned in silence. She could not move. Did her mother just refer to her as a princess? Did she say something positive in the face of Disappointment? In that moment, Sandy felt a warming sensation from the forgotten vial around her neck. Her heart received its warmth and she felt its essence. Hope made its way into her heart. Her mother did not despise her or her name as she had thought. She had pleasant memories of the Shores in the Lowlands, and she called her—a princess.

Disappointment got up in a huff. "Well, I have other stops to make tonight. I can see we're done visiting here. I'll let myself out." As she did just that, Sandy's mother sat with a slight smile, staring at the flame of a candle on the kitchen table. *Wait*—Sandy was taken aback. There was a lit candle in her home! Sandy had never seen her mother light one before. They only ever used artificial light. This natural flicker of light, though small, seemed to break through more than its usual assignment of darkness. It warmed the room with the same sense of hope Sandy felt in her chest. Sandy sat down at the table and their faces together glowed in the light of this small flame.

After a period of peaceful silence, Sandy's mother said, "I'm glad you went to the Shores. Everyone needs to get out of here once in a while. There's just something about that ocean that has always called me...Good night, dear." Then she got up, put her cup in the sink, and headed to bed without another word.

Sandy remained and stared. She stared at the burning flame and held the vial of salty water at her heart. What a day. What began as a restless adventure led her back to this familiar place in the Wastelands. Yet something within her was changed. She had rejected the invitation of the mysterious man on the Shores, but he had given her hope. And now she knew her need of it, and was being comforted by it. *"And hope does not disappoint us..."* These words of Jasper floated through her thoughts. On that note, she climbed the stairs in search of rest. She was ready for sleep and closure to this day. There was too much to process right now. And perhaps, just maybe, she would dream.

the hope in vital changed the atmosphere. even Sandy Mom got a pinch of it

7

A Surprise Encounter

Sandy slept in late the next day. There was no reason to rise early. It was the second day of the weekend, and though Sandy was usually at BIG'S serving her weekend shift by now, she ignored her current quandary of unemployment—through sleep. She was asleep in the Wastelands again, and did not wish to be awakened.

Strange music layered with loud speech seeped through Sandy's cracked window. "What's behind the door to *YOUR* future? Only *YOU* can tell…but *WE* have a *KEY* to that door…at The University of *EXCESS!*" The advertisements of the intercom cared nothing for her wishes for rest. Sandy peeled one eye open, but could not manage to lift her heavy head from her bed."Visit *US* at the University of Excess…Your *FUTURE* can't *WAIT!*"

Future… This was the one word to rouse Sandy from full slumber. It was something she must think about. Sandy swung her bare feet around to dangle off the side of her bed. As her hands clenched the mattress edge, she stared down at these feet of hers. Just the day before they were quick to carry her off to adventure. At the end of that day, they had led her back here, right where she had started. Where would they take her today? She stared at them as if they would answer, but they could not tell her a thing.

UHH! I'm crazy. Sandy set her feet down and dismissed her expectation of them. *She* must determine where they would take *hope is awaken in her so now she doung one never notice by.*

her, and some decisions would have to be made—and soon.

As Sandy began her morning routine, she felt the conflict of calm and confusion begin to battle within. It was as if she could hear the sound of waves crashing as the soundtrack of her mind, but alarming questions about her future and quest for success blared loudly too, vying for attention.

She faced the mirror. Her squinted eyes softened as she noticed her sun-kissed skin from her day at the Shores. Her usual fair skin had color. It wasn't burned, it just looked alive. Her cheeks were pleasantly rosy and shoulders and chest were slightly tanned. She sort of looked *pretty,* in her own eyes, instead of plain. This surprise had Sandy looking at herself in the mirror longer than usual. It was nice to be pleasantly surprised by her own appearance for once. She normally only glanced at herself briefly, only long enough to pull her limp hair back into a quick messy bun and scrub her face. Today, she smiled back at her own reflection. The Shores had improved her, at least for this fading moment, she thought.

"Sandy?" Her mother called as she lightly knocked on the bathroom door. "Pride came by. He dropped a note for you. He wanted to see you, but I didn't want to wake you up. There's a message from him. I'll leave it by the door."

Her mother did not wait for a reply. It was a good thing too, for Sandy had none to give. She was silenced by Pride's advancement. It wasn't like him to make the first move after a falling out of any kind. What did he want? Perhaps he wanted to rub some piece of news about *his* future in her face? Sandy was still staring at herself in the mirror's eyes, searching for the reaction she should give. After another moment or two of hard staring, Sandy pushed off of the sink that she had been grasping with both hands and released herself from this puzzled gaze. "I guess I'll just take a look at what he wrote," she determined aloud, then opened the door and grabbed the note.

"Sandy—Meet me at our spot, The Hot Shot Café, before my shift. I have tales to tell! –Pride"

Who does he think he is? Sandy's own pride rose instantly on reading his summons. *He just assumes I'll come running.* But Sandy was curious, and was even surprised he came around in just a few short days. The longer she thought about it, the less sure she was of Pride's intention, but she decided to meet him anyway. Giving into Pride in her life was typical. There was just something about his way that was hard to refuse.

Sandy finished getting as ready as she could for an encounter with Pride. As she swung her front gate open, she breathed in deeply and held it, puffing out her chest to prepare herself in posture for this appointment. She did not want to appear weak, for Pride would run all over her. She must be strong, not like yesterday when she crumbled on those shores.

No. No thoughts of the Shores today. Sandy would use this walk to the train and ride into the city to re-focus her mind on her future. She had a lot to figure out after the mess she had made just a few days before. This walk would be good. She hoped to derive some direction as her feet carried her towards Excess. She mentally focused on her goals as her physical gait increased. Sandy started to formulate her plan.

"Sandy? Sandy, is that you?" Two old schoolmates were headed her way, breaking her stride and concentration. They were Worry and Doubt. Worry was a small-framed young woman with poor posture who looked much older than she actually was. She was always bent over, looking down at her hands, which were in the constant habit of nervously rubbing themselves. She had been dating Doubt for as long as Sandy could remember. He stood upright with a dissatisfied look of disgust as his ever-ready expression. Sandy could not avoid them, as they were now right before her.

"Worry! Doubt! I haven't seen you two in a while. How have you been?"

Worry had never been one to hesitate expressing her true feelings. "Oh, ok, I guess…considering the state of affairs here in the outskirts of the Wastelands. The smog is really getting thicker, you know, and I fear our health is at risk! It's getting scarier to even BREATHE out here everyday!" Worry coughed while Sandy tried to comfort her.

"I know the smog has increased, but I hear we are going to be annexed into Excess soon, and then the Mayor should take care of regulating all of that. Everything should be fine, Worry."

"Yeah, right!" Doubt rebutted. "They are *never* going to annex us into Excess. That's all hype. We're not good enough for the 'beautiful people' in there."

Sandy was agitated by Doubt's suggestion."What do you mean? Of course we're going to be part of Excess."

Doubt scoffed. "Really? They've been talking about the annex since we were kids, Sandy, and you still believe them? They broadcast all this propaganda out here, just so we buy their goods and attempt to be one of them. But we'll never be part of 'them,' Sandy, no matter how hard we try. And if you think you can be, you're living in a dream world!"

Sandy was paralyzed for a moment before recovering with an appropriate reaction. She would not be mocked in this way. "Well, maybe we can't wait for them to make us a part of them. Maybe *we* have to go in and make a success of ourselves!" Sandy was proud of this comeback and awaited her rival's admission of her valid point.

"Go into Excess and make a success of ourselves?" Worry interrupted, "Why, people like *us* would get stomped on and *flattened* by those city dwellers. They don't stop for anyone, and would surely run you over rather than let someone like *you* rise to the top! It's just not *safe* in Excess! Better to deal with the smog of the Wastelands."

Sandy's proud posture deflated as she paused and considered Worry's warning. Was the suffocating air of the Wastelands better than risking the fierce ambitions of the citizens of Excess? Did she have the stamina for such a race?

"Well, I'm headed there now," Sandy said. "I know I'm made for more than this. You stay out here if you want, but I want a better life for myself and I'm going to make it happen. See you around—perhaps." Sandy started off, not waiting for a response, though one followed after her.

"Yes, we will see you again, Sandy! I'm sure of it!" Sandy tried to dodge the dagger that Doubt's declaration was, but it pierced her thin skin nonetheless. She made no response, and headed for the train station, looking neither right nor left. If she was going to make it in Excess, she needed to get used to not looking directly into the eyes of others. Considering them could slow her down in her pursuits. She must focus in on her own needs and desires.

Sandy boarded the train, and sat up straight. She would not relax. She would be face to face with Pride soon, and had to have some sort of plan in place to refer to in case Pride questioned her. Sandy started to work through the possibilities. More schooling… Big companies to apply for employment in…Perhaps starting her own business…But what did she really want to *do* besides be a success?

Sandy did not know and examined each possibility in her mind while staring straight ahead. At one certain curve in the track, Sandy was thrust back by her memory of a few days earlier when a man in a purple hat appeared outside her train window at just that spot. *The man in the purple hat! Who was he?* She had forgotten to ask Jasper about him! His voice was so similar to Jasper's, especially in the way he called her name, but his look was different. He was more earthy than Jasper, yet still of another world. And he must be from another world, for he called her

"Princess." Who was he, and where was he now? Sandy looked out of the window for just a few seconds to search the street outside. No sign of him now. Good. She could not afford the interruption. Back to her plans for her future—her future here in this city. She would make and live her life in *this* world.

The train stopped. Sandy departed and headed straight for her meeting with Pride. She approached her familiar potion stand, but knew she would be drinking something with Pride soon. She could wait, though a potion might give her the courage she needed to engage her challenging friend.

"I'll have one of your shots of the day." The order popped out of Sandy's mouth as she passed the stand before reason could refrain her. Sandy downed the potion, disposed of the evidence, and headed off more briskly towards the Hot Shot Café.

When Sandy arrived and entered the café, Pride was already waiting for her. "Well there she is! She returns to the big city after all!" Pride always had to make a demeaning joke of some kind to break the tension of their tiffs.

"Hello, Pride," Sandy simply said. He could sense the lack of enthusiasm in her cool response.

"Well, you look…good. Got some color! Where've you been since your big exit a few days ago?" Pride had to be in the *know* of all details of the lives of those he had a close grip on.

"I went to the Shores with Restless. Just for the day," she dryly replied.

"I see—with Restless, huh? Well, I want to hear more about that later. But I have some things I must tell you before I head on to work—some things which could affect your future."

There was that word again—*future.* What did Pride have to contribute to *her* future?

"You know, you left us in quite a tizzy the day you walked out. I had to take on all of the customers myself, and I *did* do a spectacular job, I must say. Something just rose up within me and

I worked my magic! I think everyone was enthralled with what a fine job I did, juggling ALL of those tables!"

"I'm sure you did great. And I'm sorry I left you like that."

"No, no!" Pride interrupted. "Sandy, it was the *best* thing that could have happened! Well, for me, that is. I took *such* good care of Mr. Success that day that he actually took notice of me, and asked me where I felt my future was headed. I told him I was really an actor, just working hard till my big break. 'Big break?' he repeated, then told me of a few successful theatres he owned in the city, and that maybe I should audition there. I *think* he was going to put in a good word for me. I got that feeling!"

Pride barely paused to breathe before adding, "Then I heard from the hostess that she overheard Mr. Success say something to the Mayor's daughter about being *impressed* with me, who said something to Mr. Big, who said something to *me!* Mr. Big himself told me that Mr. Success commented on what a fine job I did! Can you believe that?" He almost paused long enough for her to respond, but then continued, "Mr. Big patted me on the back, told me 'Good job!' and even said, 'I hope you make it BIG one day, son!' He *said* that—Mr. Big!"

Still, there was no room for reaction.

"So you see, I just had to thank you, Sandy. You walking out made me look really good. Well, actually *I* made myself look good, but you paved the way!"

"Gee, I don't know what to say, Pride. You're welcome?"

"Well there's something in it for you too, Sandy. If I get an acting job in one of Mr. Success's theatres, I think Mr. Big might hire you back. I could talk him into it. He listens to me now, and I can make you look good—come up with a reason you freaked out on us last week. He may be desperate enough to want you back. I just wanted to assure you I'd do my part to help an old friend out!"

"Gee. I don't know what to say *again*, Pride...Thank you?"

Pride flippantly laughed, not able to detect her sarcasm in his self-absorbed state. "You are SO welcome! Now, I must be getting on to my shift. I'll mention something about you to Mr. Big—feel him out on the subject of you working there again, and try to put in a good word. And I'll let you know what happens with Mr. Success! Next time he comes in I'm going to ask him about putting a good word in for me at the theatre. I'm expecting big things to happen for me any moment! Just had to tell my bestie, Sandy!" If this was what "besties" were, Sandy wasn't sure she wanted one anymore.

"Ta-ta, Sandy," Pride flourished a high wave of his hand while he headed out of the bell-chiming door. He did not wait for another reply, but left Sandy to ponder his glory and her shame. Why had she walked out? Why had she responded to that call? It only led her back to this place, and actually set her back in her destiny of success.

Sandy remained. She stared out at the weekend streets of Excess from behind the glass of her window seat table. Sandy caught her sad reflection staring back at her. She could not see the color she found in her reflection this morning. Were the signs of the Shores fading so fast? Announcements from the city intercom interrupted this stream of thinking. Plenty of advertisements for great companies and businesses of Excess played. She should be thrilled by the thought of working for any of these, but her attention drifted as her eyes began an involuntary search of the streets, hoping to see a purple hat pass by...

As she peered through the window against possibility, a bright glimmer captivated her focus. It was the smile of the perfectly tall and handsome Mr. Success. He was right in front of her, on the other side of the glass, talking to someone who had stopped him outside. Sandy wanted to disappear. She sank down in her chair. This did nothing to hide her. She was perfectly placed in his sightline, and though she could have simply looked down to avoid him, she could not help but stare at him. Now she wished she had mustered the strength to look away, for he did the unthinkable. He returned her gaze. The blush of embarrassment compounded her sun-kissed skin color, and she could feel her face grow hot. Sandy looked down and grabbed her mug, hoping to hide her face in it. She could no longer engage his stare. A moment later, the shop's door chimes alerted her heart to increase its pace. Mr. Success had entered. Before she could construct a façade to portray herself in any kind of suitable manner, Success presented himself to her.

"Well hello there, miss." Mr. Success stood directly in front of Sandy's table. He did not hesitate in continuing his address. "I couldn't help but notice you from beyond that glass. I remember you."

Sandy was dumbfounded. "You do?" were the only two words she could find.

"I do. *You* were my waitress at BIG'S."

Sandy looked up. Mr. Success and his striking looks entranced her. After an awkward moment of staring she remembered to answer honestly, "I was." Again, only two words were retrieved for response.

"Well you left before I could leave you a tip, my dear!" Mr. Success cocked his head and cracked a sideways smirk at her.

Sandy's eyes grew as her mouth opened involuntarily. "Tip?" Only one word rolled out this time.

Mr. Success cocked his head back now, but never shifted his gaze. "Yes, your tip. I don't expect to be served without paying for it. Hard work mandates compensation. But I recall you left before I was able to pay. So I will give you your tip right now."

Mr. Success reached into his inside coat pocket. This movement panicked Sandy into a mode of greater response. She protested, "Mr. Success! You didn't tip me because I didn't finish my job. I left. I was overwhelmed and overcome by my circumstances, which you had nothing to do with, and yet I left you! I left you and your table and caused quite a scene, I am sure, and much embarrassment to my boss, Mr. Big, for which I mean to apologize. The fact that I should walk out and leave a fine man such as you—the finest in our city, most likely—without proper service is incomprehensible and therefore merits *no* tip! I can only apologize sincerely and wish I could reverse time itself and serve you appropriately, in the way you deserve!"

He paused. Still he never removed his eyes from her, though he squinted a little before replying, "I have *more* than a tip for you." Mr. Success reached into a lower pocket inside of his jacket. "I have a *future* for you." He pulled out an oversized black plastic business card. In the center there was a brilliant picture of Mr. Success with a quote beneath it that was embossed in gold: "YOU plus SUCCESS equals EXCESS."

A simple formula, it seemed, which struck Sandy as true. Without Mr. Success's business opportunities and influence on the people of this city, Excess would not be what it was, a city of so much stuff.

"You look like a girl who desires success and all it has to offer, am I right?" Mr. Success squinted and cast a confident sideways glance at her, along with that knowing, alluring smile.

"Yes. Yes I do. It's all I dream about." As soon as the words left her lips, Sandy's heart panged, alerting her memory of the lie this was. She dreamed of things far greater.

"THAT'S what I'm looking for! A girl who knows what she's after." Mr. Success's pitch gave Sandy no time to hear her heart out. "Listen to me. The greatest success can follow failure. Not that *I* follow failure, mind you," Mr. Success chuckled, "but *your* success can come from fighting after failure. Are you willing to *fight* for success? To do *whatever* it takes? To give your *all* for the prize?"

What could Sandy do but cry, "Yes! Of course!" She had been

hypnotized by his charismatic words.

"Good, because I see something in you, and I'd like to give you a chance. I know a winner when I see one. You have potential. You just need the right opportunity and you will soar into success! I can see it!"

What? She wondered what he saw in her. How could he see anything but what a fool she had been at BIG'S? It was as if he could read her mind.

"Don't doubt the power of you! Anyone who can walk out can walk back in. It's time for you to walk back in, but not into BIG'S—into something 'bigger'!" Then Mr. success flipped his card between his fingers as a magician performing tricks might do, and presented it to her by snapping it down on the table. "Come to the address on that card, first thing tomorrow. There are positions available in my companies and I would like you to be part of my team. Together we will build Excess up all the more, proving who we are—people of SUCCESS!"

That was it. Sandy was drawn in. He had captured her. She was under his spell. Her imagination was sparked with visions of her own success. Then inwardly she chuckled at the wonder of what Pride would think. He had just missed this chance meeting with Success! Something they both had been striving for—Pride even more so! Now Sandy was being offered a position of sorts it seemed from Mr. Success himself! How could this even be a possibility after her grave mistake a few days earlier?

"Thank you! Thank you, Mr. Success. I will come by."

"My staff will expect you tomorrow, first thing! They will know what positions are available. I'm sure there will be one perfectly suited for you." He started to leave, then turned back. "I see tremendous potential in you, Sandy. Your name *is* Sandy, am I right?"

How did he know my name? Sandy grew even more amazed and enamored with Success as she thought this. "Yes. Yes, I am

Sandy," she answered.

That grin flashed again. "You know, 'sand' is what glass is made from, and glass is a substance I love! I like to see through people. I like to see what's inside. And I see greatness inside of you, Sandy! In the right environment, you could *be* that glass and all will see your greatness! You are going to do grand, successful things to make this city of Excess even grander. You are going to add so much to this world of ours—I just know it!" With a wink, he turned and was out of the Hot Shot Café.

Sandy could not move. Her mind was reeling. Mr. Success saw something in her and he was willing to help her be all she could be—clear and lovely—like glass.

Sandy grabbed her heart in elation. There, her hand found the vial—the vial of hope given to her the day before. Her elation subsided for just a second as her heart panged again in a subtle attempt to warn her. But Sandy ignored any flag of warning, dropped her hands to the table and carefully held this black shiny invitation before her eyes. A smile crept across her face as she took in the image and words on the card. Success himself bid her to come and join him in the dream of making Excess even more excessive! She had no idea what part she would play, but could not wait to find out, and begin—tomorrow! Sandy placed this golden ticket, this key to her future, in her purse's inner zipped pouch for safe keeping then rose to head home. She paused by her table in the Hot Shot Café, full of pride herself now. It felt good to her. She confidently shoved in her chair and, with head held high, pushed through the café door as its bells chimed a cheer of victory on her exit.

Sandy breathed in the air of the city she craved just outside of the café. She glanced over the sidewalks and streets to her right and left before proceeding. No thoughts of the man in the purple hat, nor of the one who gave her the vial still by her heart to distract her now. Sandy felt stronger than ever with this promise of success and new life in Excess. Weak, dependent, drifting Sandy would be no more. "Unstable Sandy" would soon be transformed into solid glass! She could not wait for her new life to begin. It would be hard to sleep tonight with the wonders of tomorrow whirling in her mind. Sandy briskly embarked on this temporary return to her home on the outskirts. The city seemed more her home already, and tomorrow she would do whatever it took to make her future the one she dreamed to live.

As Sandy settled into bed, she grabbed her journal to make a record of the surprise encounter today had offered. What began as a day she did not wish to wake to, ended as one she could not have invented. She had run-ins with Worry, Doubt, and Pride, but felt she had won out in the end. Success was calling her name! Sandy's future seemed more certain than ever.

She opened her journal eagerly to record these victories. A postcard fell out. The invitation to the Shores dropped to the ground, and her heart fell along with it. Sandy gasped and grabbed at her chest, finding within her fingers the vial. Again her heart throbbed, followed by frustration which flooded her entire being. *Why? What is wrong with me? Why do I even care about this?* Sandy picked up the postcard and shoved it in her journal, then slammed it down on her bedside table.

She made no record that night. Instead, she shut off the light and lay on her back, staring up at the gray ceiling of her room. All was quiet in the Wastelands, but not in the soul of Sandy. A wrestle waged within her. Two invitations had been given, and they pulled on her confused and divided heart. She battled her heart's suitors for hours into the night, until a truce was made with her conscious state when Sandy began to dream…

8

New Beginnings

*S*andy stood before the towering steel structure with her head tilted back and sideways, squinting to find the top of it. Her trip into the city had been uneventful, but now her heart pounded in her chest, facing the headquarters of Mr. Success's enterprises in Excess. The longer she stared, the more it seemed like the tower was moving, bending over her as if it were going to envelop her. What a strange thought. She dismissed it immediately.

She was on time, early in fact, so she took another moment to breathe in deeply and reflect on her journey there. Sandy could not deny being nervous, but was flooded with pride at the same time. "I made it!" she commended herself out loud. "I am here! I will be working for Mr. Success now. I did it!" This pride inflated her, and she did not feel as small as she had a moment ago. Sandy retrieved her access card from the day before and proceeded inside.

The lobby was spacious and surprisingly empty. It was wide with a wall of many doors opposite the entrance. The only furnishing was one long reception desk positioned in front of the wall in the middle of the lobby space. It had a sterile feel that was puzzling to Sandy. A few focused people passed through the lobby, carrying clipboards loaded with stacks of paper. These apparent employees would not look up. Each flipped through and studied their clip-boarded papers until they disappeared through the door they seemed assigned to enter. Every step of these workers echoed loudly in this hollow space. Sandy's heart felt each echoed thud. She wondered if she had come to the right place.

Just then the center door on the wall opened and a slight woman with curly blonde hair in a dark fitted dress suit approached the receptionist desk. Her bright red lipstick formed no smile but held a pursed shape as she fiddled with buttons on her desk. With one final push, loud music and words of the city's intercom filled the lobby, and the woman sat down, now catching Sandy in her sights. A red smile broke through widely with a sugary tone to match. "Good morning! Welcome to Success Headquarters, where YOU plus SUCCESS equals EXCESS! May I help you?"

Sandy pressed through her hesitation and proceeded towards the desk. "I'm...I'm Sandy." She was already upset with herself for stuttering in her lack of confidence. Then she remembered the card. This strengthened her. "Mr. Success invited me here." Sandy presented her card to the receptionist, proving her right to be there.

"I...I see." Was she mocking Sandy's stutter? The red-lipped woman looked up, then placed a pair of thick, shiny black-framed glasses on her face and studied this girl from the Wastelands. Sandy determined not to look away and stared straight back into the dark eyes of the woman inspecting her. After the inspection was complete, the woman glanced down into a book on her desk, winced, then looked up, broadening her countenance with a wide smile once again. She consented, "Of course—Sandy! This is your first day. Welcome!"

Before Sandy could reply, the door on the far left side of the lobby wall flung open. The receptionist rose and referred to the door as her right hand swept in its direction, "Step wrong this way."

Sandy didn't move. "Did you say, 'Step wrong this way?'"

The receptionist caught and covered whatever her true feelings might have been with a giggle. "Of course not! RIGHT this way, my dear—right this way!"

The receptionist led the way and Sandy followed in step behind her. As Sandy passed through the door, she caught the chant of Mayor Striver that was piped into the lobby. "Go! Go! Go! Do! Do! Do! Get! Get! Get...and you'll never escape, Sandy!"

Sandy was through the door by the time this last statement was made. As she jerked her head towards the lobby in response to these words, the door slammed shut. When she turned her attention back, the receptionist had disappeared. Sandy was alone in a small room with only a desk and a light bulb dangling above her. There was a door on the other side of this desk, and another to her right as well. The only other item in this room was an old metal speaker mounted in the left corner by the ceiling. Sandy felt a little uneasy now. She sat down to prepare herself. "Ok," she started. "Be patient! It will all make sense soon."

The door to her right opened. Through it entered a short, thick, balding man wearing a short-sleeved white dress shirt with a short, wide tie to match. His head was bent down over his clipboard, causing him to continually shove his brown plastic glasses up the bridge of his nose. "Sandy. Sandy, right?" He finally looked up, but did not wait for an answer. "I'm Rush, your trainer, and we have to get you in there, on the job, ASAP." Sandy opened her mouth to ask about her new job, but before she could, he interrupted. "These are the papers you need to fill out. You don't really need to read them all, just sign your name by the X's. They basically release us of responsibility for you and make you liable for yourself—stuff like that. Just sign them all and I'll be back in a minute to explain what you are going to do today. I gotta get to the next room." He exited through the right door again.

Sandy was left with the clipboard, thick with paper. She reached for the pen, but it felt heavy to her. She could barely lift it. As she tried, a loud crackling noise came through the speaker, followed by a familiar voice...

"So THIS is what you've been waiting for? THIS is what you've been hoping for—a cramped up room with a stack of paperwork to fill out? THIS is your DREAM??" It was the voice of Disappointment. How did SHE get to speak over the intercom in here?

"I TOLD you that you shouldn't come here! I TOLD you it was all propaganda! I TOLD you it was all a DREAM world...I told you! I told you! I TOLD you!" Doubt resounded over the intercom as an unwelcomed intruder of her thoughts...

"Oh Sandy! Don't sign those papers! They'll walk all over you! Just like I said!" Worry's words rang out as well...

"Sign them, Sandy! Sign them! This is what you were MADE for! This is ALL there is and YOU will make the best of it! You were BORN for Success!" Pride's voice was the only comfort to her now. "Oh, and get me a job there too...don't forget to put in a good word for me," Pride added. He never missed an opportunity to look out for himself.

"Sandy! You don't want to stay there. It's stuffy in there! Get out while you can..." Restless broke through.

"You'll regret signing your life away!" Disappointment was beginning to make sense now.

"You probably can't even do what they're going to ask you to do. What skills do you have to be successful?" Doubt debated.

"Oh, Sandy! They'll STOMP all over you," Worry warned again.

Sandy was paralyzed by the tension in this barrage of thoughts. The right door swung open again.

"Did you sign them?" Rush inquired, looking into Sandy's face only when there was no reply.

"No. I couldn't. I...I need to know what I'm getting into first. I need to know what the job entails," Sandy insisted. He was visibly irritated, but consented to her request nonetheless.

"Ok, Ok. Mr. Success doesn't usually refer any "questioners" to me—this is a first—but OK. I'll explain—but quickly! We have to get to work!"

Rush pulled out a pair of dark goggles and handed them to Sandy. "Put these on before we pass through this door. They will protect your vision. And stick the attached ear buds into your ears. Whatever you do, do NOT take them off, especially since you haven't signed the papers yet. Put them on and follow me."

Sandy did as instructed and followed Rush through the door opposite the one she had entered. This door's threshold served as a portal, for as Sandy stepped through, she appeared to be in another world. Sandy was awestruck at what she saw. Beautiful outdoor scenes surrounded her. To her right was a tree-lined path that disappeared into sheltering woods, alive with chirping birds and other signs of friendly animal life. Beyond the path was a grand purple mountain that ascended into lit puffy clouds overhead. To her left was a clear stream that babbled over mossy boulders. In the distance, the stream dove over a ledge, forming a cascading waterfall that descended out of her sight. There was another natural pool of water straight ahead and plush, grassy land lining its edge in front of her. The mix of scenic terrains was unreal. They each appeared perfect. She had never experienced such stunning visual variety it in her life. It was particularly shocking to observe such sights in the capital city of the Wastelands.

"Where ARE we?" Sandy asked again.

"At work," Rush curtly replied. This is where you are going to work. Now pick a terrain, and that will determine your job. Do you want to walk, climb, run, or dive?"

"You mean all I have to do is move? In one of these beautiful

places? Are you for real?" Sandy was almost giddy with shock.

"Yep! Pretty much! Pick your poison...I mean, PASSION!" Rush caught himself. *"What do you like to do?"*

"I guess I'd like to start on the path. I'd love to see where it goes," Sandy answered in hopeful wonder.

Rush chuckled, then cleared his throat to cover. *"OK. Yes. Path-walking it will be."* He flipped through his clipboard and scribbled something down. *"OK, now let's go back and sign those papers."*

"Wait. Can I try it? Can I just go over there and try it first? See where it goes? I might want to change my mind," Sandy anxiously asked.

"No! No, you may not 'try it.' This is a job and you're lucky to have it. Now come sign the papers. THEN you can 'try it' for your whole shift! Time is ticking and we have production quotas to meet!" In his impatience, Rush let this information slip.

"Production quotas? What will me walking on a path possibly produce?" Sandy found the whole situation perplexing.

"Just come with me! Do you want this job or not?" Rush threatened her.

"I do...but I just want to see..."

"You just want to see what? There is nothing to see but THIS! Beauty all around you, all the time." Rush was sounding sarcastic now. He grabbed Sandy's arm. She tried to pull away.

"I don't like the way you are treating me!" As Sandy jerked her arm again in a swift movement, Rush let her go and she fell back onto what she thought was green grass. It was not. It was concrete. The hard fall shook the goggles from her face, and to her shock, an unexpected scene was exposed. It was not the landscape she had seen through the lenses of those goggles placed on her. Instead, she saw nothing but hundreds of people robotically moving on industrial conveyer belts. They were running, climbing, and moving as fast as they could, but never "went" anywhere. They

80

were on machines, like treadmills, held in place by an intricate pulley system of steel ropes and piping. And they all had goggles on, and were being pushed somehow to strive and press harder and harder.

"What IS this?" Sandy asked in a horrified whisper.

Rush was enraged. "Now you've done it! See what you've done! You were not supposed to see this! You DIDN'T sign the papers! You could ruin EVERYTHING in EXCESS!! We can't let you go!"

Rush's words and way alarmed Sandy. She shuffled back and found her footing. She got up and started for a door marked "exit." Rush ran after her. Her limbs felt heavy. She could barely lift her feet. She was getting warm. It was growing hotter and hotter in this place. She tried to run, but everything slowed around and within her as the building heated up. She looked behind to see Rush moving in slow motion too. He mockingly laughed and continued to chase after her. Her body was stiffening now. The hotter it grew, the stiffer she became. Finally she couldn't move at all. She could only hear the blare of the intercom chanting Mayor Striver's mantra, "Go! Go! Go! Do! Do! Do! Get! Get! Get! And LIVE!" Was this the life he was cheering about? The taunting laughter ensued and now the faces of Rush and the receptionist were in front of her. Sandy could not move anymore. She was frozen like a statue. A statue of…

"GLASS! You have turned to glass, 'SANDY,'" Rush jeered.

The receptionist added, "Yes! Now we can see what's inside of you! And do you know what we see? NOTHING! Nothing, Sandy! You have NOTHING in you! Nothing to give here at all!" The only cry she could make was a silent one within. In complete angst, Sandy's heart cried, "Save me! Someone, save me!"

Her heart was unheard by her adversaries, and the volume and intensity of their cackles increased. Her fate felt certain and

81

despair was settling into Sandy's empty core when suddenly, sobriety struck her accusers with the sound of a great roar. It was a thunderous roar that overpowered all other sounds in this place. It came from without. Sandy, though frozen, could see outside of a high window in the outer wall she faced. The roar silenced Rush and the receptionist as they turned their heads to this window to determine the source of this sound. A great wave of the sea rose outside, then crashed through the glass of the window and began to flood the building rapidly. Rush and the receptionist scurried to escape. The blinded people did not see the flood coming and continued on their treadmills until the powerful wave washed over them, ripping their goggles off to reveal their fateful reality. But Sandy welcomed the wave and willingly received her salvation from this false world. As it crashed over her glass-made skin, she was shattered—and woke up...

✳✳✳✳✳

Sandy woke up, but she was still frozen. It was the morning she was to report to Mr. Success's corporate headquarters to start her new job, and she had had this dream. She wiggled her toes, then her fingers. Good. She could move. Now to convince the rest of her body that it could and needed to move as well.

What a horrific dream. No. She would not consider it another moment. If she didn't think about it, she would quickly forget it, and that is exactly what she needed to do. Sandy popped out of bed, pushing all thoughts away besides how to look her best for her new beginning in Excess. This day would change her life forever.

The trip into Excess was uneventful, and soon Sandy was standing before a towering steel structure, with her head cocked back and sideways, squinting to see the top of it. She was facing the headquarters of Mr. Success's enterprises, and her heart pounded fast within her chest. The longer she stared, the more it seemed like the tower was moving, bending over her as if it were going to envelop her. A memory from her dream last night flashed before her. She extinguished it instantly.

She was on time, early in fact, and took just another moment to breathe in deeply and reflect on her journey here. Sandy could not deny being nervous, but was flooded with pride at the same time. "I made it!" she commended herself out loud. "I am here! I will be working for Mr. Success now. I did it!" This pride inflated her posture, and she did not feel as small as she had a moment ago, although she was irritated at the sensation she had felt this way before. Sandy retrieved the business card from within her purse and proceeded inside.

The lobby was spacious and surprisingly empty. Sandy's heart pounded. It looked exactly like the scene from her dream. It was a wide space with a wall of many doors opposite the entrance. The only furnishing was one long reception desk positioned in front of the wall of doors in the middle of the lobby space. It had an alarmingly sterile feel. The memory of her dream was becoming harder to subdue.

A few focused people passed through the lobby. They carried clipboards loaded with stacks of paper. These employees would not look up. Each flipped through and studied their clip-boarded papers until they disappeared through the door they seemed assigned to enter. Every step of these workers echoed loudly in this hollow space. Sandy's heart felt each echoed thud.

Just then the center door on the wall opened and a slight woman with curly blonde hair in a dark fitted dress suit approached the receptionist desk. Her bright red lipstick formed no smile but held a pursed shape as she fiddled with buttons on her desk. *No! This can't be*, thought Sandy, staring wide-eyed at the receptionist and her every move.

Loud music and words from the city's intercom filled the

lobby, and the woman sat down, catching Sandy in her sight. A red smile broke through widely with a sugary tone to match. "Good morning! Welcome to Success Headquarters, where YOU plus SUCCESS equals EXCESS! May I help you?" Sandy could not press through her hesitation. She stood frozen a good distance from the desk. The receptionist's silent stare finally provoked a response.

"I'm...I'm Sandy." She was upset with herself for stuttering in her state of shock. Then she remembered the card. She approached the receptionist and presented it. "Mr. Success invited me here. I was supposed to come."

"I...I see." She seemed to be mocking Sandy's stutter. The red-lipped woman looked up, then placed a pair of thick, shiny black-framed glasses on her face and studied the girl from the Wastelands. Sandy strained to keep herself from looking away and stared back into the dark eyes of the woman inspecting her. After the inspection was complete, the woman glanced down into a book on her desk, winced, then looked up, broadening her countenance with a wide smile once again. She consented, "Of course—Sandy! This is your first day. Welcome!"

Before Sandy could reply, the door on the far left side of the lobby wall flung open. The receptionist rose and referred to this door as her right hand swept in its direction, "Step..."

"Step *right* this way!" Sandy interrupted. "That's what you were going to say, right? Step *RIGHT* this way?"

The receptionist paused, attempting unsuccessfully to mask her disgust at being interrupted."Of course! Step *right* this way, dear...*right* this way!"

As the receptionist walked in what felt like slow motion towards the door, Sandy stood frozen. She could not follow. This place was exactly as it had appeared in her dream, and that door on the end could lead to the end of her. But what other choice did she have? She knew of no greater or easier path to success than being employed by Mr. Success himself, and he had invited her here…

The commands of Mayor Striver over the intercom screamed out in the lobby, diverting Sandy's attention. "Go! Go! Go! Do! Do! Do! Do! Get! Get! Get! And…"

"Live…" Sandy whispered. Then she trembled, "I can't live like this! I can't! I don't know what is happening, but I can't do this…" And before the receptionist even turned around to notice, Sandy was gone.

She darted out of Mr. Success's headquarters, unable to look behind her, and burst into sobs. She ducked and dashed through the congested streets of Excess. It was more crowded than she had ever remembered, with people and their *stuff* invading her every move. She found herself bumping into the citizens and their belongings at each turn in her frenzied state. It was as if the buildings were moving in on her too. Their embellishments scraped her skin and snagged her clothing as she navigated through the narrow spaces between them. The diverse noises of the city's clamor intensified and became deafening. She felt attacked just trying to move through this city enclosing all around her. She cried and cried, trying not to notice the judging stares of these proud citizens. Their looks suffocated her all the more. She just needed space! She needed to get somewhere she could breathe. She plodded on towards the only small park she knew of, weeping all the way. What a tumultuous day. It was supposed to be her big day—a "new beginning." But now her dream was in shambles. How could this be? Whose fault was this? What was happening to her life? Just yesterday she was on top of the world. Today her world had crashed, and she did not even know who to blame.

Sandy reached the park, and ran for a bench near the fountain. She intended to collapse on it until she could regain her composure. Instead, she collided with a man who caught her in his arms. As he did, a purple hat fell from his head.

Sandy saw the hat first, lying on the ground. Her sobs were silenced. He bent to pick up his hat with one hand while maintaining his grip on her with the other. As he rose and put his hat back on, she looked up into his weathered, welcoming face. He smiled in a way that only true citizens of the Kingdom can and said, "Princess! I finally caught you!"

Sandy was dumbfounded. It had been too traumatic of a day for games of any kind. She quickly found her words. "*Caught* me?" Sandy responded. "Who are you?" Her tears changed to anger now. "*Who are you?* Are you stalking me? How did you know to call me 'Princess'?" Sandy indignantly accused him, "You went through my mail, didn't you? Pride! Did Pride put you up to this? He's behind this, isn't he? He's always trying to make others feel dumb, especially me. Was it Pride? Tell me!"

"No," the man in the purple hat replied softly. "It was Jasper. Jasper sent me to call for you, and it has been my delight."

Jasper. Of course. "Who are you then?" she persisted. "And how do you know Jasper?"

"I am Page. And I come from another Kingdom—the Kingdom you are to be part of. I'm here to prepare the way for you. I am here to declare the Prince's love for you—to ask you again to come, to be a part of his Kingdom of Love, and to make you ready."

Sandy was speechless. Every word Page spoke hit heavy, like waves pounding over her mind and heart. She could barely breathe; her heart began beating rapidly. Page led her gently towards the bench. "Sit with me, will you, Princess?"

Sandy could not deny the comfort she felt from Page's kind manner. She relaxed a little as she consented to sit with him on the bench overlooking a small fountain in a very small park in the middle of Excess. As life busied all around them, they talked.

"Tell me about your dream," he inquired gently as he leaned in, looking Sandy in the eyes. She was warmed by his way, yet preferred to fix her gaze safely on the fountain before them.

"Well," she began, "I had this crazy dream last night, about going to work for Mr. Success, and it turned into a nightmare. And when I actually got up and came to work, it all started to come true! Everything happened just as it had in the dream. So I ran away. I left. I could not bear to re-live the rest of it. And now I'm realizing I blew my chances of success! I ruined my future!" Her emotions rose again. She paused to collect herself and give Page a chance to respond.

Page looked down briefly then tenderly replied, "Not *that* dream. The dream of your heart, Sandy."

Only the surge and splash of the fountain filled their ears for the next few moments as Sandy searched for a means to communicate with this man from another world. "That *was* my dream. It was my dream to work for Mr. Success and become successful—to become *somebody* in this world!"

"No. No, that may have been a dream of yours, but it is not the dream of your heart. You dream of *another* world, don't you, Princess?" He paused, but not long enough for her to answer, even if she could have. "I know, because I belong to that world, and it is the world you belong to as well. You just haven't seen it yet—well, except in your dream."

With that, Sandy remembered. She remembered this true dream of her heart from just a few nights ago—or had it been her dream for much longer? The dream of the place where light surrounded her, where peace and joy enveloped her, and where the greatest love of her life had enraptured her. She remembered, "My Prince..."

Page smiled. "Yes, your Prince. My friend. The Prince. He is the true dream of your heart. Oh, Sandy. If you can remember but a glimpse of that dream and hold it in your heart, and believe in its reality, it will guide you through this world and lead you into the next—to your Kingdom, where you will be with him forever—in love!"

Sandy's heart ached to understand better. She recalled this dream and considered the love in the eyes of the one she now knew as the Prince. And she remembered him referring to her father, the King. But she had no father. She knew no father in this world. Could she have one in another? She had so many questions. Sandy had always lived in *this* world and *for* this world—the world of Excess and Striver and *stuff.* Could she truly be made for another? She had found no success here. Could "success" be found in this other world? If what Page was saying was true, could he really lead her there? Did she have the strength to make it there? Could she even say "yes" to go?

"Page, how far away is it—this Kingdom?"

Page took her hand and held it palm-up before her. "Sandy, this Kingdom—the one you have dreamt of all your life—it is as close as your hand. It is within your reach." Then Page got down on his knee by the bench, removed his plumed purple hat and covered his heart with it. He extended his other strong hand to Sandy and asked, "Princess, will you come? Will you accept the Prince's invitation to join him in the Kingdom you were made for? The *real* life awaits. You need only say 'yes.'"

A sudden breeze blew by, a warm breeze that wrapped around and calmed Sandy, causing her anxiety to subside. Her heart still pounded, but more with anticipation. The bold beats were like knocks she had to answer, and she wanted to. Page's sturdy hand was still opened, beckoning her. She looked straight into his eyes, which flickered with fire. She searched his face, tan and weathered with the signs of someone who knew the shore waters well. There was intensity in his look—an invitation in his eyes that was just as real as each she had received thus far. Another gust of wind splashed over her, along with the sound of a low and inviting *roar*. With this last call, clarity came for Sandy, cloaked in an undeniable peace.

"Yes…Yes. Yes, I will go!" Her acceptance spilled out with a great sense of relief. Page was elated. He threw his head back and his hat in the air, then stood, pulling Sandy in for a hearty hug. A joy washed over her, and they both laughed.

"What *is* this? What am I feeling?" she asked, still laughing.

"Your 'yes' has unlocked the blessing of hope by your heart. It has flooded your heart with faith! Your belief in the Prince, your 'yes' to his invitation has made you a citizen of the Kingdom! You get to start all over—to begin again! And Sandy, the adventure starts now. I will show you the way."

To begin again—It was a gift she didn't even know she could receive. And yet, she had. And it felt good. There was a fresh feeling in her heart. Hope indeed had seeped in, sweeping out the doubt within. For the first time in her life, Sandy felt no resistance. "All right!" she exclaimed. And all *was* right. Then with a smile she turned to her new friend and guide. "Tell me, what happens next?"

Page's eyes twinkled, revealing his delight in the assignment ahead. "I'm taking you back to see Jasper. But first, there's a stop we must make, and you will never be the same again." Page winked with a nod, stooped down for his hat, then bowed to the princess before offering his arm to her.

A surge of nervous energy swelled within her for a moment, but Sandy did not let it overtake her. She had made up her mind. As scary as change might be, her hope in what she could discover won out at last. Without another question, Sandy linked her arm with Page's, and breathed in deeply. "Ok—let's go."

9

The Way of the River

Page did not take Sandy to the train station, nor did he aim for a paved road. Instead, with Sandy in tow, he crossed over the fountain's concrete edge, traipsed over a short stretch of grass, and steered Sandy towards the park's border of bushes and trees.

"Uh…where are we going? I don't think there is an exit over here," Sandy said, stating the obvious.

Page proceeded without hesitation and confidently responded, "The King always provides a way out."

And there it was. Just as they stepped directly before the hedge, Sandy spotted a heart-shaped hole, formed by the trunks of two close trees that had grown together within the hedge. There was just enough space to pass through it, one at a time. Page needled through first, then extended his hand back to thread Sandy through the slight opening and pulled her all the way out. What she saw shocked her. They were in the woods. There were woods right outside of the City of Excess. She had never known they existed.

"Woods! Trees! I've lived near here all my life and never knew…how did you know this was here?" Sandy asked.

"I live in these woods, my dear! I prefer the wilderness over the wilder city life of Excess," Page said. "There are many surprises in the terrain ahead for you, Princess. The adventure has just begun! Now come; I will lead you by route of my favorite way." Page took Sandy's hand again and they carefully made their way through the woods. "It's a bit of a trek to get there, but worth the effort!" Sandy had no idea what Page was referring to, but resolved to trust him. Trust was something new for someone as independent as herself.

"So," she started as they walked, "You said something back at the fountain I want to ask you about. You said that *real* life awaits. What did you mean by that?"

Page looked Sandy in the face with a friendly, understanding look and answered, "Yes. Real life. The Kingdom life. You are used to kingdoms only being in fairy tales. But this is not a fairy tale, Sandy, though it is a *great* story—your story with the Prince, and his story with you. And now that you choose to live this story, you can take your rightful place as Princess! But first, before you actually get there, there is much work to be done."

His words were mysterious, but resonated with her as truth. She questioned only one word. "Work?"

"Well, yes," Page laughed. "Work on *you! In* you, and *through* you! Not that you aren't perfectly pleasing to the King...you are! But there is some 'royal training' that must take place to prepare you to function fully as the princess you are! It's the work of 'becoming.'"

"Becoming..." Sandy liked this word. It held a happy hope in it.

"Your life is about to be transformed, Sandy," Page said in gentle seriousness. "Do you trust me? More importantly, will you trust yourself to the beautifying process of the Kingdom?"

Sandy had never considered herself beautiful before. Only after her day at the Shores with Jasper had she ever felt slightly pretty. To think she could be made ready for a prince! Her childhood dreams awoke within her. "Yes!" she said enthusiastically, surprising Page and even herself a little. "I've come this far.

Let's see what he can make of me."

Page bowed. "My lady, I cannot wait to see all that you become." Then he pointed toward a clearing in the woods, adding, "And your answer comes right on time, for we are here."

Sandy followed slightly behind Page's lead, peeking beyond him in an attempt to make out his surprise. She first caught the sound of its fresh rush before discerning what spread before her in the distance: a wide, wild, and rumbling river. Page faced the great force as he pulled Sandy up next to him. "This is my favorite place in the world. And this is where your great transformation begins."

Sandy gulped in fear. The face of Pride haunted her again as it had before when she faced the waters of the shores. "NOW look at what you've done!" she could hear Pride scolding her. "You committed to come here and you can barely swim! What are they going to think of you now, *Beautiful Princess?*"

"Wait." Sandy stopped. "I...I..."

"I've got you, Sandy. We've got you. No fear, my dear. There's a bridge down the riverbank a ways. It was built by a friend of mine who lives there that I want you to meet." Page was so kind and good in his way with her. He was not forceful or harsh, yet he would see that she progressed. He reminded her so much of Jasper.

Page led her carefully over and through the final vines and brush of the woods, and made sure her footing was steady as they started down the slope of the riverbank. To their left she could see it. A wooden bridge had been constructed to welcome visitors from the wooded side of the river to the other. Sandy squeezed Page's firm hand a little harder and walked with him over the water.

"You made it! I'm proud of you. You're growing braver, looking more like the kind of courageous Princess I'd like to see as a ruler." Sandy rolled her eyes at his encouragement of her baby steps. As if he could read her thoughts, he replied, "Despise not the day of small beginnings, Sandy. Every step counts!" She consented with a partial nod, and they completed their journey over the bridge and into the yard of a charming home overlooking the river.

The surrounding sights and sounds astounded her. It was all so beautiful. Everything seemed naturally wild, yet flawlessly designed. The white painted house with its red, tin roof was nestled in an explosive garden of wildflowers that shouted a cheery welcome to any who would take note of them. A path of large, flat, gray stones led around from the front wooden porch steps to an orchard of fruit trees and berry bushes to the left of the house. Behind the home to the right, a bountiful garden of ripening produce could be seen. It spread out wide and out of sight. To complete the inviting scene, a well-aged oak with a wood-plank swing hanging from its greatest lower branch stood at the yard's front right corner, extending its offer to come and sit a while. All of this visual loveliness was backed by the soundtrack of the ever-flowing river behind them. Sandy was indeed in another world.

"Pretty amazing place, huh?" Page stated with a contented grin as he took in the scene as well. Before Sandy could answer him, a figure popped up from the garden to the left of the house. A slender, middle-aged woman with tanned shoulders, wearing a broad straw hat stood upright now, with a bushel basket of berries cradled under her arm. She spotted the on-lookers and immediately beamed as broadly as her hat.

"Hellooo!" she called with an energetic wave. Then she squinted and leaned in. "Page? Page, is that you?"

Page laughed in reply. "Yes, it's me, Carry! And I brought another friend to meet you!"

As the woman approached, Sandy whispered, "Who is she? What is her name?"

"Her name is Caretaker. But I call her Carry. You will understand who she is as soon as you meet her."

"Page! I've missed you, my friend!" Before she reached him she halted and asked with widened eyes, "Is this your princess? Sandy?"

How does she know my name? Sandy wondered.

"Well, yes—Jasper's princess. And ours as well! I know she'll be a great leader in our Kingdom."

"I'm so delighted you are here, Sandy…May I call you that? For now anyway?" the woman asked kindly.

"Of course. That's my name,"Sandy responded with a growing curiosity, feeling there was more to know of the woman's request.

"I'm Caretaker, dear. But you can call me Carry, like Page does." Carry's eyes smiled at them both. She was confident, yet warm. Sandy was not used to meeting women like this at all.

"Carry tends to the river and many of its crops. So much can grow in the rich soil here," Page explained.

"Is that why they call you Caretaker? Because you take care of all this?" Sandy asked, taking in the beauty of growth all around her again.

"In part, but more so because I *take* the *cares* of others to the King, here by the river. It's what I love most."

Sandy was puzzled now. Page explained. "Carry is a great friend of the King. That is why I wanted you to meet her. She talks to him all the time. She talks to him about the cares of others and takes their needs to him. She is a great friend to all in the Kingdom because of her service in this way."

"Wait—you talk to the King? You actually talk to him? Is he here?" Sandy was visibly taken aback as she looked around.

Carry laughed and admitted, "Yes, I do! Every day, and all through the day. Why, I was just in my garden this morning talking to him about *you*, about you coming, and here you are!"

"About me coming? Well, I didn't know this morning myself that I'd be coming. I had no plans of coming here at all," Sandy informed her.

"That's exactly why I asked him to send you!" More mysterious talk continued to perplex Sandy.

"How…how do you speak to him? To the King?" Sandy wanted to know.

"Well, through the Prince of course—and Jasper. Wait. You *do* know that you can speak to him too, don't you, Sandy?" Carry asked.

"She just accepted his invitation today, Carry. She's a new citizen of the Kingdom," Page said. "I brought her here to learn from you on the way to meet Jasper again. I thought you could explain the communications system of the Kingdom to her, having so much experience in the field."

"Oh, yes! I would love to explain. Let's go have a walk down by the river." Carry led the way to the water's edge where a seating area had been prepared near a bend with a view of some rapids. They sat and gazed at the rush of the water as it passed them.

After a few moments of quietly reflecting on the river's leaps and turns, Carry equipped Sandy with the first tool she needed to build a strong and loving relationship with her Prince and the King. "Sandy, it is all meant to flow, like this river. Communication —never ending! It's the key to any healthy relationship, they say, and this is now the most important relationship of your new life. It may start like a trickle, but just talk! Talk to your Prince, share your heart, and the flow will increase till you never want to stop."

"Wait—so he can hear me? The Prince can hear me? Talking? How?"

Carry paused, wanting to convey this lesson well. "Sandy, your new world is so much greater than the world you are used to. The one you have come from is so limited. You spent all day with voices blaring at you. Those in charge never listened to you; they just wanted to shove information into you. You are not used to *talking* because you're not used to being heard. But as a citizen of this kingdom, your voice is valued. When you speak, you are heard—anytime, anywhere, even when you don't speak out loud. You are a daughter now, and you have a good father, the King himself! He wants you expressing matters of your heart to him. And he will grant the desires of your heart, if they are in your best interest. So much can be accomplished by just *talking* to him. It's amazing, isn't it?"

"What kind of things do you talk about?" Sandy asked, trying to process these new concepts.

"I continually express my love and appreciation to him, and I ask him for help when I need it and request help on behalf of others as well. I admit my willful wanderings to him and confess wrong ways I sometimes choose. I tell him about it all, and he makes things right within me. He has a way of clearing up matters of my heart and lightening my burdens. I talk to him in all of these ways, about all of these things."

Sandy could not imagine talking about much of this. She certainly had never admitted her *wrongs* to anyone. They just didn't do that in her family. It was the way of the Wastelands to protect oneself and make yourself look good, not admit to any wrong doing. Besides, Sandy didn't do anything that bad. She had lived a pretty good life. She didn't hurt people, she just tried to keep to herself and look out for herself.

"But what if...what if you haven't done anything wrong?" Sandy instantly felt she had asked the wrong question. Page and Carry were quiet. "I mean, I haven't done anything that bad," she continued. "I don't know what I'd say, if I had to talk about bad stuff I'd done."

Page spoke this time. "This is another reason I brought you here, Princess. Part of your beautification process is to get really clean—but from the inside out."

Carry leaned in. "We *all* have done wrong things. We all have acted in ways opposite of the King's ways. You are new to the Kingdom, so you may not know his heart on all matters, but his ways are always *right* and for our *good* and motivated in *love* for us."

Page continued her thought, "The world you have come from is not so right. It is full of wrong and harmful ways of doing things. People caught up in that world live for mostly for themselves. There is no place for that kind of living here, not in the Kingdom of Love."

Sandy thought for a moment, and saw the contrast. She had never committed any "crimes" or broken important laws in her world, but she had not lived for anyone but herself. Right then, Sandy realized her own selfishness, and in truth, how miserable she had been her whole life until she accepted Page's invitation. Her heart felt heavy at the realization that she had been completely caught up in the system of that other world, a world that was not like the Kingdom of Love at all.

"I have done wrong," Sandy acknowledged. "I've *lived* wrong. I've only been out for myself and what I could get out of life. I have had such little love, but you two have so much. I want to be like *you*. I want my life cleaned out and changed. But how, Page? How can I change, Carry? Will you ask him for me? What must I do?" Sandy was feeling desperate now.

"I'm so glad you came here today." Carry leaned in and touched Sandy on her knee. "Dear, let's talk to our King together, and then Page will see that you are all cleaned up. He knows exactly what to do."

For the next while, Caretaker led Sandy in taking all of her cares and burdens and wrongful ways to the King, simply by *talking*. She told him everything on her heart, admitted all her wrongdoing, and apologized for hurting his heart by not responding to his invitation sooner. And when all was confessed, Sandy sat back and smiled. A load had been lifted. Her weighty heart was now light—and full of light! The darkness of her old ways was exposed and chased away by simply talking to her King.

"Thank you. Thank you! I feel…as if I could fly! Who knew? Who knew saying those things would bring such…"

"Freedom?" Carry finished Sandy's thought for her. "Yes, freeing hearts is a tremendous part of what he does, and it comes in part by simply talking—but you'll learn more about that later."

"Yes, there is much to learn and more freedom to experience," Page interjected enthusiastically, having waited his turn, "but I have an assignment to complete with you now. I promised Jasper I would do my part in preparing you for him. And that includes a little trip into the river. Let's wash you up, Princess! We don't even want the slightest scent of the Wastelands on you. You are now clean on the inside. Let's make it complete on the outside as well!"

So she went. And with Page and Carry by her side, the old ways of Sandy were laid to rest in the rush of that river, and she came up clean of mind, heart and body.

"Oh! I'm alive!" Sandy exclaimed as she came up out of its reviving rapids. "I feel so alive!" And then she heard something.

"Princess…you are! And I am so pleased and delighted with you."

Sandy froze in the waters. "Did you hear that? Jasper? Is that you?" She searched all around, then asked her friends, "Did you hear that?"

Carry and Page smiled and both laughed. Then Carry responded, "No, but *you* did! I forgot to tell you—he talks back!" She smiled and placed her hand on Sandy's cheek, then smoothed the princess's wet hair back over her head, while looking her squarely and closely in the face. "You can hear *him* too!"

Page nodded and smiled when Sandy looked back at him. He

confirmed, "With a heart and mind clean and free of all that clogged it, you can hear him! It's true! And the longer you journey, the more clearly you will hear. Wonderful, his voice, isn't it?"

Sandy could do nothing but giggle and look up into the bright blue span of sky overhead. She squinted, surveying the rays of light beaming through layered puffs of white clouds. Words could not come now, not out loud for her friends. The knot in her throat stopped the surge of joy welling within her from flowing verbally. But inside, quietly, she responded to him, "Thank you. Thank you, my King. To know you are pleased with me, Father, is the greatest joy of my life. I *love* you."

Sandy bowed her head and wept. Her tears added to the flow of the great river, and cleansing sobs shook her body. It was a purging of her old life—a purge of the emotions of Excess, making space for whatever was in store.

When her weeping had washed away all it could for this day, Page and Carry reached for both of the Princess's hands and led her out. The three of them dried off on the bank of the river by a small fire pit Carry had made. They talked for several more hours into the evening, sharing stories of adventures with Kingdom friends and Jasper by this river. Sandy listened and laughed and learned much from her seasoned new friends.

When the night sky had completely settled in, Caretaker invited her guests to lodge with her. "Will you both stay? I have plenty of room, and it will be better for you to make a fresh start for the Shores in the morning." Page and Sandy agreed this would be best and made their way into her warm home by the river.

Carry checked on Sandy after she had settled into her guest room. "How are you, dear? Are you comfortable? Can I do anything for you?"

"I am more comfortable than I have ever been," Sandy replied. "I'm tired, but I just can't imagine going to sleep! So much has happened in one day—and to end up here, being cared for by someone like you, and loved by him, the King…" Sandy's mind raced with thoughts and questions about her new life and this new love she was experiencing. "Just tell me one more thing, Carry. Have you ever seen him?"

Carry sighed a sweet smile. "Seen him? My heart has. It knows him well. And I see him in his children, my brothers and sisters who come by this way to be refreshed in the river to get clean and revived. The closer we grow to him, the more we look like him. But someday we *will* see him." Her eyes sparkled as they filled with tears of longing. It was as if she could see something in the distance, yet right before and even within her at the same time. Sandy admired the mystery of this deep sister of hers. She knew Caretaker possessed a wonderful understanding of the King's ways, and she felt great gratitude for the post Carry held for so long. Sandy knew it was a place she could run to and would always be cared for in the most tender of ways.

"Goodnight, dear Princess. It's been my honor to be with you on such an important day. It's a day I'll never forget."

It was a day Sandy certainly could never forget either. Life as she knew it was changed *for good*. And tomorrow she would follow that river and return to those shores to discover so much more.

10

Return to the Shores

andy woke up the next morning to the mixed smells of a breakfast feast cooking. The scents swirled their way into her memory, reminding her of another little refuge by a body of water she had visited: the Cottage Café.

"The Cottage Café!" she cried aloud as she sat up in her cushioned cocoon. "The Shores! Today I return to the Shores!" With this, Sandy rolled out of bed and searched for her clothes. To her surprise, they had been replaced with new ones: a light, airy outfit that consisted of a long, linen tunic with an embroidered neckline and loose fitting linen trousers. The ensemble fit perfectly, and was not gray in color, but rather a blend of bright colors that made her feel happy, lovely, and even regal.

Sandy skipped down the stairs, still feeling light from the events of the day before. Carry was cooking in the kitchen while Page drank from a steaming mug, reading a book at the table. "Good morning!" Sandy said, waiting for them to notice her new look.

Carry turned, pan and spatula in hand, "Good—good morning!" She beamed. "You look lovelier than I even imagined. They fit you perfectly, don't they?"

Sandy spun, looking down at herself again and agreed. "They do! But how? Where? And *why* do I have these amazing new clothes? It's so much!"

"Well, we couldn't have our Princess clad in old gray garments, could we?" Carry responded. "Those old clothes were too thick and heavy anyway. You need light clothes for this new season you are in."

Page broke in, "Get used to it, Sandy! The blessings are only beginning."

Sandy hugged Carry in thanks, then bent to share a hug with Page as well. She was surprised at herself again. "Funny…I've never been much of a hugger before," she admitted.

"Get used to it, Sandy," Page broke in again. "It's all a new road now."

They conversed and ate together, a feast that broke the fast of the night. The meal felt like a celebration of friendship. Sandy had never felt this way at a table with friends before.

"What is this? What is this I'm feeling here now, at this table with you two?" Sandy stared down with a concerned look, trying to label and categorize each new experience she was having.

"This, my dear, is fellowship—true friendship with others who belong to the Kingdom. And there's nothing like it! It's one of the greatest benefits of Kingdom living," Carry said.

"Relationship is what the King values most. Friendship with him and friendship with others are the only two things that will really last beyond anything in this world," Page added. Sandy loved the thought of this, and knew she should remember it.

"And there are many, many other friends for you to meet. Some you will meet today even, on your way to the Shores. Some friends you will have your whole life through, and some will be for seasons. But your *best* friend…our best friend, Jasper….he will be there to stay." Sandy was comforted by Carry's portrayal of Jasper as her best friend. She knew she had not been a very good friend on their last meeting. She doubted him, dismissed him and never even thanked him for her gift. With that thought, she grabbed at her heart. *Good!* It was still there. The vial of hope remained at her neck. It had taken her very, very far indeed.

"Hope doesn't disappoint, does it?" Carry observed as she

noticed Sandy holding the vial.

"That's just what Jasper said to me," Sandy said in surprise.

"He is so great at giving hope! And he is always right. I'm sure he knew that hope would bring you right back to him!" Carry stood to clear the dishes, and tucking her chair in said, "Well, I wouldn't want you to disappoint him! You two had best be on your way!"

Sandy and Page stood as well and brought their final and fulfilling conversations to a close. Carry walked them to the door of her home overlooking the river, hugged them both and snuck one last gift in before they left. "I have a present for you, Sandy…"

"Oh, but you've done enough, sweet Carry," Sandy interrupted.

"You'd better let her give it to you, Sandy," Page advised. "You'll need to get good at receiving!"

"Listen to your friend," Carry added. "You are going to need this gift." Then Carry presented Sandy with a package, tied up in brown paper and twine. Sandy wanted to squeal. She hadn't been given a wrapped present in quite sometime. Only on her birthday did she sometimes receive such a treat. "Think of it like a birthday present," Carry offered, as if she knew what Sandy was thinking. "I mean, this is the beginning of your new life, you know?"

Sandy smiled and sighed, giving in to unwrapping the gift. It was a beautiful smooth leather bag with a wide flap that covered its front. It was simple but striking with a long, thick strap made of a tapestry of some kind. The tapestry was woven with a pattern of rich, bright colors, and threads of gold interlaced throughout. The bag was fairly large, but not too burdensome to carry. It fit over Sandy's shoulder and lay at her side perfectly.

"This is wonderful! I love it!" Sandy remarked as she ran her hand over the soft leather of the exquisitely crafted bag.

"It's a purse for your journey. There is much for you to receive—and much for you to give. This is a vessel to assist you with both. It's empty for now…Oh, except for this." Then Carry put a sack of snacks into her bag. "This should be enough to get you to the Shores. We can't have you fainting from weariness along the way!"

"I…I really don't know what to say…I…" Sandy lowered her head, trying to find the right words from her heart.

"A simple thank you will always do, Princess," Page coached. "She's just doing what caretakers do best!"

"That's right! Now, let me *care-take*…and YOU two *take care*. I shall see you again soon!"

Carry removed the purple hat hanging on the hook near the door and placed it on Page's head. He lifted it in a slight bow and gave her a wink. With that they were out of the door and off, turning to wave back to Carry a few times until she disappeared from their view.

Page and Sandy walked silently side by side. Sandy was deep in thought, enjoying the sounds and scenes of river life. Page broke the silence with a daring question. "Want to walk *on* the river?" Sandy looked over and saw a colony of large rocks and boulders protruding from the water and spreading out over it for quite a stretch. "We can jump rocks! It's fun." Page had the enthusiasm of a young boy about him. Sandy paused skeptically until Page offered his familiar hand again. "I've got you, Sandy." With that encouragement she hesitated no more, and grabbed the hand of this friend who had led her to this wide-open and thrilling place.

"I can't believe I'm here," she shouted, remembering where she had come from as she leaped from rock to rock. "I can't believe I'm doing this. This is WONDERFUL! Amazing! It makes me want to SING!"

"So, sing!" Page shouted back over the roar of the river. "I'll sing *with* you!" And so they did. Off they went, jumping and leaping and singing. Page taught her his favorite songs of the

Kingdom. They were new to Sandy and beautiful, filling her brimming heart all the more. She had to sing even louder to relieve her heart of the explosive joy she felt. It was quite the way to journey.

Soon the composition of the river changed again. They came upon a new stretch where the rocks receded and the water was calmer. Page helped Sandy back to the bank and up into the meadow it ran through. They traveled on, waving to and chatting with various folks along the way. There were farmers plowing their fields, women hanging laundry and watering flowers, children climbing trees and playing tag, and older folks sitting on porches, discussing matters of the Kingdom. Page described the lives of these faithful servants and children of the King, and how each did their part in stewarding what they had, fulfilling their individual assignments given them by the King.

"Why do they do it? What drives them?" Sandy asked, still operating somewhat in the residue of her old mindset.

"Sometimes their motives get mixed with that of their old lives, but the most faithful ones do it purely for the pleasure of the King. To please him is our aim. In that there is great reward!"

Sandy thought about this. "Will I get an assignment too?" Sandy was a hard worker and ambitious. She hoped to be productive and succeed in this new world.

"In time. You will get your assignment. Jasper will let you know, but first we must get you to him! He has so much more to teach you than I ever could. My assignment with you is nearly over."

This thought made Sandy sad. She had grown fond of Page. "You mean you are not going to stay with me? When I meet Jasper, you are going back? Without me?"

"Sandy," Page stopped and looked her straight in her drooping eyes, "I am your friend, and we may share other Kingdom adventures together. But I must always follow my assignment and listen to my great friend. I have almost delivered you to him, his beloved Princess, and that makes my joy very great and complete. But now, he must become greater to you and I must become less, so that you may be *one* as he wishes."

The river broadened and deepened as it moved towards the Lowlands. Sandy and Page came upon a dock, to which a raft was attached. "Ah! Just where I left it. We'll float on this raft the rest of the way. I'll get you to the mouth of the river, where you can easily find your way to the Shores." Sandy was not happy about leaving Page, but consented with a nod and boarded the raft. She wanted to sulk at the thought of losing her friend. She had never had one so kind and committed to her. But then she thought of Jasper, and all Page had said about him being his *great friend* and hers as well. She decided to dismiss any feeling that would take away from this glorious day and last moments with Page.

Sandy leaned back on her elbows and forearms on the flat, wooden raft with her face to the sun. Page whistled a Kingdom song as he rowed them down the smooth wide river. Sandy relaxed. The rhythm of the raft and gentle lapping of water against its sides lulled her into a satisfied state. She exhaled a happy, contented sigh. Then it occurred to her. "We should talk to the King!"

Page responded in agreement, "We should!"

So for the rest of their journey, these two friends of the river conversed with the King. They listed each and every blessing they could remember, and thanked him heartily. They talked about their relationship with Carry and asked him to bless her greatly for the blessing she had been. Sandy thanked him for sending Page to rescue her out of the Wastelands, and Page thanked him for the friendship and joy he found in Sandy. They talked and talked and listened too. They felt his pleasure as they drifted along on this river of reflection and gratitude that would carry Sandy to her next destination.

Soon the raft approached the mouth of the river, which would empty into the Great Sea. Page rowed them as close as he could to the bank. "I cannot go further. I must send you off here." These words were as hard for Page to say as they were for Sandy to hear. "Goodbye, my lovely, lovely Princess!" Then Page removed his purple hat and bowed to Sandy as he had at first.

Sandy covered her face with her hands, unable to reply. Then she found the simple words he had coached her with earlier. "Thank you. Just thank you. I could never repay you for your kindness in calling me to this new life!"

Page paused, looking over this transforming one before him. "Good thing you don't have to. Jasper has already paid me in full with joy!" Then Page held his purple hat before him and pulled out its plume. He handed it to Sandy. "Here. Don't forget me. Keep it in your bag as a remembrance of your journey and a man in a purple hat who would not give up on you."

Sandy received the plume and stared at it, remembering all the times she had caught sight of it. Her eyes welled with tears as she stroked its feathery frame, but when she looked up, he was gone. Sandy stood alone on the beach. She wanted to panic, but a peace overcame her. The crash of the Great Sea called out behind her, soothing her and stealing her attention, as it should. She beheld the plume for just another moment before gently placing it in her bag. "Thank you, Page. I am forever grateful. Now it is time to find *him*. My Jasper—where are you?"

"My Princess, I am here!"

~ ~ ~

"Jasper!" Sandy froze in her gasp for only a moment, then kicked off her shoes, threw down her bag, and ran the short distance I left between us before surprising her. We embraced. I picked her up and spun her around, then set her down gleefully in the sand.

"Look at you, Princess! You look so…"

"Clean? Colorful? Light?" she interrupted.

I laughed and nodded, "Yes! All of those things. You are

altogether lovely. My, how you've changed."

"It's those friends you sent me, Jasper. Thank you! Thank you for not giving up on me. Thank you for sending Page to rescue me!" Then she looked down shamefully. "And Jasper, I'm sorry. I'm so sorry I didn't respond to you sooner. I'm so sorry for hurting you the first time we met. I'm sorry…"

I interrupted her this time, "Princess, there is no need for this. You apologized already. At the river, am I right?"

Sandy stopped, then asked, "How did you know?"

"The communication system of the Kingdom never fails. Everything you say to us is heard and considered. And Sandy, you must know that we never refuse a request to forgive! It's what the Prince is known for—his majestic mercy to *forgive all* when simply asked."

"I have so much to learn, don't I?" Sandy looked me in the eyes, then embraced me again. "Oh, Jasper! I'm just so glad you were here, right here waiting for me. You won't leave me soon, will you?"

"No, dear Princess. I never, ever will! You have me forever. I am sealed in your heart, and you are sealed upon mine! I have much to show and tell you. There was a great reason for your trip here today, so get your things and walk with me, will you? I have a surprise planned for you ahead on the Shores. Let us talk as I take you there."

She took my hand with no hesitation as one becoming used to being led. Her heart was as yielded as her hand, and with a yielded heart, I can perform wonders. My princess and I proceeded together down the beach to begin living the dream she had been born to live.

co - the 1st invitation she was curious, but was not fully ready to follow all the way so he had to send help her way to begin to peel back the pain of the past which made her lighter + more joyful. All He wanted is a intimate relationship.

11

A Surprise in the Sand

It was good to be together again. My princess was changing, "becoming" before my eyes, looking all the more like us, her family now. She almost skipped in the sand as we swung hands and headed toward the spot where we first met. She expounded on all her recent happenings, catching me up on the events of her life. I already knew, but didn't let on. The sound of her hurried, excited speech filled my heart. Sandy was becoming my friend, and that is exactly all I had desired.

"...So you see, Jasper, your gift worked! I could actually *feel* the hope in my heart keeping me going, and it led me all the way back here, to *you*, and this new life! Thank you! Thank you," she gushed.

I threw my head back and laughed, "Sandy, to see you like this—it is all I could hope for myself. Your Prince and your father, the King—they rejoice with us too. Oh, how proud and happy you have made us all!"

"Jasper, when can I meet them? I want to know them! Oh, I can't wait! To hear the way Page and Carry speak of them...I can't wait to get to know them." Sandy's eyes sparkled at the thought, as they should.

"You will indeed get to know them, even before you meet

them. And *that* is part of my surprise, ahead on the beach. Look!" I waved my hand ahead to reveal what I had prepared for us on the shore, in the exact spot of our last encounter. Four poles had been securely posted in the sand and a white cotton canopy was attached at each corner, forming an airy tent. I had set a table there, with refreshments to satisfy my Princess after her long journey back to me. The table had white linen draping over it that billowed on the sides like an inviting wave. On the table were delectables—a grand presentation of fruits, cheeses, fresh breads, and other appetizing treats, offered on a platter of silver. I had two goblets of juice and a carafe of cold water. The very beads that slid down it were mini prisms, reflecting a rainbow of promise in each drop.

"How wonderful," she exclaimed, her eyes entranced by the presentation.

"Surprise!" I simply stated. "Now come. Let us feast together. We have much more to share."

I pulled out a cushioned square stool for Sandy to sit on, and tucked her into the table with a full view of the Great Sea. Then I sat to her right, able to see her expression along with the ocean she was instantly enamored with.

"There it is. The sea," she said dreamily, looking over the breadth of it.

"Yes! It has remained. Always here, calling for you. I told you we'd wait for you," I said with a wink.

She looked over at me. "You did," she admitted softly. "And here we are, in this perfect place. My heart is so full. What could possibly come next?"

"Plenty! The surprises of the Kingdom are never ending. But you had to return here first. Now eat up. You are going to need your energy for what is to come." I raised my glass and she raised hers with a laugh, and then we both feasted on the delicacies before us, catered by Kindness and Contentment. When she had consumed her fill, she let out a great sigh. "Amazing! Just what I needed. Thank you."

"You are indeed welcome, my Princess. And now, for my *real* surprise, sent just for you from the Prince himself." Sandy's eyes widened at the mention of the Prince. Then she followed me closely with her eyes. She hadn't noticed that under the front corner of the table, under the linen, I had hidden an even greater gift, a purposeful present I had in mind to give her at just this juncture in her journey. I stooped down by the table with my back to the sea, and slid out in the sand a dark wooden chest, bound by leather and metal straps, aged with years of use.

"A treasure chest!" she cried. "My goodness, it looks like a real, authentic treasure chest! Like ones that pirates search for on a deserted islands!" The fairy tales of her childhood swept over Sandy's imagination as she marveled at it. "Can I take a closer look?"

I nodded for her to approach, and she knelt in the sand, gently rubbing her hands over the exterior of this mysterious container. "What's inside?" she asked, looking up at me at last.

"All you need for your journey. Do you want to see?" The anticipation was almost too much.

"Yes! Yes!" she exclaimed, laughing expectantly.

"Well then, it would be my pleasure to show you!" I bowed slightly in honor, as well as in practicality, to open the chest for her to discover what was inside.

"Wow..." was the only word uttered as Sandy's eyes took inventory of all they could in this red velvet-lined chest. There was a stunning variety of sparkling jewels loosely scattered throughout the chest over bulging pouches of golden coins. Steel weaponry of swords and pieces of armor shone through, along with keys, large and small, on a bronze ring. Small, colored bottles containing unknown liquids emerged through layers of unknown surprise, buried beneath this treasure she could see. And a long white strand of pearls was streaming through it all at the surface. There was so much value to take in. Then I reached down to draw out my gift for her, the most valuable of all of the treasure indeed.

"All of this is appealing, I know. But for now, this is all you need." I handed her a book. It was bound in an old leather cover with two straps sealing the cover over the pages.

Sandy stared at it with peculiar curiosity. "A book...though it looks like a treasure chest itself," she observed.

"Indeed it does. Indeed it is, though it is no ordinary book. Sandy, this book is your map."

"My map? Where am I going?" she asked plainly.

I smiled at her innocence. "Wherever it takes you, my dear. And in whatever way I whisper for you to go. This book will guide you through the terrain you will find yourself traveling in your life. If you go on from this place without the map, you will just roam. But if you study its directives, you will find yourself where you actually want to be. This map will light your path. When you study it and heed its instruction, you will never go astray. You will indeed find the Kingdom of Love and live the great love story that you were created for and long to live!"

Sandy had a perplexed look as she stared at the book, flipping it over and rubbing its closed, worn cover. "Will I understand it? I'm not used to following maps or actually going anywhere. I'm used to going only where the trains in the Wastelands have taken me. Before this journey, I've never really gone anywhere at all."

"Oh, yes," I assured her. "Just as I sent friends like Page and Carry, I will send other experienced map-readers along your journey. And you will always have me as well!"

I could see trusted relief wash back over her face. "Thank you. Though it feels like a bit of an assignment to be entrusted with such a book, thank you. I trust you know what I need, and will help me if I don't understand."

"Indeed I will."

Sandy received my gift with slight hesitation. She held it in her hands outward a bit from her body as if she were afraid to hold it close. As she turned it in her hands for further examination, she *we were to long for something more.*

perfect love cast out fear

caught a gleam of light. Sandy squinted. "Wait—I think the page edges just lit up! Am I seeing things, Jasper?"

"No, you are just coming to grips with the kind of treasure map you hold in your hands," I replied.

Sandy smiled and pulled the book closer. "A treasure map. Well, I've been waiting all my life for the adventure to begin. I suppose this is a great way to start, with a map!"

"Indeed it is. And I know of another great way to begin your adventure—with a dip in the sea!" I stood up and started for the surf, looking back to beckon my princess. She remained still for a moment, clutching her map book. "Come on," I persisted, extending my hand. "Take my hand that you might rejoice in the waves of the King's love."

She jumped up, unable to resist my reach. She laid the book on the chest and ran to meet me in the surf she had inwardly always longed for. As her first foot met the water, she squealed. Her stride set her other foot a little deeper. She held on to my arm, and laughed as loud as I had ever heard her. I drew her out a little, up to her ankles where small foamy waves rushed over her feet.

"It tickles!" she laughed. "I love it!"

"Let's go out further," I suggested.

She consented. The water came up to Sandy's shins, and she proceeded till it met her knees, hanging on, but moving out into the great waters that surrounded her. "It's so invigorating!" she exclaimed over its roar.

"Yes! Love is!" I replied as waves of perfect love washed over Sandy.

"I'm…I'm not *afraid* anymore. I'm not afraid!" Sandy danced in the sea, discovering a deep truth already, locked within the map book she had been given.

"Perfect love casts out fear, Sandy. It washes it all away!" As she considered this, a greater wave surged over her, sweeping her off her feet and into my arms. We laughed and laughed as the

115

water receded back again.

"Now *that* was fun!" Sandy was beaming, fully drenched in the love the Great Sea had enveloped her in.

"One day I will take you out even further. When you are properly conditioned, we will dive deeper. There is so much beautiful mystery that lies beneath the surface of deeper waters." Sandy nodded as she looked out, wondering what she might discover on that day. "But for now, let's dry up. I have other treasure to share."

I built a little fire next to our tent on the beach and the two of us sat before it, beside one another. I looked on my new friend's face, admiring the glow of the flame on her features.

"I feel so warm, Jasper. From the inside out, I feel warm," Sandy said, staring constantly at the flames.

"There has been a flame placed in your heart, my dear one. A fire is burning and will intensify as you grow in your journey. And it will warm your world as it continues to spread. This fire can burn away what is not necessary in your life and cause many to stare and consider the wonder of its source. It will produce great light to lead you in the darkness of the land you will travel. Your heart is full of light now. The fire will purify your heart and allow for new growth—and you will look all the more like one who belongs to the King."

Sandy remembered the small flame on the table of her mother's house, and how the glow of it created a tranquility never known in her world before. She was amazed to think she could carry such light, and therefore peace into her world—I knew her thoughts.

"Yes. You are a carrier of light now, Sandy. Within you lies this great treasure as well, for there is darkness ahead on your journey, and the world will need your light."

"So, my map is a light for me, and I am a light too?" Sandy asked. It was a lot to digest for someone new to the Kingdom.

"Yes! You are a light because you hold the Prince in your

116

heart. The Prince of our Kingdom is light itself, as opposed to the prince of this world, who rules in the dark and opposes our world," I explained.

"Wait—I don't know of any prince in this world. We are certainly not living in a fairy tale *here!*" Sandy commented.

"Oh, there is a prince of this world. He is our enemy but he can't always be seen. He's a master of disguise, and prefers to remain invisible. He doesn't want anyone to see him coming. He desires for his subjects to go blindly through their lives, in darkness, seeing life through goggles, like the workers in your dream, not realizing they are not getting anywhere at all. They are just creating power for another. But his spell is what drives the citizens of the Wastelands. He has permeated their system. He works through its people. His goal is to keep his subjects blind, in darkness, never letting real light penetrate his domain. He is controlling and tricky. He makes the citizens believe they are living for themselves, and doesn't care to be noticed as long as he keeps them from devotion to the true King. Oh, you'll see his affect on those you encounter in your journey. But do not worry. I am with you, and I'm greater," I stated confidently with a smile that reassured her, arresting any anxiety attempting to arise. "I am *with* you!"

"I believe you," Sandy said after a pause to absorb all I had relayed. "And I'm not worried. I trust you." With steady yet gentle resolve, Sandy reached for my hand and added, "Jasper, I'm ready. I'm ready for this adventure." Sandy smiled with a confidence that could only be birthed out of love and complete faith in me.

"I know you are, my Princess! I know you are!"

"I have only one more question for now." Sandy's tone softened in a playful way. "The rest of that treasure in that chest…is it for me?"

I smiled widely. "Yes. It is all for you—in time! I will deliver the tools and provisions necessary for each leg of the journey. All of that treasure and more has been stored up for you. But for now, you need only the map…Oh, and some even greater treasures than that chest can hold—new friends! Come now, Princess, let's meet some."

With that we rose and shook off the sand of the Shores, ready to encounter new friendship beyond it. Sandy had been surprised by treasure and great love, and now she would begin her adventure by finding even more.

12

Refreshment in Friends

*H*and in hand I led my princess up the beach access, and together we crossed the sandy street in anticipation of more refreshment. The Cottage Café was directly before us. Sandy paused, remembering, "This is the first place I ever tasted pure goodness. And the sweet people there made me hungry for so much more."

"Then they did their job. Come on. Let's go see what is on the menu for today," I said, and we started for the welcoming shelter overlooking the sea.

As we opened the door, the cool air rushed to greet us, carrying in it aromas that instantly flooded Sandy's memory and refilled her heart with the sweet recollection of that first day here. Salty tears of grateful joy welled up in her eyes as she scanned the room. It was the same, spots of comfort staged throughout, but this time, there were people.

"Jasper!" Kindness looked up from the table where she sat and darted immediately toward us. The rest of her company responded as well, in surprised faces, gasps and cheers. "Jasper," Kindness repeated as she approached. "You've got her! You brought this princess back again. I knew you would." Then she looked down at my girl with those kind sparkling eyes of blue. "He's hard to resist, isn't he?" She winked at Sandy, then threw her arms around her. "How *happy* we are to have you back, love!"

Before Sandy could respond, Contentment bounded through the swinging door of his kitchen. "Did I hear JASPER has walked into our cottage? Just what we were hoping for today!" Contentment approached us as Kindness drew us in closer to the others in the cottage.

"Contentment, my friend! I'm so happy to be here," I replied. "I had to bring my Princess back. There is so much to gain at your table. And I see your table is full of our friends!"

"Yes, it's been a day of rejoicing indeed. We were all just sharing stories of our adventures with you and our times in the Great Sea. And we've been talking to the Prince too, all while gobbling up the cooking of Kindness here! It's been the perfect morning with friends," Contentment said as he surveyed his comrades. "And now it is all the more perfect since you walked into the room with your Princess! Come, sit with us, please."

Sandy and I gladly slid into a space around the table in the middle of the café. All of the faces around us glowed as they smiled, lit from their own inner light. Sandy noticed. I watched as she studied their looks. She just smiled sweetly, quieted by the serenity of their collective presence.

"Princess, let me introduce you to our friends. You already know Kindness and Contentment, but these are other friends of theirs and mine, and now they can be yours too. We all travel this journey together, and you will get to know them well along your way. You might as well get started," I said with a wink. "Here we have Joy, Passion, Peace, and Wisdom. They are all great comrades to have!"

Sandy nodded and smiled at each of them. "Hello! It is my pleasure to meet any friend of Jasper's. I hope we can be good friends too."

"Oh, we shall!" shouted Joy, a dark skinned woman with a

bright white smile that shattered any despair whenever she wielded it. She could never contain her enthusiasm, and no one wanted her to. She was as pleasant and as approachable as any motherly figure could be, but with a youthfulness that would draw folks of any age. "I for one am certainly your friend to be had! I love a great adventure and look forward to journeying with you all the way!"

"Joy will be a great strength to you, Sandy. You will even find her in places you least expect. She's a delightful companion." I then moved to Joy's left to continue the introductions. "This is Peace. He too is a constant friend." Peace looked to be a young man with longer, wavy hair and a tranquil spirit that permeated his countenance. His eyes were as green as the lush pastures by the riverbank, and had a sedating effect on her as she looked into them.

"I will keep you calm, Sandy, when things go awry. When you don't understand what is going on in circumstances around you, keep close, and you will have the assurance you need to make it through anything." These words settled Sandy's nervous heart. She knew she needed him and was grateful for the gift of his friendship.

"Passion is another great support to all who journey in the Kingdom," I explained in my introduction of this strong and attractive journeyer. Passion was confident and powerful, but was mature and determined in his speech and manner.

"I am honored to travel with you, Sandy. The Prince deserves our commitment to him and the ways of his Kingdom, and with me around, you won't forget why you are traveling. I will drive you on!" Sandy felt strengthened and her calm heart remained at peace but pounded with a new determination at Passion's words.

"I have one final person for you to meet right now." I motioned towards the oldest gentleman in our midst. "This is Wisdom, and you will not make it without him." He was older, but not fragile. He looked like one who had walked many miles, with wrinkles that could tell stories for years. These wrinkles formed the kindest of expressions with each whispered word he spoke.

"I am honored to assist you on your way, Princess. And *on* my honor, I will keep you on the right path, teaching you how to read that map of yours, and one day, that path will deliver you directly to the arms of your Prince." With that last comment, the room was filled with a dreamy hush, for all knew *that* was the goal, the intended end-all of her journey, and each companion was committing in full to help see this dream of her heart come true.

Kindness broke the silence as she popped up from the table. "My dear! I haven't even offered you a drink. I'll be back with a tray of choices. My, I can't have you dehydrated before you even set foot on your journey!" Kindness smoothed over her white hair and adjusted her apron as she started for the kitchen, determined to top Sandy off with a dose of what her kitchen could serve.

Sandy was almost overwhelmed as she looked over each new friend. "I don't know what to say! To think each one of you is willing to travel with me on this new adventure—you are all so spectacularly wonderful and needed in my life! But how will we all travel together? It seems we'll need...a bus!" We all, including Sandy, burst out in laughter. The imagined sight of this unlikely caravan was funny, but in a sense, that is what the fellowship of this journey would be like—a band of brothers and sisters, mismatched as they may be, bound together in a call to reach the Kingdom of Love.

"Princess, they will all travel with you, as each has directives written within the map. And they each have gifts to give you too." Almost on cue, they each reached for vessels within their pockets and pouches to present to Sandy.

"What is this? Colorful bottles—like in the treasure chest," Sandy perceived in surprised delight.

122

"Exactly the same!" I affirmed. "Each bottle contains the essence of what these friends carry. And you will have a portion to take when needed along the journey. Sometimes you will get to encounter them face to face, but these friends will always travel with you in your heart, and you will learn and receive more from them through your map."

"Yes! Drink in my joy whenever you feel weak. It will strengthen you and give you power to overcome any obstacle," Joy instructed with fiery enthusiasm.

Passion was ignited. "From my bottle you will be recharged, remembering the source of love that beats within your own heart. This passion will serve to sustain and bolster your resolve to journey on."

Peace quietly encouraged Sandy as he offered his bottle. "If you are ever overcome with worry, fear, or the troubling effects of doubt, let my portion aid you in regaining your peace, putting to rest all that these enemies of your soul will taunt you with."

Finally, Wisdom presented his bottle and added, "I hope you grow to hear my voice always guiding you, within your head and heart, but here is a simple dose to refresh you, and to give you ears to hear in the taking of it."

Sandy accepted each bottle and studied their varied shapes and sparkling colors. "Thank you so much. I feel their effects already," she commented, examining each one. "I shall treasure them indeed!"

Just then, Kindness pushed through the kitchen door with her large serving tray full of more to drink, and approached the group of friends. "Well, I can see you have already been served," Kindness commented, noticing the four bottles before Sandy on the table. "Save all of that for later, my dear. Let us all drink up from my cups together now. We have so much to celebrate!"

With that announcement, the quiet was broken and Joy rose from the table. "I'm with Kindness. Let's celebrate! Princess Sandy is on her way. I feel like singing." We all agreed, and Joy led us in loud songs of the Kingdom as Kindness poured out refreshment and Contentment joined her to refill us whenever needed.

We laughed and talked to each other for quite some time. Sandy was happily edified by the company she found herself in. "I never want to leave here," she finally exclaimed in a sigh.

I knew then I had to speak. "You shall always hold all this in your heart, but now that you have been filled up, it is time to begin. And my dear, you shall begin in the most splendid place, where you will receive another, equally important gift. Put these bottles in your pouch for now and come, my Princess, let me take you there."

Sandy placed the bottles in four sewn-in padded pockets within her pouch for safekeeping. We then got up from the table and a hush came over all, though the atmosphere remained charged with love. "Friends! It is time for our Princess to depart. Thank you for doing your part to welcome her into the ways of the Kingdom. We shall go for now, knowing you each go with us."

"Yes. Thank you," Sandy added. "You are indeed part of me now. Thank you for your gifts, and thank you for being exactly who you are. I hope I look just like *all* of you one day!" Low laughter mixed with the sound of scooting chairs followed as each new friend rose to embrace Sandy and me in sweet goodbyes.

"I'll take her through the back door, Contentment, Ok?" I asked.

"Of course!" he replied with a knowing wink. The back door led to my next surprise and necessary stop on Sandy's journey. A lesson awaited her, so I gathered her up and whisked her past our friends.

"Goodbye, Princess," they bid with their unified voices and waves. She had been fully refreshed indeed. It was now time to learn of deeper refreshment. And that is exactly the lesson I had in mind for her, just beyond the back door.

13

Garden Path

We stepped out into the night air and down the stone steps that made up the back stoop of the Cottage Café. The light wind of the beach air mixed with the smells of fresh green life coming from the next location I had in mind for my Princess. I took her by the hand, and guided her over a narrow stone path that led directly to a hedge of tall shrubbery, which served to encircle some secret place. No wall could be seen behind the shrubs and other green and flowery life that grew there, but there was a gate, and there we stopped.

"Now, my love, here I leave you for a time."

"But…" my Princess immediately protested, "you said you would never leave!"

"I will leave your sight, but not your heart. I *am* with you—always! But there is a gift in you not being able to *see* me all of the time. Your *hearing* will get so much better! And this is the perfect spot to practice!"

"Practice?" Sandy asked, hesitant to accept my instruction.

"Yes, practice…to practice listening and loving. Your first and most important lesson as a citizen of the Kingdom, and as the King's daughter, shall be learned by you here, in the garden," I explained.

"Is that what this is? A garden?" Sandy examined all she could of the gate and the green garden wall with more willingness in her look.

"Yes, a most splendid place, where you will meet with the King!"

Sandy turned to me wide-eyed now, "The King! I will finally get to meet him?" She held her breath at the thought.

"Yes," I laughed gently, "but you won't see him yet. You must learn to hear him clearly first, and become attuned to his voice. It would please him greatly for you to learn his voice and know him from the sound of it." This was a bit complex for Sandy. She was trying hard to understand.

"I want the King to be pleased with me, but how will I recognize his voice? How will I always know it is him?" Sandy wanted to know.

"Well, first of all, you have your map. It will show you the paths of the Kingdom. It reveals the ways of the King and accounts for his words and ways with the ones who once journeyed with him here. As you study the map, you will become familiar with the voice of the one it was written about. And then you will hear it for yourself, for you belong to him too, and the map book says you can! And plus, Sandy…he sounds like *me*," I added with a wink.

Sandy reached down to her leather bag strapped at her side. She ran her hand over its smooth flap before flipping it up to remove my gift that had been placed inside along with the feather and bottles. As she pulled it into view, I could tell that Peace, Joy, Passion, and Wisdom were already having an effect on her. Their influence was obvious in her expression as she looked on the map. A grin emerged as my Princess looked straight up into my eyes. "I can't wait to *hear* what this map book has to say!"

"Well then, let me leave you to your study…with one more gift to aid you." I presented the Princess with a large bronze ring. One key was on it. It was long, simple, and perfectly formed for her cause. And as she received the key from my hand to examine it, I took leave from her sight.

Sandy studied the key, then looked up to find me gone.

"Jasper!" Sandy whispered, with a hint of fear. I sent a gust of wind to blow over her and calm her. It did. Then she looked back down to see a word inscribed on the key. "Devotion," she read. It was the key of devotion, and it would be her admission to the gate before her. Sandy had come to our garden.

~ ~ ~

With this key decidedly in her grip, Sandy stepped up to the iron gate and slipped it into the lock. The swinging screech of the hinges welcomed her in as the gate swung open. The full moon overhead lit the landscape of this intimate, lush paradise flawlessly for her first introduction to it. All was aglow. She felt life surging around her. She walked through an arbor of purple wisteria hanging overhead. Then she inhaled the scent of sweet honey-suckle growing on trellises that leaned against the ivy covered garden wall. Mature fruit trees of varying heights would provide wide covers of shade by day. By night, these peach, pear, plum, and fig trees revealed only hints of ready and soon-coming fruit under protective leaves, but Sandy caught sight of them.

Low stone walls retained an assortment of colorful coastal flowers, such as red poppies, violet anise hyssops, and lilac-blue sage. These beds lined a mossy flagstone pathway to a mini-garden within of established rose bushes encircling a small trickling fountain. Before this spot was a sturdy, backed wooden bench that invited Sandy to sit. She did so.

Breathing in the fresh scent of all the life and water around her, Sandy closed her eyes, never wanting to forget the smell of this place. This deep breath seemed to expand her heart too as it was filling up even more, although she thought it had met its capacity this day, taking in all the love it could handle.

"My love…" Sandy's eyes sprung wide open, afraid to move

her head. Then she did, from side to side.

"I'm hearing things." She said aloud. Then, "No…" she added. "I'm hearing *him*, I think…the King!" She strained to perceive more, but caught nothing. "Practice hearing…" Sandy repeated Jasper's previous instructions to her, then remembered the map. She placed her key in her pouch and held only the map on her lap. She had not opened it yet, and was hesitant to do so. It appealed to her, certainly, with its worn leather cover and secretive straps concealing the mystery within. But she was intimidated, wondering how to handle such a book, and where to start. Sandy slid her hands over the cover, front and back, for quite some time, staring down at it. Finally, she gathered the courage to undo the straps and spread the book open, somewhere in the middle, to see what treasure she might find.

It was just as she feared. She didn't understand it at all. There were words and numbers and places listed along with names and directions, but she had no idea what they meant. Her full heart was deflated and filling with fear. *Oh no. What have I done? I'm all alone on a journey with a map I can't read! I've devoted myself to someone I just met, and have vowed to listen to voices of people I can't see! Sandy, what have you done?* She could see the faces of Doubt and Worry, standing on that street days before, telling her she would be back. Were they right? But everything with Jasper had felt so right. The love of the ocean, her refreshment in the presence of her new friends—all that was real, right? Sandy wondered all this as she sat frozen in perplexed debate upon this bench.

Just as her heart was sinking deeper within her chest, Sandy heard steps behind her and, in a moment, one of her new friends stood beside her at the bench. She looked up into the face of Wisdom. "May I join you?" he kindly asked, being every bit the gentle soul that Page and Jasper and all her friends of the Kingdom had been so far.

"Of course," Sandy mumbled. The lump in her throat prohibited much sound from escaping.

Wisdom sat silently with Sandy for a moment, allowing the trickle of the fountain to calm her along with his presence. "Quite a book," he finally stated.

"Yes. I suppose it is." Sandy hung her head, embarrassed that she should not have anything else to say.

"Quite a lot to take in," he added sympathetically.

"Yes. I'm…I'm not sure where to start," Sandy quietly admitted.

"That is why I came, my dear. I can help you navigate this map of yours. I know it well. If you just ask me, every time you approach it, I will help you."

It was so simple Sandy couldn't believe it. "You mean, I only have to ask you for help, Wisdom, and I will understand?

"Exactly! That is what I am here for. That is why Jasper wanted us to be friends. But you must call for me, and ask me for help. Many examine this map and want to make their own sense of it. That often leads them astray and they never find the deepest treasure. But Sandy, I know where it all is!" Wisdom's eyes sparkled youthfully. "And I know what treasure would be most valuable to you in each leg of your journey."

"So I just have to ask?" The simplicity of Wisdom's instruction was shocking to her.

"Yes! Ask away," Wisdom responded.

"Ok…where do I start?"

Wisdom's wrinkles happily flexed as a knowing smile covered his face. "That, my dear, is easy! Let's start in the garden…" And with that direction, Wisdom motioned towards the book on Sandy's lap. "May I?" He wanted to show her the first great treasure to be had.

"Of course!" Sandy slid the book over and they shared it on

their laps. With one finger, Wisdom turned to the beginning of the map book.

"It all started in a garden," Wisdom began. "On the very first page, the scene is set with a location most precious to the King's heart. The King made a garden...much like this one, but it was perfect. There was never a weed nor anything placed within its boundaries that would choke out the perfect life and love he had intended to experience here. It was a haven of beauty, a parcel of heaven on earth, and it was all created for—"

"For who?" Sandy asked, caught up in his explanation.

"For *you*...for his children. It was intended for his sons and daughters to live there with him—*then*, in the beginning, and *now*," Wisdom explained. "He grew this garden to be a sanctuary of love and life. He wanted a place where fellowship would flourish, where he could walk and talk with his kids and they could share their hearts, souls, and thoughts with one another, and they all could be *known*. It was to be the grandest place to be. And it was, for a while."

"What happened?" Sandy asked.

"A lie crept in. The King's enemy snuck in and lied to his children, and they believed the lies. They listened to other voices of pride and doubt, and this caused them to turn from their father, the King."

Sandy's heart panged. She knew Pride and Doubt all too well. To think their ancestors had hurt the King's heart so long ago... and to think she had listened to them so much herself. She was sorry for her own mistake of listening to their lies.

"And *then* what?" Sandy had to know where this action led.

"Then the garden became a place of hiding instead of seeking. Where the King's kids used to frolic unabashedly in his presence, they now hid in the bushes, wishing not to be known at all. They hid from their very selves. They forgot who they were. The venom of the lie had cast its spell."

"What did the King do?" Sandy asked. Tears filled her eyes; she could see this scene unfolding as she examined the map.

"The garden was sealed off, as it had to be. It was quarantined, for the enemy had been allowed inside, and he brought decay with him. The King's kids were sent on their way. They had chosen another path. But the King never stopped seeking their hearts and their love. He never stopped pursuing *them*. And he had a plan to redeem it all and know oneness with them again."

"What was the plan? Is it in the map? Does this show the way?" Sandy asked, seated on the edge of the bench now.

Wisdom smiled, looking straight ahead into the fountain and seemingly into another world. "The Prince," he responded. "The Prince was his plan." A spring of love refilled Sandy's heart at the very name of her Prince. She did not know him well at all, but was here to learn of her new love, and her heart pounded at the mention of him in this story.

"Tell me more, will you, Wisdom?" Sandy softly asked.

"Yes. I love to tell his story." Wisdom took the book and flipped forward many pages, then laid the map down flat again as he pointed and explained. "There is a great deal that happened between the beginning and this section of the map, and you will have time to go back and research the ancient paths that led to this spot. But for now, I have this lesson to teach you and this question of yours to answer, so I will take you to another garden that our Prince found himself in on a dark evening much like this."

Wisdom explained to the Princess how the Prince had come to fight the prince of this world, the same enemy from the garden, and was willing to do anything to win back the King's children so the dream of the King's heart could come true. He told her of the Prince's life here, how he left his royal throne of the real Kingdom to come walk in this broken world, and did nothing but bring beauty and life, wholeness and fullness to those he encountered while here. "He was the perfect Prince. And on his last night of freedom here, before he would pay the ultimate price for the King's dream, he stopped by a garden."

"His last night? What do you mean?" Sandy asked, alarmed.

"I will get there, dear Princess, but first you must hear what he did here, in this garden,"

"Go on." Sandy conceded.

"He sought out a garden, a refuge of fellowship for him and his father, and they talked. He bared his heart, and cried out for that which they were both so passionate. And do you know who they spoke of, Sandy?" She only shook her head in silent unknowing. "You. They spoke of you—and the King's other kids. And all that the Prince cried for was *oneness* to be restored—for relationship. All the King ever wanted was to have a family and to share all he had with them. And with just their belief in one lie, his dream was broken. But the Prince, the one who had been with him since the beginning and experienced it all, came down to restore the King's dream and heal the broken hearts of all who were supposed to know their true father since the beginning as well."

Sandy could not move. She had heard Page tell her of the Prince and tales of him here in their world, and Carry had explained a trade he had made with his life in their talks by the river, but it wasn't until Wisdom clarified it all here in this way, in this garden, that it all made sense to her. The gravity of it left her paralyzed.

Then Wisdom turned to face her and leaned in, gently patting her hands, which lay lifeless on the map. "Princess, all is well! He won!" Wisdom flipped forward a few more pages. "It was the most difficult road any one in this world has ever faced, but he won! He beat the enemy and returned to his Kingdom. And now he lives to see that as many of the King's kids as possible resist the lie and live the dream they were born to live since the beginning! So you see, Sandy, it is very fitting that you find yourself right here tonight…in a garden. It is a very good place to start, and to remain."

Sandy was relieved at the victorious ending to the Prince's journey in this world, and she held great hope and joy in her heart over her current position in the journey. It seemed that the dream of her heart was merging with his, and that had to be good, she thought. But what did Wisdom mean by "remaining" here? It didn't seem like Jasper would want her to stay in one place. She was sent on an adventure, after all. "Remain?" Sandy asked.

"Yes, dear Princess. Remain." Wisdom pointed to a pear tree by the garden wall. "Do you see that fruit tree, Sandy?" She nodded. "It grows delicious, juicy fruit that Kindness uses in her pies and tarts. Guess how the tree made that fruit?" Sandy shook her head, not knowing where Wisdom was going. "By remaining. It just remains in this garden. It soaks up the nourishment of the soil and holds its limbs to the sun, and as it stands in this garden, the fruit comes." Sandy was still at a loss as to how this applied to her and this directive to *remain* when she had so many places to *go*.

"Sandy, your heart is his garden now. It is the place he seeks to know you, and the place you can seek him in return! He wants to be known by you. He wants you to know your true father. He wants *both* of your dreams to come true, for they are one in the same! True love is to be had by you both! This garden we sit in is like the garden of your heart. You must tend to this garden, allowing no lies to come in, and no weeds to take root. And as you fellowship with the King in the garden of your heart, great *fruit* will come from your life. You will produce all kinds of wonderful things to share with others. So as you go, *remain*. Remember the garden. It is within you and it is where you were made to live!"

Wisdom had a way of settling Sandy's questions and bringing her the understanding she desired. "What an amazing teacher you are, Wisdom. I wish you could journey with me all the way."

"Oh, I am never far, my dear. Just call on me, and I will make my voice heard," he assured her with a pat and a wink. "But for now, you must rest. Rest tonight in the garden. For tomorrow you will travel beyond this place into lands you have never gone. Rest up, my dear!"

Wisdom led her to a hammock in the trees, where he tucked her in and swung her to sleep, surrounding her with songs of deeper Kingdom love. Sandy was joining the dream, and would carry this place and lesson with her, forever in her heart, wherever she might journey next.

14

The Flatlands

Bird-sung breezes served as Sandy's call to wake this first morning in the garden. Before she opened her eyes, she remained tucked in her swaying bed, suspended in peace. She was conscious of where she was, yet had not encountered the garden in daylight, and was trying to paint her best guess of it on the canvas of her imagination. Sandy could stand it no longer, and popped open her eyes.

"It's a million times lovelier!" she cried in exuberant surprise. The sun's rays radiated through tree branches, giving dimension and depth through light and shadows to each exquisite creation surrounding her. So many hues of green in thousands of leaves contrasted with the brilliant colors found in petals of flowers planted throughout. Sandy scanned the garden from where she was perched. She would like to remain here always, but she knew, as Wisdom had instructed, she would go on from this place today. Hopefully the garden of her heart would grow to be just as grand.

A happy creak of the garden gate broke through her thoughts and Sandy looked over to catch the sunny face of Kindness, carrying a tray into her garden retreat. "Good morning, Princess! I figured you'd be rising about now. How did you sleep?" Kindness's tone was soothing and cheery, ideal for arousing one out of slumber.

"I had a perfect night's sleep, camping out here in the garden. What an amazing secret garden you have here, Kindness! What a privilege to be allowed in," Sandy commented.

"Oh, it's a privilege any can have. Jasper is generous with his keys, though not all accept them." Kindness dropped her head and furrowed her brow a little while she arranged plates and saucers on a small garden table.

"I can't imagine not accepting a key to this place! Why would one refuse?" Sandy hopped out of her hammock and approached the table Kindness was preparing.

"*Devotion* means time, and many traveling this way don't think they have it. They choose to walk more in the way of their old lives, eating on the run and searching their maps quickly, and often only when lost. They want to hear from the King at certain times of their journey, but they haven't taken the time to learn what his voice sounds like. They haven't sat with him here, so they can't rightly discern, and his voice can be counterfeited."
Kindness looked up with light beaming through her clear blue eyes. "But you, my dear, you are here. So you shall feast, and you shall know." Kindness fiddled about, removing the last of the items from the tray and pouring from her pot to fill Sandy's breakfast cup.

"You are so good," was all Sandy could say as she stared once again at another scrumptious meal created by Kindness.

"Enjoy your meal, my dear. And enjoy the company! I have a feeling he has much to say to you today before you head away." Kindness referred with her glance to Sandy's map, which had been placed on the seat next to her at this little garden table.

Sandy looked up and smiled. "I shall! I shall enjoy it all. Thank you, Kindness! You always draw my heart to deeper places of understanding. Thank you for that."

Kindness looked down with a shy smile. "I can only serve what I have been so richly blessed with. The King has shown such great kindness to me, and now it is my joy to share what I have known with others. Have a beautiful morning, my dear! Drink in as much as you can from this time. It will help you along your way." With that, Kindness turned, creaked open the garden gate, and carried her tray with her to refill for her next guest.

The gate closed again behind her, leaving Sandy alone in the garden with this feast for one, and the map. After one sip from her cup, she curiously picked up the map book and noticed something she hadn't before. A red satin ribbon lay between the pages, somewhere in the middle, and hung out on each side. Sandy was surprised she had not seen this before and could not resist looking to see what the ribbon marked. She opened to some words of advice. Sandy muttered the words softly aloud.

"Listen to me, my child, and do as
I say, and you will have a long, good life.
I will teach you Wisdom's ways and
lead you along straight paths."

"What wonderful words for a day such as today," Sandy observed. She read on.

"When you walk, you won't be held back. When you run,
you will not stumble. Hold on to my instructions and don't
let them go. Guard them, for they are the key to life."

"Another key—this map book…it's like another key," Sandy realized as she read. Sandy's eyes fell on another spot on the page:

"The way of those who walk right is like the first
light of dawn, which shines ever brighter till the full light
of day. But the way of the wicked is like deep darkness.
They have no idea what makes them stumble."

Slight fear struck Sandy's heart. "What if I don't know which way is right and which way is wrong? I don't want to end up stumbling around out there…in darkness," Sandy said to herself.

"Read on…" Sandy heard these words spoken to her heart. She complied.

> *"Above all else, guard your heart, for it*
> *determines the course of your life."*

There were mysteries to be solved in reading this map book. The words on the page seemed cryptic to her. Then Sandy remembered, *Wisdom! I can ask Wisdom to help me at any time.* And so she did. She asked for Wisdom to help her interpret the mystery of these instructions, and immediately she saw a picture in her mind's eye. She saw her heart as a castle, guarded by one looking much like her Jasper in full armor. No one was allowed in without permission of the guard. And the guard did searches of the castle to expel any enemy intruders that may have snuck in, hiding out to await their attack.

 So my heart must be guarded in such a way, for if I let the wrong thing or wrong person in, the whole course of my life could change. That makes so much sense. Sandy was shocked at how quickly Wisdom interpreted these instructions for her. She went on reading, hoping for more help from him.

> *"Look straight ahead, and fix your gaze on what lies*
> *before you. Mark out a straight path; stay on the safe path. Do*
> *not get sidetracked; keep your feet from following evil."*

Sandy looked up, straight ahead, just as the map had said to in this spot that had been marked for her. Her eyes caught a glimmer of light on the lock of the garden gate. It seemed to beckon to her. Sandy finished a few bites left on her plate, filling up on the last morsels Kindness had cooked to nourish her body and soul. It was time to heed the call she heard within to go. Sandy rose, placed her map in her pouch and approached the garden gate. It swung open easily as soon as her hand touched it, and presented a path to the left of the cottage that was clearly the road to take. Sandy inhaled, looked up and talked to one she could not see.

"My King, I'm coming! Although I do not see you, I trust you, and I am learning to hear you. I know you are calling me, so here I come."

And with that, Sandy started off. She was fairly peaceful and joyful as she began her journey, wondering what kinds of landscapes and terrains she would see and find herself in. The road was flat and sandy. There wasn't much to see for quite a stretch—no rich plant life to entertain her visual thirst for beauty. There was not much color either along the path she walked for hours that morning. All was tan and bland. Even the sky seemed a sandy shade of blue. "Oh my," sighed Sandy, finally breaking the silence she walked in. "I wonder where I am going." She paused for just a moment to get out her map and check her location. "Perhaps I've wandered off course. This road seems just the same over and over again." Sandy opened again to the page marked for her:

"Look straight ahead, and fix your gaze on what lies before you. Mark out a straight path; stay on the safe path. Do not get sidetracked; keep your feet from following evil."

"Well, according to this I'm Ok…" Sandy continued on, a little less aware of the peace and joy she had started with. She journeyed on into the late afternoon, noticing small changes in the landscape, but very little. She was growing tired, and searched for a place to rest her weary feet. Just as she thought this, she spotted a bench along the road up ahead, but it was not vacant. Two strangers were occupying it. As she came closer, they entreated her.

"Hey! Hey, you there! Come here," the first one spoke out. He was tall and lanky with pronounced sharp features, especially in contrast to his round and pudgy companion. "Come here, girl. We want to talk to you," he called as Sandy slowed in her advance.

"Yes?" she answered awkwardly as she grew closer. "Can I help you?" Sandy was skeptical of these two characters that seemed stuck to the bench on the side of the road. She approached hesitantly.

"Sure, you can help me. I'm Bored. And this is my friend Lazy, and we can use all the help we can get. We're *lost* out here." Bored looked around aimlessly while Lazy barely moved and stared unhappily forward, not even making eye contact with the newcomer.

Sandy was slightly sympathetic. "You're lost? Do you have your map book?" This was a good and logical question to pose to anyone on this journey, she thought.

Bored laughed, while Lazy remained unmoved. "Map book? Oh, yeah. We had one once, I think, but it got kind of heavy along the way, so we tossed it. We didn't understand it anyway, to tell the truth," Bored scoffed. "We were just hoping to tag along with someone who knew where they were going, right, Lazy?" Bored elbowed Lazy, who grunted, and looked up only momentarily at Sandy before slouching back down on the bench, crossing his arms, and closing his eyes to nap.

"Well, I'm sure you don't mean to tag along with me. I'm new to this whole journey. I'm just staying on this straight path, like the map book says." Sandy could tell her new acquaintances were not impressed with her strategy.

Bored raised his eyebrow to question, "Isn't it kind of *boring* though? Just walking this same straight road? That's what we were doing, but as soon as we found a nice place to sit, we grabbed it. I grew sick and tired of that road!" Sick and Tired—Sandy remembered the faces of the couple she had once served back at BIG'S, the couple that constantly complained and were easily dissatisfied with whatever was placed before them. Bored resembled them greatly.

"What about you? Aren't *you* getting tired? Want to sit with us a while? Lazy can scoot over, can't you, Lazy?" Bored shoved his plump companion who was sprawled out on the bench. Lazy grumbled a little and budged only slightly.

"That's Ok. I don't think I should sit yet. I feel sure that this path leads somewhere I am to go, and the map will show me where I am to stop."

Bored sneered, "You're *sure*, huh? Well, I *sure* could use a little excitement, which is NOT what this path seems to offer!" Bored then looked over at Lazy, who was drifting off to sleep, and mocked, "I need to get rid of my ball and chain, Lazy, over here, but I seem stuck with him. Can't seem to get him to do anything," Bored complained. "Just sit with us, will you? Just stay a while. It may not be exciting here, but at least we will have company in each other."

The bench was appealing. So was the thought of some company, as *boring* as these two seemed to be. Sandy wanted to sit. She was tired of traveling along this monotonous way, and considered his invitation. Then she remembered the words from the map that she had read in the garden that morning.

"...Stay on the safe path. Do not get sidetracked..."

The bench was certainly off of the path, on the side of the road. And these two did not show the signs of life that Joy, Peace, Kindness, Contentment, Passion, or Wisdom had. Bored's plea felt draining, where her friends from the café energized her. And now the words of her map were reminding her of what to do.

"I'm sorry, but I must go. I cannot stop and sit with you now. I know there is more road for me to travel today—so much more ahead. I hope you find your way—and your friend wakes up," Sandy added as Lazy began to snore.

Bored just rolled his eyes, crossed his bony arms and sunk in the bench. "Suit yourself," he retorted, shutting his eyes now too and crossing his outstretched legs at the ankles, planting his heel in the ground where they sat.

Sandy looked on them only a second more. They were not going anywhere, but she must. The road had not ended, and even though it wasn't an exciting road right now, she had peace that she was headed in the right direction. She just had to keep moving, straight ahead, leaving her Bored and Lazy encounter behind. They were going back to sleep, but she had been woken up with a call to pursue a dream. Sandy would continue on her sandy path, flat and straight as it was, fueled by the voice that spoke his love to her heart that morning, and the instructions in the map that re-enforced this love. And Sandy would guard her heart, determining not to let anyone alter her course.

15

Side Roads
and Sidetracked

Sandy forged ahead, and in only minutes, the path took a turn and color broke through the dull surroundings, bleeding green into the landscape around her. There were now more trees and grasslands about, all wildly natural along the side of the road. She was glad to see color again after trudging through the beige, bland Flatlands for so long. As Sandy proceeded down the dirt road, taking in all she could of the new setting, she began to see other trails leading off of the main road. "Interesting," she thought aloud. "I wonder where all of these little paths lead." She was curious, but did not stop to explore them, for the reminder rang in her head, "*stay on the safe path...*" and that she did for a while longer.

Sandy lifted her head and focused straight ahead, rubbing the pouch by her side that contained her treasures, reminding Sandy of those she had come to trust on this journey and of the reason she was traveling at all. She would make her way to her Prince, learning of him and her father, the King, *becoming* all the while through whatever lessons would lie ahead. Just as she was growing satisfied in this thought and regaining strength from it, she heard rustling in the tall grass ahead and mumbling voices. Sandy slowed in her approach, but leaned forward, stretching her neck to see what was moving. Two little characters popped out in front of her on the path, causing her to gasp in surprise and jump back. They looked liked twins, short and silly, dressed in oversized clown-like costumes, and wearing loud face make-up and colorful wigs. They both had some kind of rope coiled up at their sides, attached to their belts.

"Well, hello," the first one greeted loudly with a huge wave of his white gloved hand. "Whom have we got here?" he asked as he cocked his head to inspect Sandy. "We haven't met you along this way before!"

Sandy was reluctant to reply to these strangers, but did anyway. "I'm Sandy. I haven't been here before. Who…who are you?"

"Sandy…I see," the first little character slyly responded, looking her up and down, then over to his cohort who quickly cut in.

"Sandy! So nice to meet you! Pardon my brother for not introducing us! His name is Distraction and I am Diversion and we are here to lead you on an adventure,"Diversion announced boldly while tapping the rope at his side.

Sandy loved the word "adventure," but wasn't so sure of these two comical creatures before her. She politely responded anyway. "Nice to meet you. What kind of adventure do you mean?"

Distraction shoved his brother back. "We would like to take you on a tour of one of our trails! We have blazed many of the thrilling paths off of this main road into sensational domains that are sure to suit your fancy! Fulfill your fantasies! Let us *entertain* you, dearie!" He finished with a tap dance move and spin.

Something within Sandy did not trust their tone, yet she was intrigued. Diversion could sense this. "We will bring you right back. We just want to show you a good time and let you relax…have some fun! There is SO much to do on the side roads! Don't you want to have some time for *yourself* to do whatever you *want* instead of traveling along this road you were *told* to travel?"

Sandy considered his point. She had been following this path for a long time and had not taken any time for herself. What would it hurt to just head down one of these side roads with Distraction and Diversion for just a while? She could turn back at any time, she reasoned.

Distraction jumped into her pause. "Sandy, *what* do you like to do? *How* can we entertain you and show you a good time? We want to help you get your mind off of this long, boring journey you've been on and help you have some FUN! We can amuse you in whatever way your heart desires! We know all the paths of pleasure!"

Sandy searched her own heart now. What *did* she like to do? What was her "heart's desire"? Then she remembered—her heart! *Jasper!* She remembered the picture Wisdom had given her in the garden of Jasper guarding her heart. What did the map book say?

> *"Above all else, guard your heart, for it*
> *determines the course of your life."*

"Jasper!" Sandy cried. "Jasper, search my heart." She closed her eyes and felt immediately refreshed by peace. When she opened her eyes a moment later, the two characters were gone. She looked side to side. Had she only imagined them? The side roads were still there, but she had a renewed vision of heart. She had not let these two amusing strangers lure her down their paths. She was reminded of how protective Jasper was of her heart, and she was glad for this. Simply fixing her mind and setting her heart on Jasper made them disappear. With invigorated resolve, she walked on.

Sandy remembered Page and the songs they sang along the River. She began to sing and joy filled and refueled her heart. As she walked on and sang, she noticed more trails to her right and left. There were so many along the road she traveled. Soon the terrain turned hilly and she had to put more effort in her walk. Her path led through denser woods with constant trails branching off on both sides. Sandy had to concentrate all the more to stay on the path she had been set on.

Occasionally she would hear more rustling and distant voices. As her path topped one hill, she noticed a fellow traveler to her left being pulled down a path just beyond her, yelling. Right below that path, there was another person being dragged away. Sandy snapped her head to the right. She saw more trails down the hill on that side with people being pulled on leashes by smaller animal-like creatures. She stopped to assess what was happening.

"Jasper, what is going on here? I need your Wisdom to discern. I'm very confused by these woods I find myself in," she cried. "Help me understand."

Wisdom showed up, just as promised. "I'm here, Princess."

"Wisdom! Thank you for coming so quickly. I need you." Sandy was relieved and began to process with her wise companion. "These woods are so confusing. There are trails leading off of this road in every direction. And people are being taken away, far into the woods and down embankments, and I don't see them returning. Am I safe on this path? What is going on here? With so many tracks leading off of this one, how can I be sure to keep on the right path?" Sandy looked around, dismayed by what she saw.

Wisdom surveyed the woods then answered the Princess with a question. "Sandy, have you looked at your map lately?"

Sandy's head dropped slightly, realizing the simplicity of instruction in Wisdom's question. "No. No, I haven't looked at it in quite a while…not since this morning in the garden, though I have been encouraged by what I studied of it all through this day."

"If you fear being lost, you can get out your map at any time,"

Wisdom gently instructed. Sandy did just that. There in the road she flipped open the leather flap of her pouch and pulled out the ancient book. As she wielded it in her hands, a gleam of light shot off from its edges, just as it did when Jasper first gave it to her. She looked up with surprise into Wisdom's face, who quietly smiled and nodded for her to open it. Sandy looked down to do so and when she opened the pages, a most mysterious thing happened. Her whole path was lit before her in a golden hue, while the side trails seemed shadowed by a dark veil.

"My goodness," Sandy exclaimed, "It has all become so clear! How…"

Wisdom interrupted. "Read the map," he simply said.

Sandy did so, reading aloud.

> *"The King's word is a lamp to guide*
> *my feet and a light for my path."*

"That's just what happened! So that is what his words do in this map, right? They light my path."

"You are a quick study, Princess. Yes. That is exactly what the words and directives of this book do. Go on. Read what is highlighted for you," nudged her wise tutor.

Sandy flipped over to a spot that stood out and read,

> *"You will show me the path of life; you will fill me with joy in*
> *your presence, with eternal pleasures at your right hand."*

The Princess was arrested by the truth and goodness of this promise found within the map. The path of life was being revealed to her, so she was sure that joy and lasting pleasure would follow as the King granted it. "Amazingly true," Sandy replied. Then she looked up at what surrounded them again. "But what about these people on the dark trails, and the creatures that are dragging them away. What is happening to them?"

Wisdom looked at the chaos surrounding them and explained, "These travelers, my dear one, are being led astray by their own thoughts and feelings." He pointed to one lassoed traveler being jerked away to their left. "See there? That creature is Anger. He is vicious and puts a tight hold on his captives. That journeyer is being led down the side road of rage, and the road is a dead end." Wisdom pointed to another untamed creature to the right. "And there—that one's name is Jealousy. Her venom is strong and causes her victims to think murderous thoughts. She chooses Paths of Comparison and Avenues of Envy to lead her hostages away from the Path of Life."

Sandy followed Jealousy and her prisoner with her eyes until they disappeared deep in the woods. Her heart sank. Then she spotted another leashed traveler who was panicked and pulling at the collar around her neck as a bully was yanking her down another trail. "Who is that?" she asked.

"That is Anxiety. She gets hold of many and traps them in her Ways of Worry," Wisdom responded somberly. "All of them started out as you did, on the straight path, but they listened to these thoughts and feelings that the enemy attacked them with, and now they have gotten off course."

"What happens to all of them? Where do they end up?" Sandy was alarmed at how travelers on her trail could be so easily sidetracked and taken captive.

"Some get tangled in the ropes of their bondage and get stuck on their path, snagged by some obstacle along the way. Many of them end up sinking in the Swamp of Despondency. Some end up in even worse places, never to return," Wisdom said sadly.

"Can they ever get free? Do any of them ever find their way back?"

"Oh, yes. There is always hope. Just as you cried out for me to come, they can too. They can cry out to the Prince or Jasper to save them, and they always will. But many, caught up in their feelings or wrong thoughts, become skewed and warped in their thinking. And if they don't study their map books or remember to ask for help, they can get lost on a pathway that will only lead to agony. These negative feelings that all travelers encounter should never be submitted to. They will never lead where you really want to go."

"Can I help them, Wisdom? Can I do anything right now?" Sandy was growing in compassion, which was a good thing, but Wisdom knew her well, and he knew what was right and best for her at this point in her journey.

"Sandy, my dear, it is beautiful that you are burdened, and there is something you can do. You can talk to the King and Prince about your care for them while you remain on your way. But you must not set foot on their path at this time. Look what it says at this spot where we are." Wisdom pointed to their position on a page in the map book.

"My Child, do not go along with them,
do not set foot on their paths."

Wisdom's finger slid over to another spot.

"Give careful thought to your paths and
be steadfast in all your ways."

This advice resonated with Sandy, though she was still alarmed by the ease in which even citizens of the kingdom could be led down wrong roads. Wisdom could read her heart on this matter. "There is much to learn from this scene, Sandy. There is a way that seems right to a man, but in the end it can lead to destruction or even death. But you have the map and can always know the way to go! You don't have to listen to *feelings*, as real as they may seem. And just because you *think* something, doesn't make it true. Sandy, make sure every step you take lines up with the directives of this book. It will illuminate your way and keep you safe, and lead you to very great joy and reward."

Sandy was comforted by Wisdom's words. She resolved to refer to her map book whenever she had questions about her way. She walked on with Wisdom past these sidetracks and continued to learn from him as he taught her more of the map and how to approach it. Soon they had made it together through the thick woods and came to a clearing, where the road continued through fields on flatter ground again.

"We are in the clear, it looks like," Sandy stated, looking around at her simple surroundings.

Wisdom smiled wisely. "For now. The road is always changing, Princess. But the King never does! And his map is always full of wisdom for any terrain. I am going to leave you to your own study of it for now, but again, I am never far. Call on me—I'll answer you."

Sandy looked down at her treasured map, then up again to find Wisdom gone. She smiled and sighed, "Thank you, my good friend! You've led and equipped me well. I will journey on. I wonder what is next..." Then Sandy opened her map and whispered more gratitude as she browsed through. "Thank you, Jasper! And thank you, my Prince and my King. I know you are with me and I *am* finding joy in your presence. Thank you for calling me out and leading me on." Sandy was alone on the road, it would seem to any onlooker, but she knew royalty was accompanying her. She paused only to take a swig of joy from the bottle in her pouch. It gave her just the added strength and energy she needed to continue. And continue she did for quite a ways until the sun began to set and she came upon the Crossroads.

16

At the Crossroads of Broad and Narrow

The map led her into a level stretch of land, covered by a wide-open sky, hazy with the shades of dusk. In the far distance Sandy could see hills, but the land straight ahead was flat with only one obvious sight before her—the Crossroads. Sandy's slighter path intersected with a wide highway, a road many were traveling. She stopped to watch, not having seen this many people in her journey thus far. They were traveling mostly from her right on the wide road, crossing over her path to her left on that same wide road. She did not notice anyone turning her direction or continuing down the narrower path she was on. All this traffic made her curious, so she stepped in the wide highway before her to take a look in the direction everyone was headed. The sun was setting, so the light was low, but far in the distance she could make out the tiny skyline of the city she knew so well, the City of Excess.

Sandy froze, startled to see it. As she gazed upon its outline from where she stood, she became aware of the excited sounds of people around her. She was shoved about as hordes of travelers moved hurriedly towards the city, down the wide road. Many were dressed in party dresses and fine clothing, smelling of rich perfumes and spicy colognes. Some of their faces were painted with glamorous precision. Their hair had been molded and plastered to stay. Others were more casual, but clamored in rowdy cheer. All manner of folks moved in the direction of the city, laughing and joking, full of anticipation over what their travel might bring them. They all seemed gleeful and eager in their trek on this wide way.

Sandy was taken aback. She had not been prepared for what the sight of the city she had yearned so long for would do to her. Her heart, unguarded, sank within her, and she did not rush to save it. Sandy stared at the city, as the distant lights began to twinkle in the coming night sky. She was shoved again and was now off the narrow path, completely and fully on the broad road, pointed in the direction of Excess.

Straight ahead, in the corner of this crossroads to her left, Sandy noticed a drink stand of some kind. The sky was quickly growing gray, but there was something familiar about the form of the person manning the stand. Sandy decided to approach.

"Sandy? Sandy, is that you?" Now she had a voice to match the form. It was her old traveling partner, Restless.

"Restless?" She returned the question as she squinted and advanced closer. "What are you doing out here?"

"Well, I was about to ask you the same thing! But I'll go first. I started my own business...sort of. I'm running this portable potion and tonic stand as a mobile branch of 'Club Compromise.' May I serve you, my friend?" Restless lifted a clean and empty glass as if to toast her, ready to serve her a dose from his cart of Compromise.

"Your own business? How did that happen?" Sandy ignored the offer, but was curious about his new venture.

"You might remember how we talked on the way to the Shores about how I was ready for a change. After I dropped you off at home the day of our trip, I went to Club Compromise and met the owner, who happened to be there. It was Mr. Success!" Sandy's heart panged at his name. Restless continued. "He said he saw something in me and could help set me up in business. Long story short, here I am, serving up cups of Compromise to whomever might walk this way!"

Restless appeared so satisfied and fulfilled to Sandy. She had to ask, "Are you doing well?" Sandy's emotions were jumbled and indefinable. She was scrambling for information she wasn't even sure she wanted to know.

"Well, I'm just getting started, but there is a lot of traffic. Everyone wants to go to Excess, and this is the road they travel from out here in the country. I'm sure I'll do very well, serving weary travelers the tonic they need to prepare them for who they must become in the city. That's what Mr. Success says anyway. He said he *guarantees* I'll be successful!" Restless was convinced. Sandy was becoming so too. Her spirit sank further. "Sandy? You look like you really could use one of my drinks. I'll give you a friendly discount. What will you try?" Restless leaned over his cart and his smile sparkled in the familiar way that Mr. Success's had.

Sandy reached for her bag as if automatically searching for payment, then came to her senses, remembering what was in this precious pouch of hers. "No. No, thank you. I'm amazed to see you, but I don't need a drink. I'm just going to go sit down for a bit. Maybe I'll come back later." Sandy backed away, and crossed over to the opposite corner of the Crossroads, on the right side of the narrow way, but still next to the broad way.

"Suit yourself!" Restless called after her. "I'll be here all night long selling potions that can liven up any trip you are on! Come back and see me, old friend!"

She didn't turn back to respond. Instead, she spotted a bench to occupy on the opposite side. She could see Restless's stand to her left, but set her gaze on the flickering lights of the city. Sandy sat and stared, quietly taking in all the sounds, smells, and sights her senses could gather as they drifted in from the city. She heard her old music in the distance, and muffled tones from the intercom. The familiarity of it all was enticing her. She thought she even smelled the scent of bread from BIG'S, and was sure she could hear the sound of her friends laughing—the sounds of Pride and Doubt, probably, mocking her. The city she stared at still had a pull on her.

Those traveling on this broad way were here for the nightlife now; they danced and sang as they crossed by. Lights were strung up across the wide path, presenting a grander invitation to all who approached to party their way to Excess. Sandy just observed, almost hypnotized by the scene. The later it got, the more like a carnival it became. More carts of potions and portable pleasures pulled up to offer their vices to incoming guests. It was a crowded and colorful scene. Sandy did not join in, but drifted internally in neutral as she watched.

A gust of wind assaulted her with a harder blow, as it carried a newspaper page up to the foot of the bench where she sat. It was from that day's paper, and had flown in from the City of Excess somehow to share news of the happenings there. Sandy bent down to remove the sheet plastered against the bench and her leg, and when she did, she caught sight of the current events she wished she could have remained ignorant of. Sandy spotted a picture of Mr. Success with Pride of all people. They were smiling widely outside one of Mr. Success's theatres. Pride had been cast as a lead in a show. Sandy could not read on about it. Jealousy assailed her heart. She glanced on down the page. There was an ad for BIG'S, with Mr. Big looking happier than ever, hugging his glamorous wife, Mrs. Vain Conceit, at his side, who appeared unusually happy. She also noticed a social column by Ms. Selfish Ambition, listing all of the places to be in the city, if you were anyone...

"Anyone who's *anyone* is headed *that* way, my dear!" Someone took the spot next to Sandy on the bench. Sandy

154

lowered the paper and looked over. This character looked young in the face, but dressed like an old man in a loose-fitting gray suit. He had long unkempt hair topped with a fedora, and wore shoes that needed polishing. He looked as if he were trying to fit in with the scores of folks headed to Excess, but didn't quite have the right look. Sandy did not respond to him, but continued to examine this curiously strange yet familiar individual. "Yep! They are ALL going to the city. Good for them. GOOD FOR THEM," the stranger dramatically repeated, looking over the crowd.

Sandy could no longer ignore him. "Excuse me...Who are you?"

"Oh! Don't you recognize me? I thought you would. I'm Self-Pity, my dear. We've met before," he informed her with a woeful stare.

"I'm sorry. I don't recall," Sandy stated skeptically as she studied him further.

"No matter," he said dismissively as he slid a little closer, putting his arm up on the bench as he turned to Sandy. "You look like you could use a friend, just sitting here all alone, watching the beautiful people go by. Why ARE you here alone?"

Sandy knew better than to engage this stranger. He did not seem trustworthy at all, but her defenses were down. "I...I was just passing through, and decided to take a break." Sandy decided it was best to limit her answer.

"Oh! So you ARE on your way to Excess—just resting up for the exciting journey?" Self-Pity pressed.

"No. I was traveling in that direction." Sandy referred with her glance to the narrow path that ran perpendicular to the broad one they sat by.

Self-Pity chuckled, "You mean that little dirt path? Well, where does that lead? Can't be anywhere exciting! There aren't even any lights. And I don't see one soul traveling there," he added as he stretched his head, straining to prove his point.

Sandy turned to her right to look as well. He was correct. There was no one on that path, and it was growing dim in the shadows of the lit broad way. She was growing embarrassed of her commitment to this quaint course. It seemed so antiquated compared to the road that led to Excess. Sandy said nothing, but just turned her head back and dropped her gaze down. Self-Pity moved in even closer.

"My Friend, why would you choose that path? Why would you go it alone? There are so many friends to make on this way. And there is promise of *becoming* someone BIG and important in Excess!" How did this stranger know? This was indeed her old dream and he was bringing it back to mind as her dream city sparkled right before her very eyes.

Then she remembered. "Jasper...the Kingdom..." She let out these words in a whisper, unconsciously.

"Who? What? What did you say?" Self-Pity demanded. "What are you talking about?"

Sandy's face grew hot. She knew this stranger would not understand. She knew it would never make sense to anyone here. She wasn't even sure it made sense to her right now. But could she deny why she chose this path? "The Kingdom," she sheepishly replied. "I'm traveling to the Kingdom."

Self-Pity dropped his jaw in a dramatic pause, then softly echoed her, "The Kingdom. Oh, my dear. *You* believe in fairy tales, don't you?" He thought she was crazy. That was it, she thought. He thought she was crazy, and maybe she was. Self-Pity allowed no time for her to defend herself. "You know that's not a real place, don't you? There is no 'kingdom' other than what is here, and what we can see. You've been misled, my dear! If there *were* a real 'kingdom,' why would so many happy travelers be going towards Excess? You are ALONE in your thinking and ALONE in your way. I can barely see it now ahead. It looks like it is leading nowhere!"

Sandy turned again to look down her path. It did indeed disappear into the night sky. She could barely make out any of it with the gaiety of the party on the broad way. She shook her head and muttered to herself, "But I have come so far. What am I to do?"

Self-Pity took his cue. "Poor thing. You are tired. You are weary. I can tell you've traveled long and hard today on this dusty path, trying to do the right thing, only to be disappointed. Let me help you get out of here!"

The disillusioned princess could not stand to stay here, but could not imagine advancing down her charted path either. She battled a barrage of thoughts in her head. Had she been misled? Was the Kingdom really a figment of her own fantasy? Why had she not stayed in Excess, the place all of these people were happy to make their way towards? "I do need to get out of here—but where can we go? I don't think I have the energy to make it to the city tonight in this stream of partiers," she admitted.

"I know a short-cut!" Self-Pity proposed. "It's a rest stop of sorts for weary ones such as you. Follow me." Self-Pity rose, and without resistance, Sandy followed. He led her onto the broad way for just a few yards, past Restless, and then down an embankment that led to a flat field.

As she was guided by Self-Pity, she could think of nothing but how bad she felt for herself. *How could I be so dumb? Why did I let them tell me what to do? I've always been so independent, and those strangers wore me down with their empty promises.* Her thoughts turned worse, the farther they drifted. *What will become of me now? I'm ruined. I had my chance at success and ran away. I left everything I had—my home, my friends, and now I'm here to see the world go on happily without me. I don't know if I can go on anymore. I don't know if I even want to.* Sandy was crying now, tears of regret and hopelessness. Never had she felt so despondent and alone.

And there they stopped at the cusp of a great hole. Self-Pity stepped to the side, allowing Sandy to stand alone on the edge. She noticed a metal slide of sorts, rounding the hole and spiraling downward toward an unseen end. Her heart beat with fear. "Where are we? What is this?" she questioned her escort.

"This is the short cut I spoke of. It's called 'The Spiral of Despair,' and it's made for weary travelers just like you. It will lead you back to the Wastelands. Simply give yourself to it, have a seat, and you will slide all the way home, where you belong. Listen to your feelings, Sandy! I'm sure they will tell you this is the only choice you have."

My feelings... Sandy thought. She instantly recalled the *feelings* she saw on the side roads earlier. They led people astray down paths that led nowhere good at all. Where would her feelings lead her now? What had Wisdom said to do? *Wisdom!* Sandy recalled. If she ever needed him, she needed him now. But she was so weak. She stood still for a moment, looking down the dark hole.

"Well," Self-Pity prompted, "why don't you sink right down there —I mean *sit* right down there on the edge, and think about taking this shortcut for yourself. You deserve a break from the long journey. You are going to end up back in the Wastelands anyway. You might as well take the fast track home. This is the easiest way."

"The way..." Sandy repeated, and suddenly Sandy experienced a peculiar peace and strength washing over her. As if awakened from a trance, Sandy remembered her map book. If this was indeed the easiest way, it should be marked in there. She stepped back and grabbed her pouch. Her quick response alarmed Self-Pity.

"What are you doing? What are you grabbing for?" he asked nervously as she opened her bag.

"My map. I have a map book of this whole region. It should identify any shortcuts. I just want to confirm where I am." Sandy spoke with more authority than she had thus far in her exchanges with Self-Pity.

"Why, I'm sure that old book is outdated! I'm sure it can't help you at all!" Self-Pity tried to prohibit her actions.

"Let me just see…" Sandy insisted, then asked aloud, "Jasper, guide me with Wisdom." Self-Pity backed off, speechless as Sandy turned to this book that lit up as she opened it. Her eyes fell straight to this instruction:

"For you are children of the light and of the day; you don't belong to darkness and night. So be on your guard…stay alert and be clearheaded."

Sandy knew this instruction was for her. She had not been on her guard and had allowed the ways of the night to fog her thinking. Now she considered how to get out of this place she found herself in. Sandy's eyes were drawn down the page where she saw something sticking out of the map. She flipped the page to find a key placed within the pages. She had not noticed it before. *Jasper must have slipped it in,* she thought. From the glow of the pages she could read another word inscribed on the long shaft of this key. It said, "Thanksgiving."Right next to the key where it lay on the page were these words for Sandy to see:

"Give thanks in every circumstance, for this is the King's will."

As Sandy stopped to consider this, the truth of these words penetrated her thinking. Self-Pity had led her to this Spiral of Despair, but now she would test the instruction of her map and this key by doing what it led her to do.

"I thank you, my King. I thank you for the many gifts you have given me. I thank you for your devotion to me, and for the

Jesus words in Red.

kindness I have found in my journey today. I thank you for a map that lights my path and for giving me the friendship of Wisdom, Joy and Peace..."

"What are you doing?" Self-Pity whispered in desperation.

Sandy ignored him. "I thank you, my Prince, for the real love I feel from you in my heart, and the real love I have for you. Though I have not seen you, you have allowed me to taste greater love than I ever have..." Sandy was feeling renewed with every word of thanks.

"This is ridiculous," Self-Pity protested.

"I thank you for the hope I hold in my heart, and the faith that has renewed me. I thank you for true friends that encourage and for the safety I have known along this way..."

"That's it! You are CRAZY, Sandy!" Self-Pity was enraged now. He grabbed his hat to throw it off in a fit, and as he did, his hair came off with it too, revealing the true character costumed as Self-Pity—

"Pride? Pride, is that you?" Sandy was shocked to see him standing before her, exposed for who he was.

"What?" Pride was uncovered. He scrambled in his response, "I am an ACTOR, you know! Just trying to convince you to come back to where you belong! It was a role SOMEBODY had to play in your life! So are you coming or not?"

Sandy faced off with Pride once again. As she stared at his features, she remembered what had pulled her into a friendship with him. He was confident in a cocky sort of way. He acted like he knew where he was going, and he always bragged about the future they would have if she just stuck with him. But now the truth was revealed. He tried to hide under the guise of sympathetic Self-Pity and led her to a spiral of her own despair to return her back to where she had started. He was no friend to have at all.

"No. No, I will not come with you. And you should not go

either. There is no real future for you there, Pride." Sandy was unsure how to convince him, but thought she must try. "You should come with me. The King can transform you too, I'm sure of it. I can share my map with you. It will show us the way of the real Kingdom."

Her words made no sense to him, for he was still asleep. His ears could not make sense of her plea at all, so he laughed. Pride laughed hard. "Me? Me, come with YOU, as a *lone wanderer* out here on a path with NO ONE? No one to applaud you or even perform for? Ha! That is really funny, Sandy! You are HYSTERICAL!" And with that, Pride began to laugh so hard that he stumbled backwards and tripped at the edge of the deep hole where he had led Sandy. "WHOA!" Pride yelled as he now slid down the spiral of his own despair. Where he would end up, Sandy wasn't sure, but for now that was the end of Pride.

This did not please Sandy. She had compassion for her old friend, but he was not ready to listen. She opened her map book for any word of instruction or comfort, asking for Wisdom's help again. She was led to these words:

"Pride goes before destruction, and arrogance before a fall."

How true these words were. How thankful she was not to follow Pride's lead, even disguised as Self-Pity. And how grateful she was to discover the key of thankfulness that kept her from going down the spiral of despair herself.

Sandy was tired now. It had been a long day, and she had encountered more than she dreamed she could when she left the garden that morning. It was time to rest now. Sandy turned to head back to her path, but didn't know where to go. "The map book," she whispered in a smile to herself. It was beginning to become natural to turn there. She was led once again to just her spot in this unknown territory and read,

"Those who dwell in the shelter of the Most High
will find rest in the shadow of the Great King."

Sandy lifted her head and saw there above her a shelter up in the trees with a warm glow inside. The "Most High" King had prepared a place right there for her, even in the midst of this enemy territory. She climbed up the wood-plank ladder and into this safe haven for the night. There was room for a fluffy mattress on the floor with a small, low table beside the door. On the table was a basin of water and a cloth to wash up, and fresh food wrapped just for her. The candle had just been lit, and Sandy immediately knew... *Jasper. I thank you too. You are too good to me. I almost got lost again, but you never do give up on me, just like you said. Thank you, my friend!*

Sandy partook of all that had been prepared for her, and then lay down to sleep. Before she blew out the candle, she took out her map book to place it next to her, rubbing her hand over its age-worn cover. "And I thank you for this *this* light, my friend! I don't think I should doubt it again. It has kept me sound and safe today. I am indeed grateful for this gift. Good night!" With that, Sandy blew out the candle and sank under the thick comforter provided. She indeed found rest in the shadows, for she now knew where her refuge was. It would always be with her King, in special secret places he had chosen.

17

The Lodge at Love's Way

*I*n that foggy space between wake and sleep, Sandy heard the clear voice of her Prince in the morning. "*You* have the *greatest call*, my Princess..." That was all she heard.

Sandy flipped the comforter down and sat up. Morning light streamed through the wood framed windows of her refuge in the trees. She looked around. The little tree house was even more enchanting by daylight. The walls were wide planks of warm woods and the floor was wood as well, covered by a thick, woven wool rug. She felt comfort in this safe place, but was puzzled by these words she so plainly perceived. "*You* have the *greatest call...*" Whatever did that mean?

Sandy stretched and moved about in this small place, happy to be tucked away and off the beaten path of her journey for a respite. She sat back down on her mattress and noticed a small mirror above the table, between the door and window. She looked, examining the effects of the journey so far on her appearance. Her skin was peachy and rosy. Her eyes looked clearer, more blue than gray in this light, compared to how she usually saw them. And the dark circles beneath her eyes were filled in with flesh tones. Though the journey had not been easy, she did not look worn like she did after a day's work in the Wastelands. Sandy was puzzled and pleased by this at the same time, not breaking her stare until she heard the sound of singing below.

"This is the day! This is the day that the King has made—I will rejoice! I will rejoice and be glad in it..." The vigor and vitality in that tune rushed in through the open window and splashed Sandy's heart with joy. And Joy was exactly who was singing below.

"Princess! Is there a Princess up there? I have come to get you, love!" Joy's smile beamed like a sun from below and Sandy's face was lit with happiness by it as she peeked out the window to meet her friendly call.

"Joy! Joy, is that you? I can't believe you came by this way!" Sandy cried with a laugh.

"Oh, I always come in the morning, at least for the King's kids! No matter how troubled the night may be, you can look forward to me coming in the morning," she chuckled in her bright and booming way. "Now, come on down. We have places to go today, Princess! There are people for you to meet and lessons to learn!" Joy made it all seem surprising and fun. Sandy quickly tidied up her retreat in the rafters of the woods, and scurried down to join her new companion, Joy.

"Come here, girl!" No sooner did she hit the ground than Joy reached for her to offer a hearty hug. *"That's* how we greet around here as citizens of the Kingdom! Nothing like a good ole hug to fill you up on love! And that's exactly what YOU are going to fill up on today!" Joy didn't wait for a reply but grabbed Sandy's hand and started leading her back on a trail she had blazed, and up the embankment to get her young friend back on the narrow way.

They had to cross back over the broad way, the short distance Sandy had traveled it the night before. It certainly did not look like the same road. "What in the world?" Sandy gasped in a whisper, taking in the debris and aftermath of the party the night before.

The scent was atrocious, as the over-indulgence of potions made many sick as they followed and fell along the way. Sandy could see some of these travelers passed out on the side of the road in ditches and ruts. Their faces were not as pretty as the night before, as the paint had smeared and worn off. Trash was strewn about, and one lone sweeper was the only one on his feet now. The sound of his broom was the solitary sound of this morning after.

"It's never as pretty or appealing in the daylight as it is in at night," Joy observed. "When you can only see by artificial light, you have to wonder what is hidden in all that darkness…" Sandy knew this was the same road, but Joy was right. It was not alluring at all anymore.

Sandy looked behind her down the path towards Excess. People were still stumbling on and tripping over others who were passed out. She saw many "short cuts" off of the main broad road that people were taking. She did not know where they all led, but could not believe they would lead anywhere good at all, not after the *short cut* she had experienced the night before. She turned back to Joy with a tinge of shame in her eyes. "I…I almost went back. I followed Self-Pity and he led me down this path a while. How could I have strayed so easily?" Sandy asked, conveying her disdain for the choice she had made.

"My dear, you are a citizen of the Kingdom, but you have not been perfected yet! You are a work in progress, and you will make some wrong choices, but His Grace will save you, over and over again. Because you are his, and because you have said yes to this journey, the King will always offer his gift of GRACE to lead you out of any trouble you might find yourself in and set you back in the right direction!"

"But I certainly did not deserve such a gift. I followed Pride of my own free will. I deserved to fall into that pit of despair," Sandy reflected.

"We never do deserve grace. And we never can earn it," Joy

explained. "It's a *gift*, my child—a great favor granted by your father who loves you that much! It's a mysterious thing, I know. But grace is strong and amazing. You did well to accept that gift last night!"

"I certainly experienced something like that when I stood by that great gaping hole." Sandy recalled the inexplicable strength and peace that had rescued her the night before as she stood on the edge of Despair. "So that is what saved me?"

"Yes! That was grace, followed by your faith in the map and the writer of it. His grace saved you at first, back at the fountain with Page, it saved you last night, and it will save you again if needed. The King never runs out of it, and that's a good thing!"

Sandy laughed. "You have a way of making me forget all my sorrows, Joy! I so need you in my life."

"You most certainly do!" Joy playfully retorted. "Now let's hit the narrow road again and get away from this awful smelling junk!" Joy grabbed Sandy's hand again, keeping a wide distance between them and the lone sweeper as they passed by. "Watch out for that guy," Joy whispered. "They call him 'Denial.' They say he tries to cover things up on this road, making it all look better than it really is. Guess you got to wake up early enough to catch him in the act and see this mess for yourself. Come on, let's get out of his way!" They scooted on over to where the narrow path resumed, and bellowed happy songs of the Kingdom as they went.

The air was soon fresh again, and Joy was having a wonderful, freeing influence on her new friend. Sandy had never known companionship like this. Joy had her appreciating all of the simple beauty along the way. "Each little flower just shouts of the King's greatness, don't you think, Sandy? He made it so all that color and delicacy fit into a tiny seed. And then, in just the right time, after just the right amount of water, soil and sun...BOOM! A flower pops out, just in time to smile at us as we walk by. Now *that* is an awesome thing!" Joy smiled right back at the little purple flower

166

she spoke of that greeted them along their path. Sandy grinned as well, and nodded in agreement.

"He is pretty awesome! The longer I walk, the more I know that is true," Sandy acknowledged as they journeyed along at a pleasant pace.

"That is just as it should be, Princess," Joy confirmed. "And there is so much more beauty to be discovered and such amazing mysteries to thrill your soul with as you walk along. Oh, you are in for a remarkable adventure!"

That made Sandy remember those first words of her morning; "*You* have the *greatest call*, My Princess…" Sandy decided to ask her new friend what this might mean.

Joy nodded knowingly after Sandy explained what she had heard. "Girl, I am taking you to just the right place! I've got someone to introduce you to that will explain exactly what that means. You're gonna LOVE her!"

Sandy was satisfied for the moment, content with the coming encounter. They walked on at a steady pace in the brisk morning air until they saw a figure up ahead, leaning on a post by the side of the road, eating an apple.

"Peace, be still my heart," cried Joy.

"Who is that?" asked Sandy, unsure of who the stranger in the distance was.

"It's Peace! My good friend Peace—don't you remember him from the café? Oh, I am always glad to run into him!" Joy added a bounce to her stride and Sandy fell in step. They approached Peace, who swallowed his mouthful of fruit and grinned widely.

"Hello there, ladies. I've been waiting for you." Everything about Peace had a calming affect on those he encountered. Sandy experienced it immediately.

"Well, thank you for waiting so patiently, Peace! You here to walk with us the rest of the way?" Joy patted his shoulder fondly as they arrived.

"Yes. I wanted some time with the Princess after her long journey yesterday. Thought I could share some of my fruit with her." Peace tossed Sandy an apple, which she caught on the fly. "You want one too, Joy? Picked straight from the orchard this morning—lots of fruit being produced up ahead."

"Of course! I can never resist fruit from the orchard. It is the best around!"

Peace tossed her one as well and the three of them crunched into the sweet fruit as they commenced to walk on.

"It's great to see you again, Peace," Sandy started as they strolled along. "Though I could have really used your company last night," she chided in a friendly way.

"Well, you can always have me. I am available to you at all times, Princess. Joy and I both are. Friendship with us comes with citizenship in the Kingdom! You just have to remember we are there. Do you still have the bottles we gave you?"

Sandy felt her bag at her side, remembering, and responded, "Yes—yes I do. There is a bottle called 'peace' in there, isn't there?"

"Yes. It is the *essence* of peace, just to remind you that he is with you." Joy instructed. "Peace and joy are always yours, and we'll be your constant companions on this right road you walk. You just have to remember we're here—and don't *lose* us!" Joy smiled broadly as she elbowed Sandy playfully.

Sandy pondered their words and their way. As she walked between these two, she felt satisfied, as if she could never stray again. She was completely at home in their presence, walking along this narrow, dusty road. Peace and Joy were indeed the best companions to have.

Sandy was enjoying their company so much as they told stories and laughed, that she never gave a thought to where they were going. It was soon mid-morning, and the path led to a slight fork in the road. By the road to the right was a wooden plank sign, nailed to a post that read, *Love's Way.* Joy and Peace paused for Sandy to read it, then Peace gestured with his hand in the direction of the sign. "Right this way, Princess! This is the way we are going."

Sandy nodded and cast each of them a wondering glance, then proceeded without a word. She trusted them implicitly, and knew wherever Peace led her, she should follow, especially if it was marked by such a way as Love.

The path was lovely. Rich green pastures bordered it on both sides. Animals were grazing in the rolling fields. A stream ran down to her left, and the sound of its flow reminded her of her dear friends Page and Carry and the lessons she had learned with them. "Thank you, my father," Sandy burst out unintentionally as her happy heart swelled at the sights that surrounded her walk. Peace and Joy joined her, and for the next few moments, they talked to their unseen King, thanking him for bringing them to such a space, where Peace and Joy could so easily guide Sandy in her way.

The path narrowed into an uphill, tree-lined drive opening up into a grassy yard where a grand and inviting wood-sided home topped the hill. They had arrived at the Lodge at Love's Way.

"What is this place?" Sandy's eyes were wide and wondering, searching every friendly feature within her sight. There was an old well in the front yard, and flowerbeds and fruit gardens were sprawled about. The full front of the lodge was wrapped with a wide porch, furnished with multiple seating areas of the coziest kinds. The house seemed large but intimate, and Sandy could not wait to go inside.

"We are at the Lodge at Love's Way," Joy said, "and now you get to meet Ruby, the caretaker of this most wonderful place." Sandy smiled, still taking in the details of this most desirable dwelling, then looked to Peace who nodded for her to walk on. The three ascended the broad steps going up to the porch, and then Joy stepped in front to knock on the door.

A face as bright as Joy's radiated back through the screen door, followed by a cheery voice to match. "Friends! You are here! Jasper whispered you were on your way. Come in!" The door flung wide open, and so did the arms of the embracing woman who extended the invitation.

Ruby was a tall woman with bobbed, blonde hair mixed with gray that bounced as she whisked about. Her whole way was friendly and inviting. She was a woman of great compassion who desired to love all in her path. Her countenance was lit from the inside by the King of Love himself as she carried his presence. Her effervescent smile spread that light from within, illuminating dreary perspectives of visitors to the Lodge, and boosting the visions of others who would come here to grow in Love's Way.

"Ruby!" Joy exclaimed. "I'm so glad we got to bring the Princess to you today." Ruby and Joy hugged tight. They were like sisters who loved deeply and well, and shared a great history together.

Ruby reached for Peace too, and patted his back. The sight of him caused her to sigh in relief. Next she paused right before Sandy, and bent to stare her directly in her eyes for just a moment. She broke her silence with an observation. "Sandy—but not for long. I see something lovely in the making. Come in."

Sandy knew Ruby could see something deep inside of her that she could not see for herself yet, but as she followed this Kingdom crew inside, Sandy trusted it would all be revealed in due time. For now she was here with Joy and Peace, and about to explore the warmth of this delightful lodge she found herself in.

Ruby's kitchen emitted smells much like the kitchens of Kindness and Carry. Brunch was being prepared, and Sandy was led to the dining room where a banqueting table awaited.

"You are right on time, my friends! We have just finished preparing a feast for you all. You must be starving after your long walk. Have a seat and my girls will serve you in a second. I'm going to let them know you are here." Ruby disappeared through the swinging kitchen door and allowed her guests to seat themselves at the long and well-dressed table. It was covered with eyelet cotton cloth and had different china plates at each place setting. The table was fancy but friendly. Small clear glass vases of garden-picked flowers were placed in front of each plate. Clunky cut-glass goblets of various jewel-tones, along with polished silver utensils flanked the plates as well, with lace-lined napkins under each fork. Peace motioned for Sandy to sit at the head of the table as the honored guest. She resisted at first with a shake of her head, but yielded as Joy cleared her throat and nodded to insist. They left a seat for Ruby to sit by the kitchen door to Sandy's right. Peace took the seat to Sandy's left and Joy to the right of Ruby's.

As they settled into their spots in silence, Sandy lifted her eyes to a handcrafted banner that was hung above the thick wood-framed doorway she faced at the other end of the table. It simply said "LOVE." And that is what she felt—love all around. The walls oozed with it through every work of artful beauty hung about. The very air was saturated with it. Love could be breathed in this place. There was so much to take in. Every detail of the room declared love, and today Sandy would be its recipient. She wondered if this could all be real.

Ruby burst through the swinging door holding a tray, followed by her two helpers, who each had trays of their own. "We will set all this down and eat family style. It's the only way to go, I always say." They did just that, then Ruby took her seat next to Sandy, and the two other girls filled in the remaining spots. It was time to feast.

Ruby extended her hands to those sitting at either side of her, and all were signaled to do the same. This circle of strangers-made-family, thanked their King for all his provisions and kindnesses to them, including the food. When they were done blessing him back, the feasting began, but more importantly, the lessons for which they came.

"So, my dear," Ruby began, "You are here about your call."

Sandy gulped down her current mouthful and froze. "How did you know?"

Ruby's eyes sparkled like the rare gem she was named for. She was rare indeed—generous in nature, yet right to the point. Her stare was strong yet soft, not intimidating, yet intense. And most importantly, Sandy felt accepted and loved. She answered, "You wouldn't have come here unless you wanted to know… about your call. And it is the greatest call you could have." Ruby took another bite, smiling as she did at some inner knowing. It was a knowledge Sandy hoped she would share.

"What is my call?" Sandy asked. "I would so love to know. I thought it was just to get to the Kingdom, to meet my Prince and the King, but is there more?"

All at the table exchanged glances and soft smiles. They all knew the answer and were excited for Sandy to discover it as well.

"Yes." Ruby responded. "There is so much more to the journey. The greatest call…is to love."

It sounded so simple to Sandy. "To love?" she asked aloud. *That's all?* she inwardly thought.

Ruby could tell what she was thinking, "Yes, and it's not as easy as it sounds, but it is most rewarding. Your greatest call, Sandy, is to love!"

Sandy let this settle for a moment before entreating her, "Tell me more. If it is my call, I have a lot to learn!"

The guests all chuckled, but only Ruby replied, "We all do, Sandy. We will never complete all of our lessons in love. There will always be more to learn. But I will start by telling you that the reason it is the greatest call is because this call is based on the greatest rule of the Kingdom. Let me show you in your map book, my dear."

Sandy drew her map book from the bag and handed it to

Ruby, who handled it with such experience and understanding. She knew just where to turn. "See, here it says that the greatest rule is to love the King with all of your heart, all of your soul, all of your mind and all of your strength." She pointed to each word as she spoke them. "I particularly love the word 'all' in there! Full devotion is the key!" Sandy remembered the key of devotion she had been offered. She was glad she had accepted it. Ruby continued, "and the second greatest rule is like it, 'Love your neighbor as yourself.' That sums it all up. All the rules of the Kingdom are tied up in two simple instructions: Love the King and love others as yourself. It is simple, but not easy!"

Sandy tried to let this all soak in. She knew what Ruby said about it being "simple but not easy" would definitely be true for her. She wasn't even sure *how* to love, let alone love with everything in her. She admitted this to her new friend. "But why…why would he call me to this? I have never really loved anyone well myself. In the Wastelands we mostly look out for ourselves. That's all I'm used to doing." Sandy thought the King must be wrong in giving her the greatest call, if this is what it was.

"Princess, he wouldn't call you unless he would make you able. And you are indeed capable of great love. It is yours for the asking! The King is love itself and can extend his love into the hearts of any willing to carry it. You simply must ask. That's what I did years ago. I asked the King over and over, 'King, increase my capacity to love! Increase my capacity to love!' and he did just that! Sandy, this whole journey you are on is one great big lesson in love. Well-meaning travelers can get side-tracked and focused on other subjects the map book explains, but the greatest rule, therefore the greatest objective of ours should be to do everything in love!"

This resonated with Sandy, but still she was lost. "Where do I begin this love walk, Ruby? Will you teach me?"

"There's no one better!" Joy chimed in. "Why don't you show

her where the map explains what love is," she suggested.

"Indeed! I was just headed that direction in the map myself. Girls, will you clear the table so we can begin to study? We'll take dessert in the den later." Ruby's two helpers rose, content to clear dishes, while the others leaned in over the table to learn more from the map book on love. "Let's start right here." Ruby turned to a page illuminating this meaning all the more. "Ah, here it is! 'The Most Excellent Way...'" She read aloud;

"Love is patient and kind. Love does not envy,
it does not boast, and it is not proud or rude. It
does not demand its own way. It is not easily angered,
and it keeps no record of wrongs. It does not rejoice
at wrongdoing, but rejoices whenever the truth wins
out. Love never gives up, never loses faith, always
hopes, and endures through every circumstance."

Ruby paused as Sandy stared at these words, glowing in the map book. "Wow. That is a most beautiful but difficult way indeed. I've never seen anyone walk completely in that kind of path," Sandy confessed.

"No one ever does walk it completely or perfectly, but it is the way in which citizens of the Kingdom are to endeavor to walk. It's how the Prince walked when he came, and it's how the King desires his kids to journey—to love him and love others in this way."

"But how?" asked Sandy. "How will I ever love well when I so seldom feel patient or kind, and so often feel jealous and boastful and rude?"

"You can," answered Ruby "because love is a decision you make, not a feeling you have. Love is a choice, made regardless of how you feel."

Ruby went on to explain in detail how when the Prince walked in this world, he did not *feel* like making the sacrificial choices he did that caused him pain, but he made those choices to go into battle and lay down his life out of great love—for all. "He chose love, despite the pain. And because of that choice, we can know the King's love. The Prince's great choice made the greatest love available to us. And now this father of love wishes to lavish his kids with such great love that they never forget who they are, and will share it with those still unaware of who they really are. That's why the love walk is so important. The others lost about their way will know you, and come to know *him*, by your love."

Sandy understood. It indeed was simple, but she knew these lessons would not come easy. "What should I do first? How do I make myself ready for this walk, Ruby? I really want to be great at this new call of mine."

"Well," said Ruby, loving Sandy's enthusiasm, "you have the first step mastered—commitment to this way! Now remember this before we go on. There are only two things of true, eternal value: the King and people. Invest your life in that. And that investment requires your love. It will bring eternal rewards."

"And great reward here too!" Joy interrupted, "Just look around. Ruby's the most loving one I know, and this place is *proof* of what a life of love can bring. Look here..." Joy rose and led Sandy, followed by the others, into Ruby's hallway that ran from the door to the great room. Almost from floor to ceiling were framed pictures of Ruby with all kinds of people from all sorts of lands. These pictures told stories of deep friendships through many years—more stories than Ruby would ever have time to tell, though they were all rooted and treasured in her heart.

"Wow...you know a lot of people," was all Sandy could manage to say.

"I collect friends." Ruby scanned the wall with her gaze for just a moment, absorbing a bit more joy from these memories in her heart before she continued, "And I'm so thankful to add you to my collection, dear Princess! Let's go to the den."

Ruby mentored Sandy in the ways of love for the next few hours and days. She lodged there in a guest room upstairs, and walked with Ruby in the gardens each morning. Here Ruby taught Sandy from her experiences and the map book how to care for and grow the garden of her own heart. Sandy spent much time alone there too, talking to her Prince and the King. Her heart was being expanded as the King was pouring from his great heart of love into hers.

Ruby had given Sandy a journal on her first night before bed. "Here's a gift, sweet Sandy. It is a blank book now, but write your heart out in it, and write *his* heart out too! Listen for what he says. He has so much to say to you!"

Sandy treasured this gift, a record of her growing relationship with her Prince and father. She wrote down whispers she heard from Jasper as well. Writing it all down helped her remember what she heard from their hearts, and chart the progress of her own. It was a great tool for hearing and seeing the goodness of all she was learning.

On her last evening at the Lodge before departing the next morning, Sandy sat with Ruby on the wide front porch, both sipping from mugs of hot drink. They quietly enjoyed each other's company, staring at the setting sun over the line of trees at the drive. Sandy broke the silence as she asked, "So what do you see in me, Ruby? The first day you saw me, you said you saw something in me. What is it?"

Ruby looked over and smiled as she leaned her head back on the old rocker she sat in. "I see a gem," she simply stated. "I see a beautiful gem, formed from the pressure and even out of the irritations of life. I see such beauty, but I only see in part. Only the King knows in full what he is making you into. Just remain in him. He will see this beautiful work he has started completed." Ruby told her how her own life has been formed as well, under pressure and sometimes in dark places. "…But Jasper was always there with me, and he brought me out, and *shined* me up into the 'Ruby' you see today," she said with a wink, "and I see him doing the same kind of thing with you. I suppose that's part of the reason he brought you here, so you can learn from the lessons I've lived."

Sandy nodded reflectively before she said, "It's been such an honor…to be taught by you, here, in this safe and beautiful place! I could never thank you enough. You have loved me so well."

"It has been a greater delight for me," Ruby sincerely replied. "And that's the way of love," she chuckled. "You follow the rule to love, and you get filled up with joy! What a deal that is!"

Sandy nodded silently in agreement, letting this truth soak in.

Then they turned to the sunset again and Sandy continued to drink it all in. Her heart was warmed from the words of her mentor and from the love she had known in this stay. But tomorrow she would depart and forge on back into Love's Way, and allow this way to be expanded within her for the rest of her journey.

18
The Gated Community

After one final morning meal had been enjoyed under that banner of love in the dining room, Sandy and her family of friends rose to gather on the front porch and say their farewells. Joy opened the door and Peace led Sandy out, staying close to her side. Ruby came last and completed their small circle between the door and the steps. "Well, here we are," Ruby said with a sigh. "What a wonderful visit we've had!" Ruby was teary as she smiled proudly at her beloved new student.

Sandy returned the teary look. "I've learned so much from you all. I…I wish I could stay forever."

"I know," said Ruby, "but the way of love is one that must be walked out. Now you get to practice. And there are so many people who need you to pick them to practice on," Ruby said with subtle humor in her tone. "Here—I have something for you. I wrote it out for you last night." Ruby pulled from her apron pocket a small booklet made of textured paper. Within it were beautifully hand written coordinates of some kind.

"What is this?" Sandy asked.

"These are coordinates found in the map book. They all lead you to treasures in love, and wisdom needed along the way. The road ahead will be challenging in parts, and it's about to get much steeper, but armed with love, you can overcome any obstacle you face. Yes, you are ready, Princess! It's time to ascend higher so you can see more from the King's perspective."

"And the views are beautiful," Peace added. "It will be worth the climb." He nodded with an assuring wink.

"And you are not going alone," Joy added in her warm bold way. "Tell her, Ruby!"

Ruby laughed, "I was getting there, Joy. No, you are not going alone, Princess. I'm sending my girls with you." Ruby called for her two helpers to join them on the porch. "Quietness! Confidence! Are you ready?" The two young helpers swung open the screen door and joined the group on the porch. They were wearing backpacks and hiking boots.

Confidence had an extra pair in her hand and offered them to Sandy. "Surprise, friend! We're coming with you! And you will need to put these on for where we are going." Sandy received them and studied the fresh faces of these two friends she would be journeying with. They smiled back in a most accepting and pleasant way, excited themselves for the journey on which they were about to embark.

"These two have been with me for a long time," Ruby explained, "and they know the trails ahead. Confidence will lead you on. She's great at reminding you of who you are, to whom you belong, and how truly loved you are. Quietness will remind you of the power of your words, a most important point to remember when walking in love. Words can get you into all kinds of trouble. They can lead you to wrong ways of thinking and can intensify dangerous feelings, which can lead you down stray paths. Let Quietness and Confidence be your strength in this journey of love. Lean into them and yield to their promptings. They will help keep you on this narrow way that leads straight to the Kingdom of Love."

Quietness and Confidence both extended their arms to Sandy with wide, receiving smiles. She accepted their hands and the three of them huddled in a hug. Sandy was relieved to have tangible comrades with her who were young like her, yet wise and experienced in the road ahead. "Thank you, Ruby! Thank you for sending them with me. I'm so happy to not leave alone," Sandy admitted in relief. She thanked her new friends. "And thank you for coming! Your presence is a gift to me indeed." Quietness and Confidence both smiled and nodded, then looked to Ruby as she gave final instructions.

"The obstacles ahead should not be feared, for perfect love drives away all fear, and you now have a sprouting garden of love in your heart. From this growth you will be equipped to handle any hindrance. Just keep tending that garden of your heart, not allowing the *weeds* from your old world to choke out your new growth. You will need all the fruit you can possibly bear, both for your own well-being and to share with all the others you are meant to give to along Love's Way."

"The bigger your garden, the more souls can be blessed!" added Joy.

"Indeed," confirmed Ruby. "The greater the love, the greater your call can be heard. Many are intended to be fed from the garden of love in your heart, dear Princess."

Sandy still did not understand all that was said to her, but she nodded, knowing in her heart it was true and right instruction. Ruby continued, "Let love be the motivation for all you do. Be motivated by your love of the King, love of others, then love of yourself. Never be driven to action by fear of any kind, but be moved by your faith in the King and by his love. Do everything in love!"

Confidence spoke up to assure her as well, "And remember, we *can* love, because the King loved us first! Isn't that a good thing to know?"

Sandy considered her words as she paused then added, "Yes. It is so good to be loved. It is so good to be really loved, and for no reason at all. I didn't do anything to deserve it!"

"None of us do, Sandy. None of us do, yet it's who he is and what he does—He loves! And we get to be just like him as we grow up," Ruby added with a gleaming smile on her face.

Just then, a group of kids ran up Love's Way and waved to Ruby from the yard below before breaking out in a game of "hide and seek."

"What are they doing here?" Sandy was shocked to see children show up at just such an important moment in her journey, interrupting her goodbyes.

Ruby waved back at them, smiling broadly as she watched them play. "Oh, they come by every week to see me and just to love on me! Today they are going to help me pick apples from the orchard. I have so much fun with them. No one loves so freely as children. You'll see more along the way and glean so much from their ways. I learn from them all the time."

Sandy remembered Jasper speaking the same way about children on her first visit to the Shores. She was still slightly skeptical, but held her tongue. Sandy glanced over at Quietness, who nodded and smiled as well. Sandy was glad she had kept quiet, and opened her heart and mind to learning from these kids in one way or another in the future. For now she turned her attention back to Ruby and the beautiful friendships formed at this lodge.

"Well, there's so much more I could say," Ruby sighed, "but you have a whole lifetime to learn it. You have your map book, these guides, and the Prince's love that have paved your way. And of course you have our Jasper! I imagine you'll hear him loud and clear as he whispers the way of love as you walk along." Then radiant Ruby reached to pull Sandy in for one final, heart-filled hug for this visit. Sandy relaxed under the love, peace, and joy of this moment, as they all embraced one another in a send-off of affection.

When the cluster relaxed, Sandy stepped back to express her gratitude. "Thank you. I have been refreshed, renewed, and encouraged by you all. Peace and Joy, I know you remain here, but go with me too. You are a part of me now, and I promise to share the joy and peace of our King with others along this way as you have taught me." Joy and Peace both smiled and nodded silently in agreement.

Then Sandy looked to her mentor. "And Ruby, I hope I can grow to be as lovely of a person as you. You glow with love, and light up the world around you with it. Thank you for teaching me, and mostly just for being who you are and allowing me to live life alongside you these many days. You are a treasured friend and teacher. I'm so happy the Prince saw fit to prepare a place for me here with you for this season. Thank you…and, well…goodbye!" Sandy did not know what else to say, but knew it was time. Confidence headed down the steps, followed by Sandy and then Quietness. They made it to the path, then turned to see the three they left on the porch, all waving back.

"Live a life of love, Princess! Just imitate our loving King and live the grandest life possible," Ruby cheered. Sandy nodded, then turned with her two companions to cross through the children playing in the yard and down the tree-lined drive. They walked silently together down Love's Way, each reflecting on the lessons in love they had learned and anticipating what would lie ahead for them.

Soon they reached the main road again, where Confidence broke the silence. "Here we are. The narrow way is to the right. Here we go!" They all giggled and then began to talk and share, exchanging ideas and guesses about what adventures they would have. The three girls got along in a beautiful way, and Sandy was so happy to be provided such friendship. Her heart was instantly connected to theirs, for they shared a common love for the King, the Prince, and Jasper. As they walked along for the next few hours along the country dirt road, they spoke of their Kingdom encounters, and felt the Prince's pleasure as they did so.

The hours passed by quickly in the midst of this company. Sandy did not mind the hills or the heat nearly as much when accompanied by such pleasant and positive friends. She thought of her old friends for a moment. Pride would have resented the long walk, demanding transportation be provided for any sort of lengthy trip. Restless could never have the patience for a leisurely stroll such as this. And Doubt and Worry would have questioned every incline and side road, taking the joy out of the journey for sure. Sandy was quite content to have Confidence and Quietness for companions now. These Kingdom friends were quickly becoming the sisters Sandy had never had and always unknowingly longed for.

"We should be coming to the mountains soon. That's where it gets exciting," Confidence informed the other two as she looked ahead. "This hilly path has been a good warm up for what is to come! I know it is going to get harder but there is beauty to be seen ahead." Quietness and Sandy only nodded and walked on.

Quietness led for a while, allowing Sandy to reflect and also talk privately to the Prince in her heart. She asked him to prepare her for the unknown path ahead. She asked for strength to keep up with Confidence and Quietness when the way would get difficult. And she thanked him for the safety and peace they had enjoyed so far. More peace flooded her heart as she expressed these things, fixing her thoughts on her beloved Prince, whom she had never met, yet loved so much. She heard him reply, "Remain in me. If you remain in me and my words remain in you, ask whatever you wish, and it will be given to you. Now remain in my love..." Sandy gasped at the clarity of his voice heard by her heart. She recalled reading similar instructions in the map book earlier that week when studying it in the garden. It was so sweet to hear these words of his rise within her heart at just the time she needed them. She said nothing to her friends, but pondered this instruction in her heart, and committed to indeed remain in his love. There was nothing she wanted more.

Soon the road turned, and the three travelers saw a bench up ahead on the right side of the road. A stout and miserable looking man was plopped in the middle of it. His feet were firmly planted in the ground underneath, and his arms were crossed. He stared straight ahead with a furrowed brow that hung over his pouty cheeks and lips, and he would not look up, even as he heard the girls approaching. Confidence nudged Sandy to speak to him. It was time to practice what she had been taught.

"Hello, there," she started in a cheery way. "How are you today?" A grunt was the only reply from the man on the bench, who still refused to meet her gaze. Sandy looked to Confidence who nodded for her to continue. "Are…are you Ok? Anything we can do for you, Sir?"

Her additional prodding had lit a fuse within him now, and the man exploded in angry speech, "DO for me? What could you POSSIBLY *DO* for me? You don't even KNOW me! And even if you DID, I don't need help from ANYONE who travels along *this* way!" Sandy was taken aback. Part of her wanted to return the attack, as it was unfair to be treated this way when she was only trying to be kind. Quietness could tell she was ready to defend herself, and touched Sandy's arm gently, shaking her head as a signal to refrain from making a hasty response. Quietness had gotten out her own copy of the map book and simply pointed down to the spot they found themselves in.

"A gentle answer turns away anger."

These were the simple instructions she read. Sandy calmed down and resolved to respond correctly. "I understand. You don't know us. And I'm sorry for any pain you've experienced along this way."

The man was silenced by her words this time, and a calm of sorts even washed over his face. He looked up and stared at her for a second before furrowing his brow again and staring back at his fixed spot. "It's Ok," he muttered. "I've just been stuck here for a very long time, I'm in pain, and it makes me grumpy!" He paused for a moment before adding, "I'm not used to people along this road caring at all!"

Sandy was perplexed. "But, I don't understand, sir. This is supposed to be the *narrow way* we are on...the *way of love*, the *most excellent way*. How could you possibly feel like this?"

The man jeered, "'Love'? The 'way of love'? It's *narrow*, all right! Everyone who travels here is *narrow-minded*, but I have not known much *love* in this way, that is for sure!"

Sandy was even more confused now. She was so enjoying this trip. What could have happened to him? Confidence spoke up. "May I ask your name, sir?"

He looked her in the eye. "Grudge. My name is Grudge. And I have been done wrong so many times along this road. As soon as I try to get anywhere, someone comes along and shoves me out of their way. I've been walked on, used, beaten up and mocked, and I'm just SICK of it! So I'm staying right here," he added with a humph.

Sandy was not sure how to respond. How could someone have made it this far in the journey, traveling the same road she was on, yet have a countenance and disposition like this? What could have happened in his journey? Before she could find words, he added, "Just you wait! You all are young, but you haven't seen what I've seen! You haven't met whom I have met. There are all types on this road, so I just decided to stay right here, and out of their way."

He seemed immovable. Sandy saw nothing but hardened hurt in his eyes that spread to stiffen his face and whole body now. Grudge was stuck to this bench on the side of the road, and Sandy did not know how to help. He had dismissed her for her youth, and it was true she hadn't been on this road long, but she had to try one more time. "Well, sir, do you know what the map book says about where you are and where you should turn? I know the King wouldn't want you stuck here forever!" Sandy could feel her words falling flat as soon as she spoke them.

"Ha! Why don't you ask those travelers up ahead on this road what THEIR map books say! They sure don't seem to be living by their maps at all! Oh, they say they do and sing all about it, then shove others around who don't look and sound just like them! They could care less about me and where I end up! So I'm just staying here. Just leave me be!" With that, Grudge turned his head away from them, crossed his arms all the tighter, and dug his heels further in the ground. Quietness motioned for them all to move on, so they left him on the bench and passed by.

When they were out of his view, Sandy broke into quiet tears. "Why couldn't we help? We tried to love and tried to help. Why couldn't he see that?"

"He wouldn't look past his hurt, Sandy," Confidence answered. "When you spoke of the map and the King, he couldn't get his eyes off of the people who had hurt him to think on truth itself. We haven't been where he's been, it's true, but the King and the map are the right place to turn."

"Let's ask Jasper, the Prince, and the King to pursue him still, as they did us! I feel that is all we can do and must do for now," Quietness suggested. And they did just that. They paused in the road to plead for the case of this man. This indeed was best course of action for now, Sandy concluded, for it seemed a "grudge" could only be unstuck from the inside out, and matters such as these in the heart could only be changed by the King.

The three traveled on, more sober in their journey, observing others along their way. There were plenty of Kingdom citizens to meet as they proceeded. Most were friendly and loving. Some were more reserved in their manner. All moved at different paces. Some sat along the roads, looking at their map books. Some sat in groups, eating and laughing. Others sped along alone, hyper-focused and intense in their journey. No two travelers looked alike, but all were headed in the same direction along the same narrow way.

Sandy and her friends stopped when necessary to eat food Ruby had packed for them, or to take a swig from the bottles Sandy had been given for refreshment in the journey. They found

186

their way interesting and pleasant, learning much from observing the walks of others and interacting kindly with them. However, they were careful to constantly refer to their map book to make sure they would keep to the right way.

They were getting closer to the foothills of the mountain range, when they turned yet another bend to find a woman sitting by a well. To their pleasant surprise, I was with her.

~ ~ ~

"Jasper!" Sandy could not contain her cry and ran to embrace me.

I laughed with glee and twirled my Sandy girl around. "Princess, I'm here! Though I've been with you the whole way. And I must say, I am so proud of how well you girls are doing. You are progressing beautifully and learning so much."

"Yes, Jasper! I love this way! It's so interesting. And I could sense you with us every step of it," she added with a twinkle in her look. "But it is so good to see you again!" Then Sandy looked behind me at the woman by the well, and questioned me with her look.

"Oh! Girls, I want you to meet a very dear friend of mine, and a big sister to many in the Kingdom. This is Teacher." I stepped aside so they could approach my friend who sat with a pile of books and a shovel next to the well.

"Hello," she addressed them. "It's very good to meet you young travelers. Are you thirsty?" The woman looked to be twice their age, but was beautiful and strong in every way. Her deep, soothing voice beckoned them to listen to every word she spoke, and just her invitation to drink made them aware of their thirst.

"Yes! Yes we are," Confidence spoke for all. Teacher smiled and grabbed her bucket to lower it into the well.

"I have a pet name for her as well," I informed them. "'Digger.' I call her, 'Digger' for she digs these wells in just the right spots to find the freshest waters for those traveling by."

Teacher pulled up her pail.

She smiled at me then offered them a drink. "Here you go. See if this satisfies." They all drank from her dipper and sighed.

"Wow!" Quietness could not be contained. "This is so refreshing. Thank you!"

"How do you know where to dig?" Confidence asked.

"Many years of studying the map," Teacher answered. "I love this map. Ever since Jasper first gave it to me, I have found no greater delight than studying it and learning from every page of its instruction. The fascinating thing is, the more I study, the more places I discover to dig, so I can share my fresh discoveries and create watering holes for other citizens of the Kingdom." She clenched the oldest of her books in her hands, her map book, close to her chest. "This has been my assignment and my delight."

The girls looked with respect at this Teacher as they drank more from her well of refreshment and life. I explained as well, "This one has heeded her call to dig wells and has been used to revive many who will stop to drink. The King's kids have many gifts, all different and useful, designed just for them, but we should always be thankful for the ones who love to dig and will labor to do so, that others might have the nourishment and refreshment their bodies and souls need to journey on even farther."

"What made you decide to start digging wells, Teacher?" Sandy asked.

Teacher looked into the distance and smiled, remembering. "I once encountered the Prince. He asked me for a drink, when all I had to offer was brokenness. I gave him all the pieces of my life, and he made me whole and filled me with new life. He knew everything about me, and loved me anyway. He saw a vessel in me, one that could be filled up and used to pour life into others. So I dig wells and tap into his deep sweet living waters that flow far beneath the surface. And now I am used to give those he loves most a drink, and by doing so, I love him back, and demonstrate the gratitude I have for the purpose he saw in me."

These were profound thoughts from an insightful woman who knew deep love and healing. My young girls were moved by her words and ministered to by her way. They drank their fill as she taught them mysteries of the map book for the next long while at the edge of that well. When they had all they could absorb, she provided them with canteens and filled them up with water to further them in their journey. The girls were grateful for this rest and refueling, but soon it was time to move on. More came to approach Teacher for a drink, and she was compelled to serve them.

"Don't be timid in digging yourself," Teacher offered in final instructions as she bid us farewell. "No effort is ever wasted when searching this map for the treasure it leads to. When you seek, you will find. It is promised within." With that she turned to the others who came, and lowered her pail to gather more water to share.

I led the girls on, for I had something to give them too, something Sandy would need to make it in the climb ahead. We hiked on towards the foothills together, discussing their adventures so far, what they had seen, and questions they had.

"Jasper," Sandy asked, "what about that man Grudge? How could a citizen of the Kingdom who has traveled this road be stuck to a bench and so miserable along this way?"

I loved the innocence in her assumptions about how all should travel. Though some would think her naïve, I knew she was pure in heart. Indeed, travel along this road *should* be as she perceived it should be but, "People always have a choice, my dear," I answered her. "When you fix your eyes on *man* alone, you will be disappointed. Others often fail us, and hurt us, even those along this road, for they have not been made perfect yet and can operate out of selfish ambitions and pride." Sandy knew Pride and Selfish Ambition all too well, but did not think they would have influence on this higher road. "Citizens can become weak in their walks and even disabled, like Grudge, if they allow Pride to wound them—or if they have any pride of their own to be a target of attack. People will disappoint, Sandy, but hope will not! So keep your eyes on the Prince and hope in the promises of the map and where it is taking you, and you will not be derailed in your journey."

This answer seemed to satisfy and all my girls walked on silently, allowing the truth of it to sink in and water the gardens of their hearts. More growth would come as they chose to heed this word, fixing their eyes on their Prince, their King, and me instead of looking around at others. It would take discipline, and this is the key they needed next.

We passed by a rock garden along our path, and I paused to deliver the next gift from my chest. "Have a seat for a moment, girls," I instructed, and they each chose a large rock to sit on. I leaned up against a boulder and began, "Up ahead you will run into more travelers like yourself, but not all will progress. You will see various groups parked along the way, and some will stay for good. There are many reasons for this. Some may be hurt, like Grudge. Some may have self-inflicted wounds caused by choices they make contrary to the map. Some will still be tainted by friendships and partnerships with those in the Wastelands. But *you* are meant to go on—to climb higher and to see things from a Kingdom perspective. And I have a key to give you that will admit you to these higher places. The road ahead requires it, so I give it to you now."

Sandy reached out her hand to receive a key that I placed in her palm. She pulled it close and read on its shaft, "Discipline." Sandy looked up with a serious stare, to which I responded with a great smile to lighten her mood. "It's a good thing," I declared. "Discipline is your friend. It's a facet of my nature. It gives you access to places that others cannot go. The key of Discipline is you doing all *you* can do so that I can do all *I* can to get you where you need and want to go!" Sandy returned a look to me that showed she understood in part, but not completely.

"Trust in me," I said. "I shall never lead you astray and I know what is best. This key unlocks many gates, so many more than you could now know. Discipline is your friend, as I am your friend. Embrace this key. It leads to freedom and fruitfulness if used as I direct."

Sandy nodded and placed the key on the same chain that held the vial of hope by her heart. "Then I should keep this key close and use it when I hear you say to, Jasper," my Princess replied quietly and confidently, yielding her way all the more into mine.

"I am so very pleased with you, my dear. Now go on your way—and know I am ever near." With that I disappeared from sight, but watched on. The girls looked at each other, smiled and took no time getting right back on their path.

~ ~ ~

This key would be needed only a short distance ahead. Their path rounded a corner and they faced a large camp at the foot of the mountain. To the left of the road were tents and campfires with lots of people scurrying about. To the right were fewer tents, but people could be seen there also. The girls could not make out any words from the distance they stood, but they heard great noise. There was loud talking and yelling, and even crying. They looked at each other, and proceeded down their assigned path.

As they got closer they could see that this camp was made in the midst of a messy, overgrown garden of sorts. There were bushes, tall grasses, and vines strewn about, but all were withered, dried up, and dead. Nothing but green weeds thrived there. There was a stone wall right beyond the camp, encircling the mountain. The only way to the mountain was through a gate that joined and completed this wall, straight ahead on the path.

Confidence led them on towards the camp, careful to stay within the boundaries of the path. As they approached the gate, the community of people who lived in front of it came into clear view. The inhabitants of this campsite looked rough and forlorn. Some of them looked over at the fresh faces of Sandy and her companions, but some chose to ignore them. One of them with a bit more energy approached.

"WHO may I ask are YOU, and WHERE do you think you are going?" the wide-eyed, wild-haired man asked, looking the girls up and down over the bifocals he wore.

Sandy stepped forward to answer him in a sweet tone, "Why, I'm Sandy. And these are my friends, Confidence and Quietness, and we were sent on this path by Jasper."

"Ha! Jasper? You think JASPER sent you here? What makes you think Jasper would send you this far? And for what reason?" the man mocked as he asked.

"Well…He told us himself. We're supposed to follow this path and climb the mountain," Sandy answered.

The man howled at her statement, causing others to gather. "Come here, everyone! You have GOT to hear this," he jeered.

"What is it, Judgmental? Who are these girls and what are they saying?" Gossip had come over to inspect the situation.

"They *say* they heard JASPER speak to them. As if *he* would talk to *them!* Who do you think you are?" Judgmental questioned them in a scolding tone.

"Let me address these outsiders," interjected Self-Righteous, a taller and more pious looking man who looked down on the girls as he spoke. "Young girls. I'm sure you are imagining voices in your head. Only experienced map-readers and teachers like me could possibly hear Jasper at all, and I haven't heard him in quite some time. You may want to re-think your path…or come this way and I will teach you where you should go. You certainly can't hear Jasper for yourself!"

"Self-Righteous," a younger and seemingly friendlier man named Hypocrite interrupted, "let me take care of our guests! You are too important to waste your time on such young ones. I'll teach them the basic ways of our camp here, and return them to you for 'higher learning' later!" Self-Righteous nodded and walked away with his nose in the air, leaving Hypocrite to guide the three girls. "Whew! Glad HE'S gone! What a pompous snob," Hypocrite sneered as soon as Self-Righteous was out of sight.

"He's so enamored with himself," Gossip chimed in as she moved in closer next to Hypocrite, happy to have new people to spew her latest news to. "They say he stares at himself in the mirror for nearly three hours a day, he's so in love with himself. That's what I heard, anyway."

"Wow, really, Gossip? That's fascinating. Now why don't you go get the Mayor so we can find a place for these three young ladies who have made it all the way here," Hypocrite instructed. She immediately left. "What a BORE that woman is," he said to his guests. "She says the dumbest things that everyone already knows. Loves to hear herself talk, I think. Anyway, what was I saying?" Hypocrite paused to look at each of them.

"Um…something about getting the Mayor and finding a place for us. But we don't need a place. We're going to be climbing that mountain."

"Ha!" Hypocrite let out a little laugh of disbelief. "Sure you are. Now let me just introduce you to a few friends around here that are more your age. Can't have enough friends, right? And I'm a friend to EVERYONE, so let's see…Anxious! Anxious is your age. Oh! And Selfish! She's the best…well, really the worst, but you'll get along. Oh, and REJECTION! Many kids your age associate with him…until they get rejected, of course. He's on the other side of the road…"

"We really don't want to stay. We're just passing through," Sandy interrupted Hypocrite as Confidence nudged her on.

"Don't want to stay? Well, you may not have much choice, girl. The road pretty much stops here. This is where the path you chose leads! And this is the life you will live! Better learn to make the most of it," Hypocrite lectured in false cheer, spreading his arms out as if introducing them to their newfound home for good.

Just as Confidence was about to protest this time, Gossip returned with an older gentleman. They assumed he was the mayor Hypocrite had mentioned.

"Ah! Mayor! Girls, this is Mayor Negativity. He runs our beloved town at the bottom of the mountain. I'll let *him* get you settled in. I'd love to stay, but really can't. It was such a pleasure to get to meet you. I hope we get to hang out again soon. Bye bye!" Hypocrite then rushed off, glad to offload this responsibility to another.

"Hello, Mayor," Sandy respectfully addressed the older gentleman who returned her courteous greeting with a scowl.

After a pause he spoke, "They get younger and younger, and I don't like babies. You three are mere children. How have you gotten so far?"

"Our map books led us here." Sandy decided to stick with that part of the truth, and leave mention of Jasper out of it.

"I didn't think folks your age read anymore! Mostly looking for a party and fun, light instruction if you want any at all, am I right?" Negativity asked with a sarcastic tone.

"No," Sandy responded boldly, needing no help from Confidence this time. "I love my map book. Its words are life to me." Sandy slid her hand over her pouch, pulling the book closer and receiving comfort in knowing it was there.

"Oh, I see. You are one of those show-off young upstarts! Think you know everything! Well, you don't. We've been camping here a very long time at the bottom of this mountain, and we won't have an arrogant girl like you come in and think you can tell us what to do!" The Mayor was harsh in his rebuke of her.

"But I…" Sandy was taken aback.

Self-Righteous returned to back up the Mayor. "You aren't seasoned enough to know what we know, girl. But you are too PROUD to see that. Maybe you should camp for a while on THAT side of the road." Self-Righteous pointed to the tent where Rejection had been said to live. Sandy was shocked and dismayed at this treatment.

Quietness stepped in to her friend and whispered in Sandy's ear, "Don't say anything. Remember, we have the key. We have the key of Discipline that Jasper gave us. We can unlock the gate and climb as he said. Just don't say anything and let's go."

Sandy quietly nodded, turned her head back toward the gate, and walked on towards it with Confidence and Quietness right beside her.

"Wait!" Self-Righteous yelled. "No one leaves us! *We* say when and where you go!"

"Wait till I tell the town about *this*," Gossip clamored, running off to find someone to tell.

The Mayor sighed. "This is what you can expect from young people today. No respect! No respect for their elders or anyone at all. Good riddance!" And this lot of campers, who used to follow the narrow way, returned to their dying garden at the foot of the great mountain before the garden gate. They had made it out of the Wastelands, but seemed to be creating their own country version of it, right along the narrow path. Sandy did not know their destiny, and it was not hers to define. She only knew she had been given a key and instructions to climb. She had begun to exercise this key already by grabbing on to it and silently walking away. They were almost to the gate, and now it was time to extend that key again and obey the voice of Jasper, confirmed by their trusted map. It was time to set their feet on a new terrain and climb.

19

Trail of Trial

The key was a perfect fit. Discipline opened the gate, and it swung wide for all three adventurers to enter. They paused at the base of the great mountain before them, taking in the natural beauty that surrounded their trail. The incline was immediate but not intimidating, as bright, blossoming rhododendron bushes invited them in with their pink trumpet-shaped blooms. Yellow wildflowers lined the path and danced throughout the grassy mountainside, celebrating this mountain life. Even the rocks seemed to welcome them as they created boundaries on either side of their way and foretold of the solid ground they were about to stand on. "Yes! We were made for this," Confidence said. They each took a swallow from the canteens of water Teacher had given them, and began their ascent.

The air was growing cooler and was fresh but thin. "It's getting harder to breathe," Sandy observed aloud after surmounting their first steep incline. "I'm getting out of breath so quickly!"

"We must depend on our King all the more as we climb in these high places! We could never make it on our own," said Confidence.

"You are right," Quietness added. "It is good to be aware of our dependence on him as we progress."

Sandy agreed with a nod and talked to the King of her heart, "I do depend on you, my King. For every breath I take, I know comes from you. Thank you."

The girls hiked quietly upward, careful to conserve their energy for the climb. Before long, they heard the sound of thumping below them on the trail. Someone was coming up behind them at a fast pace. They paused and moved over to the side to see and make way. A very fit couple was running up the mountain. They did not stop, but smiled pleasantly and politely nodded. The male called out as they passed, "Keep going, girls! Your lungs will get used to the air in these heights." Then they ran on out of sight, scaling the mountain almost effortlessly.

"Who in the world was *that?*" Sandy asked, shocked to see anyone able to run on such a trail.

"Oh, Ruby told us of people like that," Confidence answered. "They must be Forerunners. Jasper prepares certain citizens of the Kingdom to run ahead and prepare the trail for others. Sometimes they must cut new roads or repair the old ones. They are trailblazers and way-makers for others like us who are called to climb. We should be thankful for their gifts and contributions to the Kingdom."

Sandy was silent. She knew she should be thankful, but felt a twinge of jealously in her heart. She wondered why Jasper hadn't chosen her to be a forerunner. Did he think her too weak?

Confidence was wise and could read Sandy's face. "Sandy, we all have our calls. And yours is the greatest, remember? To love!"

With that, Sandy recalled what Ruby said about the never-ending lessons in love, and that when she felt a shortage of it in her heart, she should ask for more. Sandy stopped right there to talk to her father. "My King, increase my capacity to love! I just felt envy creeping into my heart. Forgive me. I want no obstacle in my way of loving well. Increase my capacity to love, and fill me with more of your love for all of your other children. Thank you for loving me so well." And with those words, Sandy's heart was refilled. She released all resentment and received a new lot of love. To seal this work all the more in her heart, she blessed them by speaking to her father again, "And Father, watch over them and help them! Make their way smooth and protect them from all trouble. I ask you to give them courage and I thank you for their gifts that will benefit the citizens of your Kingdom. Thank you."

Quietness heard her conversation, although Sandy had spoken discreetly. "That was the perfect reaction, Princess. I'm so proud to be your friend!" Both girls smiled and continued the climb.

Just then, loud whoops and hollers could be heard right behind them. A band of boys dressed up as various adventurers bounded on the trail below them. Sandy and her friends paused and slid to the side, leaning up against a large boulder that towered behind them. The boys charged up the path with their own maps and swords made of sticks strapped to their sides. They had shields of wood, and makeshift helmets garnished a few of their heads. They were unaware that these three girls were observing their playful battle until they reached the path right in front of them and froze.

"Hello!" Sandy greeted the panting gang who had halted before her.

"Hi," the one in front finally returned. "We didn't know anyone was out here. We're usually up here exploring alone."

"You are?" Sandy found this cute, amazing and curious all at the same time. "What are you doing?"

"Practicing," the boy replied. "We're in the King's army, and we're practicing for battle. Never know when he's going to need us to fight for him."

Tears of surprise stung Sandy's eyes. All of the boys stared at her with determined passion. They were not kidding. Sandy knew she had something to learn.

"Tell me what you mean. How are you practicing?" Sandy wanted to know.

Another boy spoke up, "Well, we all have maps and are hunting for treasure. And while we do that, we practice using our swords on each other, so in case trouble ever comes we can get out of it! The King gave us shields and a bunch of other stuff to protect us, so we just run around here using our weapons. It's fun!"

"Yeah, and sometimes Jasper comes to play with us! That's the best," the boy next to him said with a front-toothless wide grin.

Sandy laughed aloud, "That *would* be the best! You guys know Jasper, huh?"

"Oh yeah! He's our leader! He tells us where to go. He's like our best friend," the biggest boy in front relayed. The rest of them nodded and muttered in agreement.

"He *is* the best friend. He's my best friend too," Sandy admitted to them. "I'm glad we all know Him. That kind of makes us *all* friends in a way, you know?"

The boys looked at her with confused faces. They weren't sure about this big girl wanting to be their friend. They just stared at her not knowing what to say. The leader spoke up, "Sure, lady. I guess any friend of Jasper's is good enough to be a friend of mine." Then he extended his dirt-covered hand for her to shake. She did so with pleasure.

"Well, we don't want to get in your way of battle. You all go on up ahead, and look out for any enemies lurking about. Keep this trail safe! I'm glad to know we are on the same side." The boys didn't waste time in doing just as Sandy had said. They took off, grunting and howling as young boys do, waving their weapons, ready for the fight.

"Now *that* is confidence!" Confidence observed. "We could use more of *that* kind!" The other two nodded agreeably and proceeded uphill.

The road grew even steeper and narrower, and they traveled long and hard. Sandy felt herself losing her footing, slipping in places on the incline. She was getting scraped up, and needed to lean on her friends all the more. Even with many stops to rest and eat and check the map, Sandy was growing weary. Her leg had gotten injured in one slip, and now she was moving forward with a limp. Their provisions were running low too, and Sandy was growing fearful of not finding anything to eat on this mountain. The old familiar way of Worry whispered in her ear. "What if you don't make it? What if you get stuck on the side of this mountain and pass out? What is going to become of you, Sandy?"

Sandy tried to brush these thoughts away. As she pushed on, a deep moan was heard from ahead on the trail, followed by the sound of sobbing. Confidence motioned for them all to stop to assess the situation. The girls could hear brush being trampled through, then footsteps on the path just ahead. A moment later, two young women, a little older than Sandy and her friends, appeared, descending the path. One had her arm draped over the shoulders of the other, and could put no weight on one leg. Her friend who supported her looked miserably weighed down. Both groaned and grumbled as they hobbled down the mountain.

"Are you Ok? Sandy asked. Can we help?"

"Do we *look* Ok?" The stronger one, named Bitter, snapped. "I would suggest you just help yourselves and turn around now. This trail is impossible." The girl resentfully aided her friend, called Wounded, who could only whimper and snivel as they staggered down the mountain.

Quietness, Confidence, and Sandy exchanged silent looks after they passed. Confidence finally insisted with a nod to the trail ahead and said, "Let's go."

Quietness fell in step behind her right away, but Sandy lingered, besieged by Doubt. Quietness could see this doubt on her friend's face and walked back to grab her hand. Confidence turned back too and grabbed Sandy's other hand. They didn't speak, but Quietness and Confidence rallied Sandy to continue on by their reach.

Doubt continued to reach for her too as he attacked her mind. "Sandy! How much longer can you make it? You already have a limp! You are weighing your friends down. What a burden you are! You should stop now. It's only going to get harder, and you are weak already. This kind of climb is not for the faint of heart. And what are you climbing after anyway? What is the purpose of going on—in pain? Turn around and run!"

Sandy considered these doubtful thoughts and began to cave.

She broke free of her friends, and collapsed on a rock to the side of the road. Her body went limp and she refused to go on. "I just don't know, girls. I don't know if I can make it. This climb…it is getting so hard. I'm worn out. And the mountain is so big. It seems we have so far to go." This is what Sandy admitted out loud. Inwardly she was forgetting why they were climbing at all.

"Sandy, I know you can do it. You were made for this." Confidence tried to revive her with words of encouragement.

"Yes, Sandy, don't talk like that. You know Jasper would never call you to do something he would not equip you to do," Quietness added.

Just then, Sandy remembered her pouch and the colorful bottles she had been given in a previous moment of refreshment after the long journey back to the Shores. She mustered up just enough energy to reach into her pouch and grab the first bottle she could get her hand on. It was the one marked "Passion."

"Jasper," she whispered under her breath, "I certainly need more passion for this journey. I'm forgetting why I chose this road, and am worried I don't have what it takes to make it." As soon as she expressed this need, her request was heard and provision was made. One of Jasper's friends from the Cottage Café appeared on the path below and approached.

"I hear I am needed, my young friends." Passion had come to her rescue. His voice was strong and appealing. He had a way with words, but they were sincere and gushed out with vigor from the core of his heart. He brought another friend with him as well. Sandy greeted him first.

"Passion—my friends, this is Passion. He is a friend of Jasper's and a friend of mine," Sandy explained.

Quietness and Confidence smiled. "Oh, we know Passion," Confidence said. "He is a great friend of Ruby's as well."

Sandy was embarrassed that she wouldn't have made the connection between Ruby of Love's Lodge and Passion. Of course

Ruby would know one who operated in such intense love as Passion.

"Yes, I know you all, but it appears this is a good time for us all to get reacquainted and know each other in a deeper way. And I brought along my sister, Faithful. We walk hand in hand on trails like these. So what is wrong, Princess? We both want to help."

Sandy nodded and gave a slight smile to Faithful, then confessed, "I'm just weary. Honestly, I'm tempted to give up. This climb is long and hard and I'm getting beat up. I'm just not sure I'm made for this. And I..." Sandy hesitated before she opted to honestly admit, "I sort of forget why I'm climbing."

Passion paused before replying, studying Sandy's face. "It's because he knows. He never forgets what he's making you into. He knows what kind of strength you need to build up, and he knows just how to transform you into the citizen capable of performing your call. And Sandy, I am told you have the greatest call. You are called to love, are you not?"

"I am," Sandy quietly answered, feeling the gravity of Passion's poignant words.

"Well, what better way to learn the walk of love than to travel through trails of trial in the company of friends? Learning to walk in love's way, no matter what the uphill battle is, brings such strength and dignity and authenticity to your walk." Passion's explanation did make sense, but it didn't make Sandy *feel* any better in the moment. Then she remembered Wisdom's lesson about feelings, and how they couldn't be trusted. They could trap you and lead you down wrong paths. She also recalled Ruby's words about love being a *decision*, not a feeling. She knew she would have to make a decision right now, for her feelings were not lining up with this narrow way. She needed more assistance from Passion. He knew this, and looked her square in the eyes.

"Sandy, remember the dream of your heart. Remember your Prince, who is drawing you with each step towards your destiny with him in his Kingdom of Love. Remember that there is joy set before you, as there was for him. He endured even greater opposition so that he could be seated with his father in high places, and you are headed to those heights as well. Sandy, look up! Keep your eyes fixed on him, the love of your life and the dream of your heart. He has blazed these trails before you, proving that all can be overcome!"

Passion had a way of moving Sandy's heart, and it was stirred. She remained pensive, considering his advice, when Faithful spoke up to add, "Dear Princess, you must draw near to the King, sincere in heart and full of faith! Hold unswervingly to the hope you have professed, for he who has made so many promises to you is indeed faithful! Here—give me your map. Let's look back at how far you've come and recall the promises of what is ahead. Reviewing the map will help you remain faithful as you remember how he has been faithful!"

Faithful led Sandy back through her journey, from her life in the Wastelands to here. Recounting the King's faithful supply of all that was needed and remembering the great joy and peace she had known revived her passion once again to go on.

"He has done so much for me. I must go on. I know I am weak, but…"

Confidence interrupted in excitement, discovering something in the map she had been studying in order to assist. "Look here, Sandy. Look what it says at this spot where we stand!"

Sandy read aloud the promise of the Prince, quoted long ago by a fellow follower of his way:

"'My grace is sufficient for you, for my power is made perfect in weakness.' Therefore I will boast all the more gladly about my weaknesses, so that the power of the Prince may rest on me. That is why, for his sake, I delight in weaknesses, in insults, in hardships, in persecutions, in difficulties. For when I am weak, then I am strong."

Tears rolled down Sandy's face now, as she stood despite the pain she still felt in her body. A wave of new strength rushed over her now. "'When I am weak, then I am strong.' Mysterious grace once again," she remarked softly to herself. "Come on, my friends! Let's lean into our strong and perfect Prince! I'm ready to move on from here." Sandy added, "Thank you, Passion and Faithful. I thought I was done for before you came along."

Passion responded with words he knew from the map, "'Because of the King's great love we are not consumed, for His compassions never fail. They are new every day! Great is His faithfulness.' May we become just like him!"

"He certainly has been faithful and loving in bringing me companions such as you," Sandy said shyly, looking over each one. "I'm grateful."

"It looks like it's time to continue the journey, Princess," Passion cheerfully prompted as he stood up straight and lifted Sandy up along with him. "I will leave my sister, Faithful, to escort you for the next leg of this journey. And I will stay with you in spirit!" With that, they each drank from the bottle of passion within Sandy's hand, then Passion topped it off, as he had even more with him to spare. When he had finished refilling Sandy and saw she was strong, Passion cheered them on as they took their leave to scale the remainder of the mountain.

Having a fresh dose of passion renewed Sandy's vision for the climb. She was so glad he had reminded her of the purpose of her journey, and of all her Prince who had called her there had done. Sandy's two friends and Faithful continued to spur her on as well, reading the map whenever they wondered about their way.

"Look, Sandy," Confidence pointed out. "It says the Prince thinks of you as a gazelle, a beautiful creature made to progress by leaps and bounds! And it says he will make your feet like that of a deer and set you upon high places! What a promise that is! Can you imagine moving like that?"

They all encouraged each other along the way, finding

promises in the book that brought them great hope. The path was still hard, but felt easier to Sandy with hope in her heart and passion restored.

They continued their climb until they saw up ahead a woman's back at what seemed to be the end of the road. She was holding a walking stick to her side and stared straight out. As they drew closer, they realized that they had arrived at an overlook.

"My! What a view," gasped Sandy as she slowly approached the overlook, standing slightly behind the woman to her left.

"It is indeed," the woman replied without turning, her eyes scanning the scene stretched before her with a light smile in her voice.

"Have...have you been here long?" Sandy asked, curious as to how she had arrived at this high place and what knowledge she could offer about it.

The woman turned. "I've been here a while, taking it all in." She was an older woman who looked to be about the age of Ruby or Sandy's own mother. She was lovely with long and thick wavy hair that billowed from her forehead and temples and was tied at her neck with a strip of cloth. She wore a soft flowing shawl that she grasped with one hand while she maintained a firm grip on her walking stick with the other. Her face showed signs of stories in the wrinkles that lined it, but grace was the foundation that covered it all.

"My name is Sandy, and these are my friends. We've been traveling all day on this trail. It's quite a challenge, isn't it?" Sandy was growing in confidence and searched for a way to engage this woman she was becoming fascinated with.

"Nice to meet you, Sandy. I'm Long-Suffering, and I've been traveling these trails for a very long time."

Sandy was all the more intrigued now. She didn't want to be rude, but found the way so difficult, she just had to know how someone would survive a long time on it. She looked to Quietness as if asking permission to inquire. Quietness shrugged, wanting to learn from this lady as well, so Sandy continued. "How long of a time do you mean? I can't imagine one could survive up here for very long, at least not alone."

"Oh, I'm not alone, dear. I've never been alone, though it has felt that way at times. And yes, you can survive much more and much longer than you can imagine. I know many of these trails, the narrow safe one and the dangerous side ones that branch off. I've been back up this mountain time and time again, and yet I never tire of this view." Long-Suffering peered back out and over the far-reaching valley below, understanding the value of this height far more than her younger fellow travelers could at this time.

"Would you tell us about your journey?" Sandy finally asked in a straight-forward manner. "We are up here to learn, and it seems you have much to teach."

Long-Suffering turned to face the young Princess, then nodded in agreement. "Let's sit right over here. I would be glad to share my story with you, if it will help you along your way."

The small company of travelers sat on rocks and stumps to the side of the overlook. Long-Suffering sat with her back to it, so they all could take in this reward of their climb as she told her tale. "My story begins much like I imagine yours did. I received an invitation to be part of the Kingdom, and after an initial struggle to leave the Wastelands, I consented and came. I walked the narrow road for many years, but remained in the Flatlands below. I often got sidetracked and distracted, but somehow the King would woo me back and I'd journey on. I thought I was headed in the right direction, and I was, but I moved at my own pace, choosing to grow in my own time and way, or so I thought. I also kept up with some of my friends in the Wastelands, and they still had their influence on me."

Sandy thought of her own friendship with Pride and how hard that alliance was to break, even in her thinking. She wondered if Long-Suffering meant friendships like that.

"I thought life was just fine. On the surface, everything appeared to be going well for me, until sudden tragedy struck and all was shaken in my world. I couldn't just stroll along in the Flatlands anymore, reading my map occasionally 'when needed.' I needed it all the time now. I had to move to higher ground."

Sandy, and the others were captivated and said not a word as they stared at Long-Suffering, signaling for her to continue.

"So I began the climb, but more trials came. I experienced more trouble, more disappointment, and greater losses in love." Long-Suffering went on to explain these losses honestly without any sign of self-pity.

Sandy commented on this. "It's amazing you went through so much and you don't seem to feel sorry for yourself at all."

"Oh, I did at one time, but I learned long ago that Self-Pity only leads you to misery and despair, and that's no place to go." How true Sandy knew those words to be.

Long-Suffering continued, "Over and over I would start up the mountain and another storm would come." She spoke of tragic illnesses, the loss of loved ones, and many dear ones closest to her falling from the heights and running back to the Wastelands. "I've known rejection and pain from many people I have loved, and have often stumbled about due to my pain. I once headed back and remained at the bottom of the mountain for quite some time in the Cave of Isolation. That's when my old friend, Kindness, would come by to see me, sharing treats and treasures of the King's love, trying to remind me of his everlasting goodness. Eventually she drew me out and encouraged me to do what I was made to do—climb! First, I spent a lot of time at the Shores with Jasper. I fellowshipped with other citizens at the Cottage Café and learned lessons from Contentment, like how to be content in all circumstances. Then I began my journey all over again in that garden and became truly devoted to the King.

"I talk to the King all the time now, and I know him in a way most of his kids don't. He's had to nurse my heart so deeply, but

207

he has healed its brokenness and continues to strengthen it still. I have grown to know his touch so well, through suffering. Many of the requests and pleas I have made have not been answered. He has not given me all I want, but he has given me his love and that has satisfied my heart in a way I never thought possible, for he has filled it with himself. And what joy I have found in his presence within me."

Sandy was astounded. Long-Suffering was one of the most beautiful friends she had met. Her joy was not as bubbly or effervescent as Ruby's, but it was deep, like still waters, and so was her peace.

"If there is one lesson I could leave with you that you may not have learned if this is your first time up these slopes, it is to never look back. Don't look behind you. Keep your eyes on the path ahead. Views even greater than these await." Long-Suffering turned to the view once again and stared out. "All of the problems of the valley seem small from these heights—and they are. Seek his perspective on everything. You were made for this higher way of living, whether you believe it or not, so believe it! And the sooner you believe, the better!"

They all stared out for quite some time, allowing Long-Suffering's lessons to sink in. Faithful broke the silence at last, affirming their new friend. "I can feel the King's pleasure upon you. How well you have served him in your perseverance. It inspires us all."

"Thank you. His pleasure is all I seek. It is all that satisfies me now," Long-Suffering simply replied.

"And now it is time for us to continue our own walk," Faithful instructed. "Will you join us, Long-Suffering?"

"You lead them on, Faithful. I believe you know his ways as well as I do. Besides, we all take this journey at our own set pace, for we all have different assignments. Part of mine for now is to encourage others as they come along this way, and then send them on. But before you go, I do have a gift for this one." Long-Suffering extended her walking stick in the direction of Sandy. "Here, my dear. You can lean on this when your way gets tricky and your foot starts to slip. And you can use it to ward off any wild creatures from the enemy's camp that you may cross your path. This rod will be a great comfort and weapon to have."

Sandy protested, "But what about you? Don't you need it for your climb?"

"I'll make another—or Jasper will bring me one. I never can give something away without him coming to visit and giving me back even more! So you take this one. I've whittled on it, coordinates from the map book. If you get stuck or lost somewhere, or just need extra courage to go on, look up the coordinates engraved. They will help you to persevere along this way." Long-Suffering passed the weathered stick on to Sandy, who took it within her grip, rubbing the worn wood made smooth by miles of travel by this beautifully tenacious beautiful woman who would never give up.

"You all go on now. I'm going to sit here a spell and visit with my King. But you run on. There are lovely surprises waiting for you on the road just ahead!" She winked at Sandy with a knowing smile, then turned back and returned her sights to the overlook.

Faithful quietly signaled them all to proceed, and they stepped back onto the trail. Long-Suffering had filled them each with courage, more than enough to finish today's climb and assist them in days to come. Evening would soon come and Faithful would make sure they found shelter for the night. For now this company of climbers hiked on in quiet confidence, assured once again that all provision would be afforded to those who obediently persisted, and that reward was at hand. They couldn't wait to experience what surprises awaited them next.

20

Fear, Fights, and Freedom

*T*he trail resumed through dense woods, and it was growing dark. Faithful had packed a tent and they set up camp for the night. The four travelers convened by a small fire to rest and recount the events of their travel so far. Sandy opened her pouch and passed around the beautiful bottles given to her by her friends at the Cottage Café. They each took whiffs and swigs, and were refreshed by the spirits of joy, peace, wisdom, and passion of which they all partook.

The night air was brisk and calm, but held a hint of mystery in it for Sandy. She had never been in such high and unknown territory, and certainly not at night. As they each settled into their bedrolls in their tent, sounds alarmed Sandy from outside before she had the chance to find sleep. She looked over to Quietness, Confidence, and Faithful who were all sound in slumber. Sandy's eyes were wide, scanning the shadows she could see on the walls of her tent, created by the moon overhead and high objects of nature without. But as her imagination was triggered, the shadows crept in, and took the form of a formidable enemy, Fear.

"BOO!" blurted Fear, coming up behind Sandy's head at the wall of the tent. Fear moved mysteriously in the shadows, never tangible, yet appearing so real. "Aren't you SCARED, young Sandy? Up on this mountain in the dark of night with only other weak girls like you? You can't even see what is out there! And didn't Jasper tell you about an enemy hiding in darkness? You must be CRAZY to camp out here like this! What if wild beasts attack you? What if raging storms come? What if disease comes to sting you? What if you've no strength to run?" The rants of Fear persisted and Sandy tossed and turned, coiling up in her blanket in attempt to escape.

"No," she finally let out in a low, determined whisper. "I will not be afraid. What was it Jasper taught me when I faced fear at the Shores? That's right—'Perfect love casts out fear,' so I will love as perfectly as I can, and remember that I am perfectly loved."

Sandy recalled the words to a song that Page taught her as they walked along the River. She had read some of these words in the map book too, and was reminded of them now. She decided to sing them lowly in her tent at as a love song and proclamation to her King.

*"You are my hiding place. You always fill
my heart with songs of deliverance. Whenever
I am afraid I will trust in you..."*

By Sandy choosing to do this, Fear went away. Peace hovered over her instead, and soon she was asleep.

The next morning, the four hikers of these high places rose, ready for new vistas and views ahead. Faithful fixed a quick breakfast and they discovered a mountain spring behind their camp, from which they filled their canteens with fresh water to drink for the journey that day.

As they finished their breakfast, they examined the map. Confidence observed, "Looks like we are nearing the top. I wonder what we'll be doing once we get there."

Faithful replied, "I'm not sure, but on the map today I saw these instructions,

*"In his heart a man plans his course,
but the King determines his steps."*

"I suppose we can't plan it all out for ourselves, even if we try," Faithful concluded.

"I read that same page," Quietness added. "It also instructed,

*'Commit to the King whatever you do,
and your plans will succeed.'*

"So I guess it will all turn out well if we keep committing our way to him!"

"*Succeed...*" Sandy hadn't thought of this word in a while. It was one she related to Excess and the world she had come from. It was a word she associated with Mayor Striver, and Pride, and Mr. Success, of course. But could "success" be part of what the King had in mind for her as well? *I have to remember to ask Jasper about this later,* she noted. For now, they had to pack up camp and proceed on their path for this day.

Not long into their morning hike, the four hikers bound for the top heard rustling off to their left at the ridge ahead. Before they could even question each other about the source of it, a gang of gangly, malnourished, and battered rebels invaded their way.

"STOP right there!" the tallest and filthiest one shouted, staggering slowly down the center of the path. "Just where do you little ones think you are going?" His eyes were wide, wild, and beet red where they should have been white. He was a scary sight indeed, and smelled ten times worse than he looked. His stench alone drove them to back up in retreat.

"We...we are daughters of the King, and we were called to this path. We're following it wherever it leads," Sandy answered, backed by Confidence as she spoke.

"Daughters of the KING," this creature-like man mockingly

repeated in a sing-song manner. "Did you hear that, fellas? We have some PRINCESSES coming our way today!" The gang of five behind him took his contemptuous cue and laughed along loudly. The leader then cut their merriment short with a stomp to the ground, and sobered his face with an insidious stare. "Well then," he whispered with a taunting tone, "since you are *royalty*, I suppose you have payment for us as a toll on this road!"

Sandy was shocked at this brazen assault, and was growing fearful again under this demand. "No," she answered. "I have no payment. None of us have anything to offer you."

"Well, what is in your *bag*, little Princess? Let me see!" With these words, the leader reached for her pouch and snatched it from her side before her reflexes could respond. The gang swarmed on their leader and they ripped into her purse.

"NO!" Sandy yelled. "STOP! Give me back my pouch," she tearfully cried out in panic. Confidence, Quietness, and Faithful rallied to her side. The gang paid no mind but got out her bottles, her map, and even her prized purple plume from Page and waved them all before her, baiting her to return their attack to retrieve them.

"What's the matter, Princess," the leader spoke for all, "going to miss your precious belongings? Afraid your daddy, the King, won't give you any more? Don't think you can make it without this old MAP?" He held up her map book and waved it about, then took it in both hands as if to tear it in half.

Sandy froze, staring at her attackers in shock and fear. Confidence prodded, "Lift up your eyes, Sandy. You know where your help comes from! The King of this mountain will send aid. Cry out to him!"

"JASPER!" she cried. "Oh, Great King and Prince of my heart! Rescue me!"

And we did.

~ ~ ~

In an instant, the band of boys from the day before descended on the path above them and let out their cry of war. Girl warriors had joined them as well, and I was in their midst. The boy leader looked towards Sandy and demanded, "Use your rod, lady!" With that Sandy came to and the battle ensued. Sandy struck from down below on the road, and the army of children surrounded the gang from the top. The boy leader cried out, "In the name of the Great Prince, you have to flee! Give back what you've taken and get out of here!"

Then they wielded the weapons that seemed only toys the day before, but today they whipped their enemies with them. The men of the gang had seemed so much larger to Sandy, but in fact, they were not. Led by me, the child troop had the advantage as they attacked from above, and were well prepared. With words from the map flowing off of their tongues, they swung their swords and blocked with their shields, throwing each and every rebel off the side of the ridge, sending them tumbling down to the valley below. Sandy had gotten in a few blows, cheered on by her companions, but the battle had mostly been won by the kids.

When the dust had all settled, Sandy came to. "What in the world just happened? WHO in the world were THEY?" Sandy questioned, still half dazed.

"Those, my love, were the Rebels of Resentment Ridge. They are all wounded way-followers, turned criminal, crippled by their own unbelief. Their leader is Intimidation, and he is followed by every form of fear. They are thieves, out to steal your joy and your peace, and more than anything they want to destroy your means of making it to the Kingdom of Love."

"My map…" Sandy whispered aloud, recalling the fear in her heart she felt when she saw it threatened. It was growing so precious to her now, a priceless possession she did not know how she could make it without. "And these children…How? Where…"

"Amazing, aren't they?" I smiled as they gathered around me. "I told you! So much to learn from them!"

"What is your name, boy?" Sandy asked the leader of them who had led the charge.

"Brave," he simply replied.

"And you are so brave," Sandy affirmed. "What is your name, dear one?" She asked the tallest girl, who led in the battle as well.

"Fearless," she answered, looking Sandy square in her face as she threw her arm around my waist and leaned in.

"Brave and Fearless. Are your names not one in the same?" Sandy questioned.

"No," Fearless answered. "I'm not afraid of anything anymore. Brave fights whether he's scared or not. The important thing is, we fight—and we don't put up with those fear guys at all."

Sandy was in awe. "How...how did you become this way? How did you overcome your fears?"

The children all looked at her with squints and puzzled looks, then looked up to me. I nodded for Brave to answer her.

"Haven't you read your map, Lady? It says all the time not to fear." I cleared my throat in slight correction of Brave's blunt and youthful way of explaining, though what he said to the Princess was true. Fearless finished his answer.

"We just know who we are and know what the map says. He left us power in Jasper to do anything—You've read that part, right?"

Confidence and Quietness giggled at this frank and candid exchange. Sandy smiled as well. "What my kids are trying to say is when you *believe* and apply the words of the map, along with my direction and aid, you will have power to overcome anything. Just as unbelief and disregard for my map crippled your attackers, true faith and knowledge of it empowered these young ones to overcome them. They know their maps, and they will win their battles."

Brave looked up at me at that moment to inquire, "Think she

215

can make it the rest of the way? We were going to go play in our forts."

I smiled and released them. "Yes, be free. I will come and play with you later. I will finish escorting these ladies to the top." And we all waved this small army off as they scampered off on a trail to hide out and prepare for whatever battles would lie ahead.

"I just can't believe that children came to my rescue! I can't believe what they know! What in the *world* will they be someday?" Sandy asked.

"All kings and queens, my dear. They are being prepared to rule and reign." My princess didn't understand me fully, but that's Ok. She was seeing the value of my kids. Soon she would learn to be more like them. For now, I had another lesson to teach and another key to give.

We walked and talked with ease through the rest of the wood lined path that morning. Right before I knew the terrain was about to change, I stopped my Princess and her friends to ask, "Do you have the key ring I gave you at the garden, my love?"

"I do," she replied, and fiddled about in her pouch. "Here it is. I have the key of Devotion, the key of Thanksgiving, and the key of Discipline, which I wear on the chain by my heart."

"Take your key of Discipline now, and place it on this ring. I have another to add to it now, and you will use it along with Discipline, so I want you to have it handy." After Sandy followed my instructions I said, "This new key I'm giving you, my girl, is one the Prince and I so greatly rejoice in. It is the key of Freedom."

Sandy received it and stared at its size. It was the biggest key so far, and on it was a tag: "*It is for FREEDOM he has set you FREE.*"

"What do I do with it?" Sandy asked me with a blank look in her eyes.

"You will see straight ahead." I finished leading this little company through the thick trees they had been so used to being surrounded by, and watched their faces as the line of trees ended and a lush grassy meadow broke out before them. Space. Wide space spread out before us, and smiles spread out on their faces, just as wide. They burst out in laughter and ran. These four women ran, danced, tumbled, and twirled as children, as if they had been doves released from a cage, or great dancers on a stage! No one had to tell them to go; they just knew. My path had led out into this wide-open Field of Freedom and it was theirs for the taking!

Oh, how I enjoyed watching them enjoy themselves, no longer cramped by that previous leg of the journey. They had grown so strong on that trail, and now they could run and play and rejoice all the more in their newfound mountain top freedom! Finally, still laughing breathlessly, they returned to me.

"Jasper! Oh, Jasper! It's so lovely up here. It's so spacious and green with life. The air is so fresh and the view is incredible!" Sandy said. We paused to take in the scene. It was far grander than the overlook, with a magnificent view encircling them. "It's breathtaking!"

"Indeed it is, my Princess. I hope it was worth the climb!"

"Oh, yes! It was worth it," Sandy responded. Quietness, Confidence, and Faithful nodded in agreement, all still smiling and breathing heavily from their exercise in their newly discovered freedom.

"But I have a question." Sandy cocked her head as she held up the key ring. "Why do I need a key for this place? I see no door to unlock, only *freedom* at hand—everywhere!"

I paused and relaxed my smile, then soberly informed her, "Not everywhere. Not everyone is free up here. But they can be." Then I motioned to a grove of trees at the edge of the field to our right. I walked slowly towards it, and the group followed. As we proceeded I explained, "The Prince *loves* freedom. He created this field of his life-giving grace as an expression of his love for it. But he is so often misunderstood and even lied about. He is thought to be one whose rules strip citizens of their freedom. This

217

is not the case at all. His rules are always motivated out of love and for our best; they lead to a truly free life. But there is a lie that has been spread up here from down below about what freedom is. I will show you the results of that lie now."

The grove of trees served as a barrier, blocking from the view of the meadow that was just beyond it—a slope of cells. There were small prison cells everywhere, spanning the sloping mountainside, as far as the eye could see. And within these cells there were people, individuals trapped in cells that held only them.

"What is this, Jasper? Who are these people and why are they imprisoned like this?" Sandy asked in horror. The cells were nasty, covered in rust and slime. The people were of all ages, genders and backgrounds. The only thing they had in common was that they were trapped and miserable, and in a place so close to beautiful freedom.

"They are citizens of the Kingdom, Sandy, who found a certain level of freedom, but then became enslaved again. They have been ensnared by wrong choices made, contrary to the directives of their map. They are trapped by their own bad habits as well, thus creating 'habitations' for themselves that don't allow for easy escape. Many arrive here, bringing with them habitual patterns from their old lives, back in the Wastelands and Excess, and decide to settle into those ways up here. But they find themselves back in bondage, experiencing much of the same discontentment they had down below. It seems they wanted to change enough to journey a while, but wouldn't let the journey completely change them. The taste of freedom was not enough to see their transformation through, so the walls went back up, and they became slaves all over again."

Sandy stepped closer and noticed that the doors to most of the cells were cracked and that even the shackles on their hands were not locked. "Jasper! They *are* free! A lot of them have doors that are open and the shackles of most could be shaken off. Why don't they just leave?"

"You are right," I replied. "They are free indeed. They have been set free by the Prince, as he won the keys to their freedom in a battle long ago, but they just don't see it. They are free to go at anytime, but their choices and habits have them stuck inside."

"What must they do?" Sandy cried out, desperate for them. "How can they be free again?"

"They have to see it. Many of them are closing their eyes, and falling back to sleep up here. Others are just staring at the prison bars and shackles in lament, so focused on their bondage, that they can't see the truth that his grace has freed them! If they would fix their eyes on this truth, and set their affections on the Prince more than on what holds them in bondage, they could run to their Prince and out of these prisons of their own making. They would no longer 'hold on' to what does not truly hold them. They would embrace Freedom itself if they would run with all their hearts, soul, and might after the King. And the keys of Devotion and Discipline can double-lock those prison doors behind them for good."

"You've given me this key, Jasper. It must be for a reason. I want to help." Sandy looked around and her companions all nodded in agreement to join her. "We all do."

"I knew you would. Free people desire to *free* people. You have just had a fresh taste of freedom, and are living the story that these falling-back-to-sleep people really dream to live too. Use your story of finding freedom as the key to unlock their hearts, so I may come in with my grace that transforms. That's how their freedom will come. That's how yours did, when I won your heart. Tell our story, Sandy—your journey with me and this map. I will help make you bold and brave. You will help many overcome as you tell this story and remind them of their truest love, breaking their bond with what holds their affections right now."

With a love for these captives and a passion for freedom budding in her heart, Sandy nodded and started right off, carrying her map book in hand. She and the others went from cell to cell, administering hope from her vial and sharing about its impact on her. They spread the essence of needed wisdom, perfect peace, renewed passion, and break-through joy to the prisoners around them from the portions they possessed. Sandy spoke of the mysterious power of the King's grace she had experienced which had saved her from despair's pull on her own journey. Her story threw courage on many of the captives to believe again, and their faith was revived. The citizens of the Kingdom were waking up and remembering who they were and *who* they belonged to. They remembered their great loving King and allowed once again for his right and pure ways to be established in their hearts, causing true liberation. Soon the great sound of creaking and clanging echoed over the mountain range as prison doors flew open and chains fell off, and the people ran free! The meadow was filled with dancing, and sounds of rejoicing reached the skies. And my Sandy burst into tears at the sight of it all and from the overwhelming pleasure she felt from her King.

"You have made us very, very proud, my girl. Well done," I whispered in her ear as I stepped up beside her, my heart bursting with hers over this joyful, redemptive scene.

"So this is love—this is what real love can do," she whispered back as she kept her gaze on the great dance before her in the field. "I like it. I like my call, Jasper. I like it a lot." Tears lined her eyes as they did back at the Shores, the first day she looked on me. But these tears had transformed and were now tears of joy. She was experiencing the joy of "becoming." Sandy had changed so much on this journey, and was now being used to change others. But the work was not over. There was still work to do, in her world and for mine. My Sandy Princess was becoming key in our Kingdom. Little did she know how much more of this freedom and love she would soon know, and how much more she would have to offer.

21

Higher Yet

The rejoicing continued on the mountain well into the night. Campfires were built all about the mountaintop where small groups of the free men and women now sat together, exchanging stories of their lives before, and now after. Joy, Peace, and Passion arrived on the scene, making their rounds to each and every assembled group. Wisdom showed up also and walked through with Sandy, distributing new maps for those who had lost theirs along the way. They stopped and sat with many—instructing, equipping, and encouraging these liberated citizens in the ways of true freedom.

The hilltop air was charged with zeal and vigor. A delightful mix of laughter, proclamations of praise to the King, and songs of his deliverance were all offered up out of the overflow of the free people's hearts. The King received the sound of it all as one might inhale a sweet fragrance. Sandy shared in his pleasure, and had never known such fulfillment. She wandered around for a little while alone, just watching. Her heart was as full as it had ever been, knowing she had played a part, partnering with others in making this scene of freedom possible.

All camped out for the night under the clear, sparkling, mountaintop sky. All rested in peace and no fear could come near, for perfect love blanketed each soul that now rested after their battles had been won.

Early the next morning, Sandy rose first. She made her way around the camp, still basking in the glory of all that had transpired. She then lifted her eyes once again and noticed in the short distance ahead an incline that led to an even higher place on the mountaintop. Curiosity nudged her to go and find out where that trail would lead. Sandy was excited for this additional invitation to ascend when she thought she had reached the top already. Little did she know that the climb would never be truly over. There was no end to the heights she could climb.

This trail produced a steep incline, but Sandy had been conditioned for it by her previous journey, and found this morning hike invigorating. She also found a surprise as she rounded the hill and came to the top. Before her eyes, at the uppermost point, was a lovely log shelter, set upon a great rock. Its logs looked golden, almost glowing in this highest place on the hill. Sandy stood breathless and stared, wondering how such a place could even be built here in such a remote location. She continued on and followed the path all the way to the two oversized yet simple plain wood doors with two rounded and smoothed wooden handles. There was no lock on this door. Sandy somehow knew this was on purpose. She proceeded inside.

Sandy's breath was taken away. She drank in with her eyes the most magnificent scene of her life. The entire wall before her was made of glass, supported only by two cross beams made of logs. The sun was still rising, emitting brilliant colors that covered the canvas of the landscape both near and far with hues that spanned the spectrum. Sandy drew closer. As she stepped into this sanctuary, she was overwhelmed with a royal presence. "The King and Prince surely reside in this place," she said to herself. She had never experienced their presence so tangibly—not since her dream.

Sandy found the strength, though her knees were weak, to proceed towards the grand view. She gazed out, marveling at the majestic beauty before her. Mountain ranges spanned from her far left to right. There were so many high places out there, so much beauty to behold. Closer, she enjoyed individual objects of nature. Towering trees of weathered strength that had withstood the winds of these heights framed the scene before her. Down below and far in the distance, she saw valleys. She could not make out people from this high place but caught tiny glimpses of evidence they were out there. Their buildings and creations were but specks from this height. What a contrast this perspective offered. Instead of being caught in the shadows of the man-made towers of the valley, Sandy was squinting to define their existence at all. She had been brought so far.

Sandy lifted her eyes again to the horizon as the dawning of day appeared over the range of mountains within her sight. Her body now felt overcome by the unearthly power she felt once again—more grace. She was overwhelmed as a wave of great love washed through her in this high place. She took one more step and then fell to her knees in this sanctuary of the King's presence. She understood in a moment that she was fully known, and yet fully loved. "My King...my father! My Prince," she cried as she poured out her grateful wonder. "You are here! You are here! Have I arrived where you've destined me to come? Where could I go from here? I have never known such joy as I do now in your presence! I can't imagine knowing any more. I doubt my heart could handle another drop of your love. I feel it might burst! Oh, Father, thank you! Thank you for leading me here. Thank you for leading me through every trial, distraction and pain. Thank you for letting me see things from this high place, from this view I have here with you. Thank you for giving me more than I ever even knew I wanted. Oh, my beloved Prince, I want to reside here with you forever!"

As those last words left Sandy's lips, spilling out from her sincere and grateful heart, he spoke. "Go..."

"What?" Sandy asked aloud. "What did you say, dear Prince?"

"Go. Back to the world you must go." His voice was clear, and

Sandy dropped her head. This was my cue to comfort.

~~~

"Princess," I whispered, "I'm here."

"Oh, Jasper!" My Sandy collapsed in my arms as I knelt down by her at the great window. "Jasper, why can't I stay? It's perfect here. I feel him so near. I have never known my father's presence or the Prince's love like I have in this place. I want to stay—I want to remain here now, after this long journey. But…but he has told me to go. Why?"

"My precious one, how happy it makes us to share this outlook with you, here in the King's High Place, for you to see things more as we see them, in truth and with proper perspective. But you must take what you have learned from these heights and your journey here and share it down in the valley below."

My Sandy girl looked up with sad surprise in her eyes. "I have to go back?" she weakly asked.

"Yes, my girl. The King is calling you to go. There are more lessons to be lived and learned in the valley, to better equip you in using the keys you've been entrusted with. This journey cannot stop for you here. You must go into the world, exactly where I lead you. But Sandy, you will get to come back!" I then pointed to the other mountains in view before us. "And you will get to climb other mountains as well, and see far grander sights. And never forget Sandy, I will always, *always* be with you, till the end of time."

Sandy breathed in deeply and sighed. She had consented within. She looked up at me with a slight smile returning to her look, and then leaned in for a hug at my chest. "I hear your heart, Jasper. I know you would never mislead me, and something deep within me knows you are right. As long as you go with me, I will be all right. Besides—there's more treasure from that chest I haven't seen yet." Now my Sandy was back, smiling and joking with me, though there was much truth in her words.

"Yes, Princess. There is MUCH treasure to bestow on you still. Are you ready for it? Let's rise! Let's go from this place and gather your friends and return to the valley. There is a village I want you to stay in a while, before I send you to the depths of the valley. I have friends waiting to train you there. It will be a most delightful stay. Come. Let's go."

My Princess rose and we gazed out of the glass at the magnificent splendor of the vision in front of us. Sandy had a new vision in her heart, and now it was time to heed it and "go."

Faithful, Quietness, and Confidence were waiting for us as we made our way back down the hill. They all nodded and hugged Sandy, knowing from her sober, tear-stained yet radiant face that she had just had a glorious but difficult encounter. I turned to give her a gift of the encouraging kind, just what she needed at this moment before her descent.

"My love, this road you now tread on is the Road of Success." Sandy was visibly stunned by my words and revelation. Her mouth opened, but could not speak. I continued. "I have the Key of Success to give you, so you may unlock the many gates and doors along its way." I pulled out from my pocket an impressive yet simple key, inscribed on both sides of its shaft. It said "success" on one side and "always say yes" on the other. "Success, dear Princess, is always saying 'yes' to me, the Prince, and your King. You can be successful each and every day, as long as you say 'yes' to every step we ask you to take. You will have what your heart has always desired—true success—as you follow me in this way."

Sandy received the key with a huge smile. "So that's what the map book meant when we read it on the trail below. If I commit my way to the King, I will succeed."

"You will indeed! Always say yes to me, in big things and little, and you will know the success you were made for," I assured her.

Sandy was refilled now, strengthened by this mystery solved

within her. She had vision and purpose, and resolved to follow, now knowing truly where every path led—exactly where she needed to go, whether she knew the way or not. She was ready to adventure again and so we departed.

I led them back down on the other side of the mountain, a different way than we came. We journeyed down the very steep side, and each hiker was careful of their every step. They concentrated on watching me, just as they should, and no one slipped an inch. We reached a flat rock, and all were relieved. I was eager with excitement for the surprise I had planned for them next.

"Girls! Over here," I called. They all gathered, looking up to where I stood. "You have climbed and now have descended so well. I feel I should reward you with a delightful surprise. It's time to soar, girls. You've earned your 'wings' as those willing to take risks. And now you should experience a fast-pass of 'fun' to carry you to your next destination." They had no idea what I meant, but all turned and giggled with one another in wonder.

"I'm up for it!" Confidence responded first. "Whatever excitement you have to offer, Jasper, I will gladly receive."

"Then step right up!" I placed on Confidence a harness, and attached her to a zip line above. "This line will take you straight from this mountain range to the one over there. I have a friend waiting for you there to guide you to the village where you will stay a while. But first, you must *fly*. Are you ready?"

"Yes! I say '*yes*,' Jasper." With that, I released Confidence, whose immediate happy holler echoed throughout the mountain range.

"Who's next?" I asked. Quietness raised her hand and let out a laugh as she popped up before me. I fastened her in and sent her off. She laughed gleefully all the way.

Then Sandy and Faithful looked to each other. "You go first, Princess. I'll bring up the end," Faithful suggested. Sandy

226

consented and looked at me with one of the most loving looks so far. Tears rose again as she stared at me the whole time I secured her harness.

"I love you so much, my friend. Jasper, I trust you completely." Then she looked out and smiled in a laugh, acknowledging, "and now I get to fly! You are awesome."

I pulled her in for hug and held her close, then placed my hands on each side of her face, and stared her in the eyes, only inches from mine. "You were made to fly, Princess. Now GO!" With that I pushed her off, and she flew off in a merry burst of squeals. My Princess had taken off!

22

The Wastelands Revisited

Once Faithful had landed along with the others, they all celebrated together, relishing in their experience of flight. "That was pure exhilaration...and so much fun," said Confidence.

"I think I should like to fly some more," Quietness admitted. "I could get used to that kind of quick travel from height to height!"

"I think we all could. But Jasper said we were going to a village in the valley now. I wonder who will come this way to lead us..." Faithful added as she looked around.

Just then, a new face greeted them from the path behind them. It was the kind, rosy face of a man who looked to be strong, but not overbearing. His countenance was friendly and his way was gentle as he spoke. "Hey there, young ladies. You look to be the band of sisters Jasper sent me to meet."

"Yes," Sandy responded. "He told us he was sending us a friend to lead us to a new village." Sandy introduced herself and her friends, and then asked him his name.

"I'm Humility, and I'm honored to meet you. You all have completed quite a journey. Are you ready for the next part?" Humility's manner was soothing and encouraging at the same time.

"Yes! Yes we are. After that flight from the mountain top, I feel like I could do almost anything!" Sandy bubbled in answering him.

Humility laughed, "Well then, let's walk this way. It's a bit of a journey to our village, but there are some really lovely views, along with plenty of streams to drink from and places to rest along these ridges. Follow me."

With no hesitation, the women followed Humility's lead. Their new journey even surpassed his description. Waterfalls of refreshment greeted them along the road at several bends. Sturdy bridges crossed over splashing, rapid streams that spurred them on in enthusiastic travel. Grassy patches spread beside them occasionally for resting grounds, along with pools to clean up and splash in for needed revival. It was a most pleasant path indeed, and the girls appreciated the steady gait of their humble leader.

After a good while of mountain travel along the ridges, the path took a steep decline, then turned off to a low ridge that revealed a scene Sandy had not expected to see. Spread out in front of her in full view was a territory she once knew well. It was the Wastelands. Sandy froze from the shock of this familiar, yet now foreign, sight. A thick cloud of darkness hovered over it, like a spell. How had she never seen this before? Just then, the scent of it reached her nostrils. A subtle stench rose from the landmass. The smell that had once drawn her in was now making her sick. She had been washed clean of its effects, and now her lungs were filled with the air of the one who had breathed new life in her. She had smelled heavenly aromas, composed of the incense of Kingdom communication expressed by other freemen and hikers she journeyed with. This was the only air she craved now.

Sandy could only stand and stare, reflecting on how she ever lived in such a place of darkness, now that she had experienced the heights. "We'd better move on," Humility nudged. "There's still a ways to go before we reach my town."

"Wait," said Sandy, not moving her eyes from the cityscape ahead. "Could we travel just a little closer? I'm from that region, and I'd like to take a closer look at what has become of that place."

"That would not be wise," Humility responded. "Jasper wanted me to get you ready first."

Sandy was becoming hypnotized by the dark spell of the land. "I...I only want to take a look. My mother. My mother is down there, and I never even got to say goodbye. She must be worried sick. Let me at least go tell her where I have been and what has become of me. I need to convince her to come if I can! I know I'm the only one she'll listen to." This seemed a logical request. Sandy was grasping for reasons to give Humility so he would grant her leave.

"I cannot keep you, Sandy. You always have a choice to stay on this path or not. I can only tell you what Jasper instructed me, and he did not mention making stops at this time." Humility spoke plainly, yet his tone remained kind.

"Why don't you ask Jasper yourself," Faithful suggested.

"Or ask Wisdom what to do," Confidence further counseled.

"You should get advice, and not make this move on your own. Your thoughts and feelings could lead you into trouble, Sandy," Quietness concluded.

Sandy dismissed them all. "I will. I will ask Wisdom along the way, and I'm sure Jasper trusts me and will be fine with it. I just want to see my mom. You all wait here, will you? I will not be long!" And without waiting for another word, Sandy departed, off of the path and down a rough embankment. She didn't look back to see their shocked and sad faces, but proceeded towards the Wastelands with determination. Determined for what, she did not exactly know.

The Wastelands still had a pull on her indeed. She didn't fall along this uncut rough path, but stumbled for sure. Soon she hit the man-made pavement on the edge of town, and proceeded towards her home built into Wall of Excess. Sandy looked up at that wall, composed of all kinds of *stuff*. It was having a mesmerizing effect on her already. How quickly she grew bedazzled by the shiny objects artistically placed in the wall. Sandy was fascinated once again and began to think of what she might contribute to her section on the wall. *Wait!* Sandy caught herself. She had come to see her mother, and see her she must. Sandy had acquired such strength and beauty, and wanted to show that off to her mother and perhaps others she might see.

She hurried through the town with the focus she once knew, never looking into the faces of others. It was amazing how quickly her old patterns of interaction were revived. Sandy was glad to make it to her mom's home without any run-ins with old friends. She planned on returning to her friends on the ridge as soon as possible, after she made this one and only detour.

Out of new habit, Sandy pulled for her keys from her pouch when she reached the gate. "That's right. This gate requires no key," she remembered, and returned the keys to her bag. Sandy swung through the gate, pounded up the porch steps and bounded inside, knowing in her heart how excited her mother would be to see her.

"Who's there?" A shrill voice met her ears as she entered the house. But it was not the voice of her mother. It was Disappointment.

"It's me," Sandy replied, trying not to display her own deflation at having to encounter this old family friend.

"Well, I declare! WHERE have YOU been? You have had your mother and this whole town sick, up in arms, searching for you!" Disappointment's tone was harsher than ever, giving Sandy a verbal thrashing that stung her heart.

"I...I..." Sandy did not know how to begin to explain the journey she had begun and the new life she had started. Thankfully, her mother came into the room.

"Sandy! My Sandy! Thank goodness you're alive!" Sandy's mom ran and threw her arms around her, sobbing with relief.

"Mom...I...I...I'm sorry. I should have sent word. I should

have let you know…I'm all right." Sandy's heart was in a throw of emotions, those of her old life mixed with the new.

"Yes, you should have. I'm just glad you're Ok. But where have you been?" Her mom asked as she released Sandy to tend to her sniffle.

"Yes, young lady! *Where* have you been?" Disappointment could not contain herself, dwarfing them all with her booming and accusing voice.

Though Sandy felt herself slipping, she had not regressed completely, and found the confidence to address her mom's friend. "If you don't mind, Ms. Disappointment, I'd like a moment with my mother alone." Sandy stared unwaveringly at the old sour woman who returned her stare back in awe and shock.

"Why, I never! What impudence! *Who's* been the one here attending to your mother while you've been roaming the country-side? I have! And now you stroll back in and think you can dismiss me just like that? What have *you* to say, my friend? Will you stand for this?"

Disappointment left the call to Sandy's mom, who took a moment to reply. When she did she said, "You may go now. I need to hear my daughter out."

"HUMPH! Ousted again, I see!" Disappointment turned on her heels, much like Pride had been known to do, and lifted her head to proceed out of the door.

After the clamor of her stomping footsteps receded into the distance, Sandy sat with her mother on the couch in the front room. "Mom," she began. "I don't know where to begin in telling you what has happened to me. Some things had started to happen even before I left."

"You mean, at the Shores?" Sandy's mom surprised her with this insightful question, catching Sandy off guard.

"Well, yes, a lot happened there. But even before. See, I had this dream one night, and then got this invitation to come…" Sandy's mom dropped her head and listened. Sandy explained as best as she could the recent events of her life. Her mom sat still, allowing Sandy to express all she wanted, not interrupting with one question or thought. Finally, Sandy concluded, "So you see, I just had to go. It changed everything for me. Jasper has changed everything. And the journey is not over, but I had to come back. Mom, I had to come back and see you…and ask you…will you come?"

Sandy's mom lifted her eyes and fixed them on Sandy for one sad moment. Then she rose without a word and headed to her bedroom. Sandy sat silently, not knowing what this meant. In just a few moments, her mother returned. She held something in her hand.

"Sandy, I am familiar with much of your story. I took a trip to the Shores once too. I had been invited. And I met someone who wanted to walk me out into the Great Sea. But I refused him." Sandy could not believe it. It was her same story. "He had the face of love itself, a face that has been burned into my memory ever since." Sandy's mom looked off with a sad, remembering smile slightly gracing her face. Then she lost her smile and dropped her gaze down to her lap before presenting an object to Sandy. "He gave me this."

Sandy's mom held out a small glass vial, bound by a golden rope. It had a corked top and there was liquid inside. On the bottle was inscribed one word. Sandy read it aloud. "Hope." Sandy's eyes darted up and her one free hand flew to her chest, grasping her own vial. Her mom spotted the bottle, just the same as hers; their eyes locked in a stare.

"Mom!" Sandy cried in a desperate whisper, "What happened? Did you ever go back?"

There was a very long pause, and Sandy could feel the anguish rise within her mother and permeate the room. Finally she cried in a low whisper, "No. I never did. I found a substitute for that love instead, and then became pregnant with you. But I named you Sandy for the love I felt on those shores. In the sand I refused the greatest love of my life, but in holding you, I hoped to cling on and always remember something of it."

Sandy was speechless. They both sat in sad silence for the next few moments until Sandy found words to express her deepest wish at this time. "You can come with me now. Come with me now, Mom, it isn't too late! I know it isn't! I know this one you met...Jasper...and this gift of hope he gave you never expires! Come with me now! You can find him again! Will you come?" Sandy felt hope flooding her heart as it pounded against the glass vial that lay up against her beating chest. The pause was long, and Sandy would not break her stare until her mom finally moved by shaking her hung head.

"No...no, I can't. I can't go. I belong here. I fit in here just fine. I'm too old to change my ways. I missed my chance." Then she looked up at Sandy, "But you go, my dear. I'm glad you found love. I'm glad you have changed. You look good. It works for you. But I must stay here."

Sandy argued with her mom, trying to convince her from every angle, but her mother's heart remained unmoved. The longer they debated, the firmer her mother grew in her resolve. Sandy recognized the stubborn resistance. It was just how she was, only her mother had many more years of hardened habits and choices to break through for a change in perspective to occur. Finally, in utter frustration, Sandy got up to go.

"I don't know what else to say. I love you, Mom, and I want you to come, but Jasper didn't force me, so I can't force you either. I'm going to go on, but someday I'll return, and I'll ask you to come again." Then she turned to her mother with one last request. "Just do me one favor. Do yourself one favor. Put the necklace back on." Sandy's mom looked up and paused, then nodded.

"I will." She looked at Sandy, studying her daughter's face for a very long time. "You are beautiful, my girl. You are a princess. I'm so glad you can journey where I cannot seem to go.

Goodbye." Then she rose and quickly headed for her room, closing the door behind her. Sandy knew her mother was crying and did not want to be approached. She granted this unspoken request. Sandy was drained, but summoned the strength to raise her own body up, laden with heaviness, and take her leave.

Sandy descended the steps, passed back through the gate and returned to the streets of the Wastelands. She wasn't sure which way to go, having lost her sense of direction after losing this battle with her mom. That is what she came for. "Now what?" Sandy thought. She stood at the gate, trying to remember just how she had gotten there from the ridge where she had left her band of fellow journeyers. As Sandy peered about, an overdressed woman with a brisk and pronounced gait approached her directly.

"Well, HELLO!!" the oddly tall and familiar person began. "It's Sandy, right? I never forget a face!" The woman stared Sandy up and down with a broad and toothy smile, bordered by the brightest shade of red paint on her lips.

"I'm sorry, I don't remember meeting you," Sandy replied, trying hard to suppress her urge to gawk in shock at this comically dressed and odd-mannered lady.

The stranger persisted, "Oh, we met at a party at Pride's house once, I think. I'm Flattery, dear, but enough about *me*. Look at YOU! You look so GOOD! Been to the beach? You have so much color in your face! You look just lovely!" The lady poured on compliment after compliment, waving her arms and head about in flamboyant gestures. There was no gap in her gushing for Sandy to respond. Finally there was a pause after she asked, "Have any of your friends seen you since you've come back?"

Sandy now had a chance to answer, though she wasn't sure how to explain. In an attempt she replied, "Well, I'm not really here to stay. I just stopped by on my journey."

"Journey? What kind of journey do you mean? I hear you've been gone for quite some time. Isn't it time you came home? You are so *bright* and *cheery* and *lovely* now. I can tell your trip did you good. But don't you think you should share that all here? I think some of your friends could use some of that *sunshine* you have! You really should just come into the city. *Shine* your light —show off a little! Don't you want them to see how you've changed?" Flattery batted her eyelashes as she leaned into Sandy and waited for her to respond.

Sandy pondered Flattery's words. She had indeed changed, and it might be good for her old friends and acquaintances to see that, she considered. "They have never seen me like this. Perhaps I could make them want to come on the journey too." She also secretly loved the thought of them seeing her look pretty and confident, proving she wasn't the failure she feared they thought her to be. She wanted them to see her looking good and strong. Sandy conceded.

"Ok, I'll go. I'll go with you into the city just to say hi. Maybe I can make a difference in their lives before I return to my friends on the journey." Sandy expressed this as her reason, though Flattery had hooked her by stirring up mixed motives within her that were not quite so pure.

"PERFECT! I'm so glad you decided to go! But I can't join you, my dear. I have places to go and people to deceive! I mean, 'see'! Ha-ha-ha!"Flattery tried to cover her gaffe with a hearty loud laugh. "You'll have to go into the city alone."

Sandy brushed over the blunder and nodded, feeling confident in her return to the city, especially after being so built up by Flattery. She justified the trip further by telling herself how close she was, and that a little slip into the city would take no time at all. She just needed an hour or so to find Pride, and maybe others from work. She wanted them to see how she had changed, how happy she was, and maybe they would want to change too! Isn't that what Jasper had relayed to her on the mountaintop? She was needed in the valley to set people free! And the City of Excess was deep in the valley. She knew she must be needed there.

As they parted ways, Flattery leaned in to kiss Sandy once on each cheek. Her puckered lips smooched only the air on both sides of Sandy's face, then she pulled back to bid Sandy one final farewell. "WAIT till they see you, Girl! You're going to blow them away as soon as you get into the City!" Then Flattery spun on her heels and stomped off down the sidewalk in a flurry of false praise she spouted to everyone she passed.

Sandy remained for a moment, trying to regain her direction again. Her inner compass was off, so she allowed the last words of Flattery to guide her. "Into the city…Yes. I need to go there," she convinced herself. The next moment, she resumed her journey in the direction of Excess.

As soon as the train doors opened within the big city, Sandy was hit with a whiff of regret. The smell of this place sickened her, weakening her at the same time. She recalled the view from just hours before on the ridge, her clear view of the smog and perspective of darkness. She was repulsed by it then. Now, she was in the thick of it.

But this regret was not strong enough to alter her course. Sandy descended from the train and stepped into the city that had once held her heart. She felt strangely out of place, yet slightly sucked in. The glamorous sights of well-dressed people and sparkly shops full of glittery objects had her jerking her head from right to left as she tried to process each one. Suddenly, Sandy felt plain and earthy again. Her simple linen outfit seemed drab in contrast to the fitted shiny suits so many on these streets wore. Sandy wished Confidence was here to back her up. She could use her dear friend now.

Sandy wasn't sure where to go first, but decided to pass by the Hot Shot Café on the way to BIG'S. Surely she would run into Pride and others she knew between these two spots. She gathered her thoughts as she walked, trying to construct the perfect approach to convince any she might see to return with her to the ridge and meet her friends. Sandy planned speeches in her head, failing to confer with Wisdom, Jasper, or even her map for guidance.

Before she was completely prepared, the moment met her. As Sandy was rounding the corner just before the café, she walked right into Mr. Big and his cohorts.

"Oh, I'm sorry!" Sandy cried as she bounced off Mr. Big. She was jolted by this run-in in more ways than one.

Mr. Big stared down and barked, "Watch where you are going, young lady!" Then he caught sight of her face and realized who this obstacle in his path was. His eyes widened in a surprised stare.

"I...I...I'm sorry," Sandy stuttered, looking up briefly, then looking down again. Her composure was lost. So was her speech.

"Isn't that your old employee, Bigs, dear?" Mr. Big's wife, Vanity, whispered up to her husband while watching the girl with one raised eyebrow. "Isn't she the one who ran off when serving us some time ago?"

Sandy's spirit sank even further, shamed by her reputation. She knew this would be difficult to overcome. Selfish Ambition chimed in as well, leaning in next to her sister. "Looks like she wasn't made to make it in the city." Selfish Ambition scanned Sandy's tanned skin. "She looks more like a country girl now—a *simpleton* for sure!" Her comments, though not made directly to Sandy, were not lowered to keep her from hearing them at all. They stung Sandy's heart just the same as if that was her aim.

Sandy was dejected, and found no words for response. This crowd had no time for one like her, as Selfish Ambition confirmed before departing, "Let's go. We don't have the time of day for such plain folks. We have important people to meet."

As they moved past the limp and spiritless girl, Sandy caught sight of the shiny shoes of one last member of their company—Mr. Success. He turned and cast a glance back at Sandy as they brushed by her. "You always run away, don't you, girl? What a shame. You really could have been somebody." Then he sealed this final jab to her heart with a nod and flash of his insincere grin, before lifting his gaze and walking off.

Sandy was shattered again as she examined herself through the eyes of the leaders in this realm. They did not see her beauty. Her ways made no sense to them and she was not appealing to them at all. In fact, they made fun of her. She came in wanting to make a difference, wanting to surprise this world with her change and share all that had been revealed to her, but this would not happen. She was not received, and now she would need mending instead.

Wounded, Sandy walked aimlessly down the streets of Excess, lost in her hurt and disillusionment. What good would *her* changing do if she could not bring about change in others? She had no influence on others here, it appeared. Even her own mother refused her. Tears of frustration and confusion splattered the pavement as Sandy moved on with no end in mind. Fortunately for her, her steps were guided, even when she gave no thought to them. When Sandy finally looked up from her tearful travel, she had come to the small park in the middle of town with a fountain and a bench. I had saved a seat for her there beside me.

~ ~ ~

"Jasper," she whispered as she stood still a slight distance off, wilted from the scorch of her encounters this day.

"Come," I simply responded, reaching out for my princess to sit next to me. She hesitated only one moment in shame, then relented, collapsing on this same bench that she sat on once with Page earlier in her journey.

Sandy sobbed and sobbed. I let her, simply stroking her hair gently as she leaned fully into me, unloading her heart in tears. When it was nearly empty of the grief that could be expressed in this way, Sandy sat up. She sniffed and sighed, remaining quiet a little longer, staring at the continual flow of water before us.

"That fountain," she observed. "It flows so powerfully and happily, refreshing all at the sight of it." She paused, then added, "I flow weakly and sadly, unable to make any difference at all." Her lips quivered again in despair of herself.

"Oh, Princess," I whispered as I pulled her in again. "That fountain is functioning as it was made to do. You, my dear, chose your own way." Sandy was surprised by my answer, though she didn't feel scolded. That would not be my intent.

She looked up at me and studied my face before speaking. "I made a mistake, didn't I? I was not meant to come here, was I?"

"You were not led this way, Sandy. It was not time to come back yet. I'm not done preparing you. There is still more to learn."

"But I thought I was the only one who could help my mom *see*. I thought she needed me to come set her free, like the prisoners on that hill," Sandy countered.

"Only the King can really know one's heart. And she is not ready," I answered.

Sandy could see this plainly now. "Oh, Jasper, I'm sorry. I didn't even ask you. I just figured I was so close, so it made sense to come. Why was I so foolish?"

"There is wisdom in the counsel of those trusted ones you travel with," I gently responded. "It would have been prudent to heed their advice." Sandy nodded her head to agree. "And you were being led by one of my finest friends, Humility. He would never be forceful in holding you back, but he is a wise friend for you indeed, quite the opposite of your old friend, Pride."

"Pride," reflected Sandy with disgust in her low tone. "I'm surprised he didn't show up to gloat at my failure."

"Oh, but he did. You just didn't recognize him," I stated. Sandy looked up at me, puzzled by this revelation. "Pride disguised himself once again—as Flattery this time. He appealed to the pride within you, and led you right back into the city."

Sandy was shocked before letting this realization sink in. "I knew there was something familiar about Flattery. How unbeliev-ably sneaky he is!" Sandy was appalled by Pride's deceit and her own lack of discernment.

"You must be careful of compliments and their effect on decisions you make. '*To flatter friends is to lay a trap.*' The map book reveals this ploy clearly, dear." Sandy shook her head, in greater disgust at herself. If only she had referred to it before she chose to listen to the logic of a stranger.

"Oh, Jasper. He did lay a trap. And I was sucked in." Sandy looked all around. "This city…Its spell started to get to me once again. I didn't think it could, but I found myself fascinated with all of the *stuff,* the shining objects and *things* it presented along the way. I must admit to you, it made me want more again. I'm so ashamed."

Sandy dropped her head again in guilt, but I found fertile ground in which to impart a seed of my wisdom. "Sandy, it's time you realized something. There is nothing inherently wrong with *things.* I enjoy giving you 'things' myself. It's only when things crowd in, taking hold of your heart and affections that they pose a problem. When they consume your thoughts and overtake your focus, that's when they become excessive. *Things* are meant to serve a purpose. You are not meant to serve them."

Sandy looked up and a little relief washed over her face, so she turned to me again. "So…so you're not mad at me? You're not disappointed in me?"

"No!" I laughed. "As long as you love me *first* and *most,* I will not be disappointed at all!" My smile relieved her.

"And you're not ashamed of me? You still want me to follow you? I haven't drifted too far away?" Sandy was still not convinced.

"My Sandy, I am never but a turn away. As *lost* as you may sometimes feel, I am always just behind you. Many strive, seeking me, feeling so distant and far. But all who seek me must simply turn from their own ways and stare into my face. I am always right there behind them. It is never a long journey home."

"Home..." Sandy repeated in sad but sweet longing. Then she looked up. "You are my home, Jasper. I never feel as settled as when you are near...when I know I am with you."

"And that's just as it should be. This world is not your home, Princess. You were made for another. And every step with me is a step closer to the one the Prince is preparing for you. Your mother, these others...they think they are home, but their souls find no rest. And *home* should at least offer that. So while you walk here, we will walk hand in hand, and *home* you shall always be!"

Sandy's eyes held tears again, but this time tears of amazement. "How did I ever find you?" Sandy asked, shaking her head slightly in wonder.

"You didn't. I found you, remember? And I called you to come, and you did! It has become quite the adventure—one that is not over. So, Princess..." I rose, then knelt and extended my hand in the same manner our dear friend Page had, asking, "will you come?"

Sandy let out a much-needed laugh, threw her hand over her heart as she leaned back in delight before accepting my offer. Then she took my hand with both of hers and kissed it. "Yes! A thousand times yes! Lead me on, my Jasper. You are the one my soul loves and the only one I trust to lead my way. If you can get me back on track, please do!"

And with that, we rose and walked through the city, hand in hand, not concerned with any who stared our way. My Princess had her confidence restored, for she had found her security in me. I would lead her back—always—to the road she was made for, the one she could always return to with every simple "yes."

23

A Stay in Simplicity

I led my princess out of the city to the edge where the great gaping gate in the wall was open. "This gate never really closes, does it, Jasper?" Sandy asked as her eyes scanned the broad width and height of the rounded entrance to Excess.

"No, my love. It is always open. It does not discriminate over whom it will allow to enter and marvel at what it has to display." I paused, waiting for the lessons of the day to settle in Sandy's heart. "But you, my Princess—you were made for *more.*

"*More?*" Sandy questioned again. "More" was the chant of the mayor of *this* city we stood on the edge of, and that I was leading her out of. She was confused as to what I could mean.

"Sandy, where I am leading you next is truly a place of *more.* But not more *stuff.* You will discover *more* of everything you have truly longed for. And Sandy, there is always *more!* Your father is very, very rich." I smiled and nudged her as I leaned in to reveal this mystery to my girl in a playful whisper.

"Just where are you leading me, Jasper?" she inquired.

"You, my dear, are going to have a stay in Simplicity!" Before she could react, her ride had arrived.

A charming, antiquated bus of sorts pulled up on the road next to us. In the driver's seat was Humility, and Sandy's gang of friends from the journey were all seated behind, along with a pretty petite lady and a couple of lively young children.

"Hello there, Jasper! I hope you haven't been waiting too long," Humility beamed as he rolled down the window to greet us.

"Perfect timing, my friend! I was just informing the Princess of her next stop. Thank you for heeding my call so quickly. I believe Sandy is ready to go now," I answered Humility before turning to my precious one. "Are you ready, love?"

My Princess smiled back. Her face had a lovely glow that matched Humility's. "Yes, I will do exactly as you say, and I will not try to forge ahead of you again! At least, I hope I will not, dear Jasper. I'm so sorry for barging ahead in my own way before," Sandy added, dropping her head slightly.

I lifted her chin with my finger and spoke directly into her eyes, "Hey! None of that. You are forgiven and free. It is time to move onward!" I then lifted my eyes to the bus full of friendly faces peering out at us. "And what better lot could you find than *these* traveling companions?" Sandy nodded in relief as she looked on each face. "Go! Humility will take you to his village. It will be a season of preparation. A time 'on the bench,' as I call it, to observe and absorb every lesson you can. And when you have acquired what you are meant to learn there, I will see you again. Until then, remember…I am *with* you!"

Sandy reached up to grab my neck for one tight hug and then released me with a wave and a look that let me know her heart was yielded and she desired the "more" I spoke of. Humility opened the door and her friends welcomed and embraced her, and their chatting quickly ensued. The bus took off and I waved them away. She was off to learn secrets that would strengthen and prepare her for the rest of her journey.

~ ~ ~

On the bus, Humility introduced Sandy to the lovely woman at his side. "Sandy, this is my wife, Gentleness. She was driving along looking for us, since we were running later than expected, and picked us all up."

"Oh, it is so nice to meet you. And I'm sorry for causing you any worry. The delay was my fault." Sandy felt a twinge of guilt again, thinking of how her actions had affected so many. She wished she had been more conscious of others at the time she made her decision to leave the group for the Wastelands.

"It is Ok, my dear. I wasn't worried. I just felt nudged by Jasper to go out and fetch everyone, so I did. I don't believe much in worrying. It does me no good." This woman was a darling indeed, so mild in her manner. Sandy was impressed by her calm disposition.

"Well, I am grateful. I'm glad to catch a ride and be amongst my friends again," Sandy responded, as she looked each familiar friend in the face. Then a small child's face popped up before hers.

"Are you going to stay with us? You can stay in my room with me! I have bunk beds!" This little wide-eyed girl did not even know Sandy's name, yet was thrilled at the thought of sharing what she had to offer.

Sandy smiled at her and said, "I would love to stay with you, but we'll have to ask your mom. What is your name, love?"

"Faithie. But you can call me Princess Faith! That's what Jasper calls me," Faith announced with delight.

"Oh, he does? He calls *me* Princess too! He says that's what I am *becoming*," Sandy replied playfully.

"You are? Well we can play 'princesses' when we get home with my sister!" Faithie was overwhelmed with excitement and introduced the other little girl in the bus, Hope, to Sandy too. Hope was younger, and much smaller. She looked quite different than other children and had an impediment in her speech. She was hard to understand, and hobbled as she moved about. Sandy thought she must be disabled and began to look on her with pity, but then noticed the sweet joy and contentment Hope had, and that those in her family had too. Faithie certainly did not treat her sister differently at all, so Sandy suppressed any judgments or pity, and just observed the girls' cheery interaction for miles. Gentleness tended her girls with such peace and sweetness too. Sandy knew she had much to learn from them all and was growing excited about the lessons to come.

The bus of adventurers laughed and conversed all the way down the smooth country road until Sandy could see a village up ahead. "This is it! Home sweet home," Humility said, "You are now entering our Village of Simplicity."

Faithful, Confidence, Quietness, and Sandy all strained to see out of the windows on either side of the bus. It was a most pleasant scene indeed. There was a wooden sign hung overhead on two posts at either side of the road, marking the village with only the word, "Simplicity." Children could be seen playing all about in a wide-open field in the center of town. Sandy noted how children were rarely seen playing openly in Excess. Unless their parents closely escorted them when traveling, the children of Excess were usually inside, plugged into the systems provided by the city. It was nice to see these children running freely outdoors.

As they drove around this town square, Sandy saw a fountain in the center of it, with a much higher and more powerful spray than the fountain in Excess. Inviting benches surrounded the fountain's pool. *Well, if I am to be "on the bench," this is the right place to be*, Sandy surmised. She deemed the park perfect and was quite happy to be provided such a splendid space for pondering important matters of the heart.

Small homes could be seen spread out amongst the trees, along streams, and set into hillsides. The terrain was not completely flat in most of this village, but the inclines made the landscape interesting when looking at the placement of homes and buildings. Nothing here was fancy, but simple and sweet. Humility drove past the square and through a grove of trees up a hill. Set upon the next knoll was their small stone house.

As they pulled up, Sandy sighed in delight. There was something about this home that was reminiscent of the others she had stayed in along her journey. Signs of life buzzed all around. Flowering bushes surrounded the home. Butterflies flew from bush to bush along with bees and hummingbirds. A small creek ran through their back yard, wound down the right side of their house and then turned off to share the joy of its flow with neighbors. The home had a stone stoop and a round wooden front door through which the newcomers entered.

The inside of this house was just as inviting as the outside had been. A stone fireplace was shared by the kitchen and living room and sturdy wood beams supported the entire open living space. A long wooden plank table with benches on either side separated the kitchen from the living area, and a few doors led off to other rooms on each of the walls. Sandy could sense that this was a place that people would want to come and stay for a while. Hospitality was the spirit of this home, and Sandy felt welcomed right away.

"You all have a seat in the living room. I'm going to fix us a snack," Gentleness said. All consented and sank into the cozy couches and chairs, worn from many similar invitations to sit.

The group spent the afternoon getting acquainted, and the lessons, whether intended or not, were immediately being taught and learned. Sandy watched the way Humility served his wife. He would not allow her to do all the work alone, but observed when he could aid her best. Gentleness always thanked him, and patted him kindly. He would smile and pat her back, showing love in his every look and manner. They always looked at each other in the eyes, and put on no false airs that Sandy could sense. Their interaction was a beautiful dance of humble and serving love. They treated their children with the same respect and patience, even when they could have easily justified frustrated responses at times. Their shared life was a great example for Sandy to see.

After observing and interacting for several hours, everyone was growing comfortable and relaxed with one another. Finally, Sandy had to ask, "How do you do it? How is your family so...nice?"

The whole room laughed, but all of the guests were curious as to the answer, for they were just as amazed as Sandy at this family's kind way. "Well, if you see anything good, it is the work of Jasper in us. When Jasper came into my life and picked me to be his friend, I was a pretty rough character. I come from the Wastelands too, Sandy," Humility revealed.

"You are kidding?" Sandy remarked, shocked that such a gentleman could have known life in the Wastelands at all.

"Yes. I was very ambitious and arrogant. I was egotistical and selfish and only cared for making a name for myself, wanting to make it in Excess however I could," Humility continued. Sandy was stunned at the parallel. She knew this story well.

"One day I felt this urgency to go to the Shores, and I met Jasper. I was wandering and restless, and Jasper changed everything. He became my best friend and changed my perspective completely. He changed the way I did everything, and how I treated everyone." Then Humility looked at his wife with eyes that smiled and seeped with love. "And it's a good thing. *This* one would never have had me the way I was!"

Gentleness lightly hit his arm then embraced him from the side and continued the storytelling where he left off. "Jasper had gotten a hold of me too. He had a lot of work to do, as I had a mouth that would not be silenced! I had a sharp tongue and a critical spirit. I made fun of people and judged everyone. I hurt others, and actually hurt myself, for I doubt I was enjoyable to be around at all. But Jasper became my friend and brought me friends like yours here." She pointed to Quietness, Confidence, and Faithful, before adding, "They made all the difference in my life and saw me through the transformation needed to be the kind of friend, wife, and mother someone might benefit from."

Sandy was soaking in every word as instruction. She too wanted the beauty they had in her own life. She needed to understand even more. "How? How do I get this way? How do I change? I do have these great friends, but I know I am still so drawn to the ways of the Wastelands. I couldn't believe how easily it pulled me in today. I am weaker than I thought, which makes me doubt I can change as much as I'd like to."

Humility grinned as he sat on the stone hearth of the fireplace. "I know the feeling. Let me tell you something that happened once between Jasper and me. I was sitting on a bench out here in the country somewhere, talking to the Prince. I was actually telling the Prince how *useful* I could be in his Kingdom, and how he should promote me and send me back into the city right way. I told him he should give me a *'big name,'* and that I could get many to follow me out of there. But he saw things differently. He told me he wanted me to have *'no name.'* He told me I would be more useful to him if I sat there on that bench and just remained with him. I was upset. I protested, 'How can *sitting* produce anything for you? I want to be *used,*' I argued." The Prince went silent. He wouldn't be argued with. He had spoken, but I didn't understand his ways.

"I sat there longer, frustrated in this life I had chosen, but knowing something was wrong on the inside of me. I knew what I felt inside my heart was not the King's intention. I asked Jasper for insight, and he came right way. He led me through the map in the paths of humility, showing that its ways lead to true wealth and honor and life. Then he summed it all up by saying to me, 'Your posture is to be one of humility. I do not want you operating in a posture of pride any longer. Just as I resist pride, I want *you* to resist pride. I give my grace to the humble.' That was it. I had experienced the power of grace, and did not want to live without it. I wanted more of it. I wanted nothing to do with anything he would oppose, so I determined to resist pride in its every form, and Jasper's promise held true. He has given me much undeserved favor and mercy and power to overcome. And now I only care to make *his* name great. I care not for my own, for what can *I* do? He has done everything worth anything in my life. I only want to reflect his greatness and make his name known."

After a slight pause in which everyone was pondering this story, Gentleness added, "I believe humility is the most attractive quality a citizen of the Kingdom could possess. Only true and mature people of the Kingdom can fully appreciate its beauty. But our King always does, and that must be our aim—to please him above all."

Sandy and her friends had a good long stay in Simplicity and began to adapt to its ways. They each stayed in different neighboring homes in this tight-knit community, but Sandy remained in the home of Gentleness and Humility. This family was leaving its mark on her life for certain. Each day provided new lessons as she observed and interacted with them in the daily routines of life. Soon she felt part of their family.

Sandy aided in the care of the children, though in truth they cared all the more for her. She was a student of their child-like ways. She loved to watch them create wonders from scraps, and employ their vivid imaginations in acting out great stories and tales. Sandy got caught up in their worlds and began to *play* in a way that her mindset of *work* would never have allowed her to do in the Wastelands. In becoming more like a child, her heart became all the more pliable and open to wonder. It then pleased her father to make even more of his wonders known to his teachable girl. Sandy's heart blossomed, due in great part to this time with these precious girls.

Sandy was particularly fascinated with Hope and the affect she had on her family. One day while the girls were napping, Sandy and Gentleness were baking bread, and the subject of Hope came up. "It's amazing to watch Faithie with her sister," Sandy started. "She's so good with her."

"She is indeed! We are so blessed in that. Well, we are blessed in every way with Hope," Gentleness added. "But we didn't always feel that way."

"Really?" Sandy responded. "Has it been hard having a child with special needs like Hope has?"

"It has had its physical and practical challenges, but thankfully we have overcome our most difficult hurdle—our disappointment at first." Gentleness was honest and genuine in her reply. "When Hope was born, we were shocked by her condition. We expected a 'perfect baby,' like Faithie had been. I was devastated. This wasn't how I envisioned our family being. I worried a lot and wondered how this would affect us all. But what I've learned over the years is that the King's greatest blessings sometimes come in packages that we question at first and don't understand. Now her diagnosis has lost its sting and I can't imagine our family without Hope exactly as she is! Her amazing spirit has made us all better people. She cannot speak well, yet her very life teaches me daily. She has helped us enjoy life in simple ways I never thought possible as we try to see things through her eyes. She is the most perfectly created toddler on the planet! Hope has blessed me beyond what I have deserved. I now believe I know what true beauty is!"

Sandy's eyes welled up as Gentleness wiped her own tears of gratitude. It was a sweet, deep moment shared by these two new friends, that turned to giggles as two sets of eyes popped over the counter, staring at them, topped with messy strands of hair.

"Mama!" the first set of eyes cried out before revealing the precious face of Hope.

"Can we get up now?" the second sleepy girl asked, still mostly hiding.

"Come here, you two sillies," Gentleness summoned her girls. Their laughter was ignited and both tumbled into their mother's arms the very next moment.

Sandy watched the scene in wonder. *How does the King do that? How he delights in taking our disappointments, and by hope, turns them into such joy.*

Lessons like these seemed never ending in the Village of Simplicity. From the smallest objects or slightest interactions, the Prince taught Sandy's heart astounding lessons that transformed her thinking. It was the richest season of her life.

One evening, after a satisfying dinner, they all sat by the fire, staring at the flames. Sandy was feeling reflective and found herself going through her pouch, examining all of her tokens from her journey. She showed each one to the girls and explained what each gift had meant. When she got to the key ring, she told the girls in simple terms what each one could do. "My dad has a big key!" Faithie declared.

"He does?" Sandy asked. "Of course he does," she then realized.

"I do," Humility answered without being asked. "And I've been waiting for the right time to give it to you. This seems to be the perfect moment." Humility rose and went to his wooden desk near the door. From the single drawer he drew out a key that would fit perfectly with the others on her ring. He crossed the room and handed it to Sandy. The word "Humility" was boldly inscribed on one side of the shaft. The words "Trust in the King" were engraved on the other.

"The key to humility, Sandy, is knowing where to put your trust. Your trust belongs to the King alone, for he is the only one completely worthy of your trust. If you put your hope or expectation in people, you will be disappointed and provoke your own pride within. Trusting in *yourself* is pride as well, and will lead to a fall. Our understanding cannot be leaned upon. But trusting in the King with all your heart is an act of beautiful submission. That is humility. You will not always understand his ways, but your *trusting* regardless of your human understanding, is a great sign of faith. This pleases our King. And that is our aim as citizens of his Kingdom, to please him and bring his heart pleasure. When we humble ourselves by laying down our own ways to trust in his, he promises to lift us up. There is great reward in a life of complete trust and humility. This is the key to that treasure."

Sandy received the key with gratitude, and then began to reflect on the many times she opted to trust herself or put her expectation in others. She had sought after reward and treasure her whole life, but had bought into her alliance with Pride as her key, never giving "humility" a thought. What an upside down world this Kingdom was. *Jasper was right*, she concluded. *It is a world of opposites indeed.* Sandy's stay in Simplicity proved this more each day. And she had never been so happy.

The next day, Sandy went to the square field in the center of Simplicity and took her pouch with her map and journal. She wanted to record this key lesson in humility along with many others she had learned in her stay. She sat once again on a bench, in *this* season of lessons, and withdrew her beloved map book first from her bag. As she rubbed her hands over its smooth cover, she recalled how in the beginning of her journey the words within felt foreign and even abrasive to her soul. It seemed a book of unsolvable riddles and rules, yet with Wisdom's help she began to understand these sacred words, and they made their way into her heart, creating gentle waves of calm and comfort. Her heart was becoming a deeper place. Everything was changing. Everything in Sandy's life was beginning to be colored by the words in this book—the words read and repeated in whispers to her soul. This book of mystery had become her most significant possession.

"It is indeed a treasure chest," she marveled, looking at this well of wisdom she could hold within her hands. She stared at it for a moment, remembering the hesitancy she first received it with. Once she had thought it so weighty, wondering if it would slow her down in her journey. Now she would choose it over anything else she would carry if she ever must make that choice.

What change of heart had transpired within her. Sandy was transforming. She was not the gritty girl guided by her own ambitions and whims. The water of this well was smoothing out every edge of Sandy's earthiness and was preparing her. She was becoming a princess. The refinement was not only necessary; it was stunning. With the singular focus of a bride making herself ready for that one day, Sandy yielded her heart to her Prince and King as she held the book close. "I feel I can almost see you in here," she whispered with the map gripped tight at her chest. Sandy was beginning to make out what the King and Prince really looked like, or at least what their hearts looked like as she was learning of their character and ways through the record of their journeys in this book. She held it out again and stared at its leather cover. In thoughtful satisfaction, Sandy inhaled deeply, savoring the map's now familiar scent. She then exhaled, and let out her gratitude. "Thank you. Thank you for this gift. I see you now in part, but someday I will see you in full. I love you, my Prince and my King! Oh, I can't wait for that day. Until then, thank you for this." She squeezed the map tightly once again. It was her treasure, her light, the voice of her love, and it had led her this far. She had no doubt it would lead her beyond this appointed place to whatever adventures were planned for her next, and then all the way home, to the Kingdom at last.

24

A Glimpse of the Kingdom

Sandy finished up her time by the fountain and made it home for supper. To her surprise, a guest had been invited. Peace was at the table with the rest of the family when she walked into the room. "Peace!" Sandy gasped, delighted by the sight of him. "You are the perfect ending to my deeply reflective day," she announced as she circled the table to embrace her old friend.

Peace chuckled at her greeting, "Well that's a good thing to be, I hope. A 'perfect ending' can't be too bad anyway, I assume." He rose to hug her back, then kept his arm about her shoulder while she told her family about her day.

"It's been a good one. I've just been remembering. I've been sitting by the fountain, recounting my lessons from this journey and reviewing my map. My, what a journey it's been."

"It certainly has, Princess," Peace interjected. "And the Prince is so proud of your growth. And more than that, he adores your heart of devotion. He sent me to express this for him in a tangible way. He knew you might like to see me." Peace pulled her in while he winked at the rest.

"He is always right! How long can you stay?" Sandy wanted to know.

"Oh, at least for this evening…or forever. However long you'll keep me around." The family laughed at his response.

"Well, have a seat, you two," Gentleness instructed. "I hope you are hungry. Humility has grilled up a feast. It is time to eat."

Dinner was devoured in no time, followed by Sandy's friends popping by with dessert. It had now become a celebration of sweet fellowship, as one story after another was being relayed, stitched together by laughter and whispers of praise for how good this season had been. When the conversation had come to a lull, Peace got his fiddle out and played old and even ancient tunes of the Kingdom. The music further soothed and settled Sandy's happy soul, saturating it with the Peace that played it.

As the fire flickered and the mellow music played on, the only weight Sandy felt was in her eyelids. Rest was beckoning her to come. She rose and hugged each one in the room and excused herself to bed. "Please continue to play, Peace. You can send me off to sleep, which won't be hard."

"I will indeed," he replied as he paused. "And I'll see you in the morning. I've been invited to stay, and remain I will. Especially with the promise of pancakes in the morning."

Sandy smiled and nodded, then exited to her room where she collapsed on her bed in peace. Sounds of the Kingdom washed in waves over her as Sandy drifted off in a dream…

*****

The songs of Peace repeated and were joined by other harmonious sounds. Sandy was not asleep anymore, but found herself alive in a way she had never been. Her very cells felt revived and made new. She felt no weakness in her body; only joy unspeakable expanded within every cell.

Sandy had entered the world where she had first awakened to the true dream of her heart. She remembered. The peace, the light, the vibrancy of color was there, but even brighter yet. Sandy was different now. Her soul was more familiar with this world, though it was no less spectacular. It was the greatest possible privilege she could conceive of to walk here.

Amidst the beauty of all that surrounded her in this this

heavenly haven of peace, Sandy sought no other sight but that of her Prince. His face was all she longed to see. She turned her head in search of him. The next moment, he was there. Again, as in their first meeting, Sandy felt faint in the wave of love that encompassed her.

The Prince reached for her and embraced her with a laugh. "My Princess! You are here!"

He released her to look in her face and combed her hair with his hand, smiling all the while. She saw such pleasure in his look at her. She could do nothing but stare back. His face shone like Jasper's, Sandy recognized as she studied it. The transparency of light he emitted was unmatched. His whole being glowed. In his light, she was enveloped. In his light, she felt exposed, yet every dark shadow was burned away. She had never felt so clean. One moment in his presence had completed a work within her. She felt transformed, and she was.

"My dear," the Prince started as he took both of her hands, "I have something to show you. You must now see who you are."

Sandy said not a word, for what could she say? She simply followed again, as her Prince led the way. He took her to view a great city. It would be indescribable to any in her world below. There were no words to explain its brilliance, its majesty, and its light. Nothing on earth could compare with its splendor. Sandy just gazed with her mouth slightly open and her eyes wide, drinking in all she could of this glorious city before her.

"I am building this...for you," the Prince revealed as he held her hand, looking over his work.

For a moment Sandy could not speak. Then she mustered up sound and replied, "For...for me?"

The Prince turned and looked on her with great love in his every response, "Yes. For you...and for all who will choose to come and return to our father, the King of this great city."

"Who wouldn't want to come?" Sandy thought, though she still strained to speak any thoughts aloud. She wondered how she

could have ever been in awe of Excess in light of this place. "One would be a fool not to come here, if they only knew about it," she further surmised.

The Prince knew her thoughts and replied, "You are right in your thinking. If they only knew, they would come. Princess, it is time for you to see yourself in the role I see you in. It is time to see what you have 'become.'"

Sandy answered him only in a nod and by squeezing his hand. He then led her even closer, and brought her before a gate.

The gate was unlike any on earth she had known. It was perfectly round, made of a single pearl. Sandy stood before it with her Prince at her back. She could see their reflection in its opalescence. She was in awe.

"My Princess, it is you! You are Sandy no longer. You are now my Pearl." Her Prince let the reality of his revelation settle for a moment before he explained further. "Your mother on earth named you for what she knew—the most glorious ground she had walked on. But your father is giving you a new name, for this is how he sees you. This is what your journey has transformed you into...a pearl. As you have hidden yourself in that secret place with him, he has changed you, my love! He has made you into an exquisite jewel of the sea. Sure, there is still a bit of that sand, that earth, within you, but I have always seen you for the jewel you were becoming, and for that jewel, I would—and have—paid any price. You are my treasure. You are my Pearl!"

"Oh, my Prince..." Princess Pearl faintly replied, overcome by a swell of emotions. She turned and embraced her love. "You have changed everything! You have transformed my thinking, my ways, and now my very name! I'm overwhelmed by the beauty of it all, by the mystery of it. I feel so complete...and...rich!" This is the best word she could find as she gazed on this city, made of everything precious and valuable.

"And you are! All this is to be yours one day...and besides all of that, you have me!" The Prince smiled the sweetest smile yet

on his beloved Princess Pearl.

"You…you are my very great reward!" Pearl whispered back to her beloved. After staring into his eyes for a very long time, she asked the question that people of earth so often ask. "So what is next?"

The Prince laughed, knowing her well. She needed to know her mission, and it was time to give it. "Next, you take all of this to your world below. You help build my Kingdom there, and make your life a gate to it like the one you stand before now, so that many might enter into this one someday. Someday soon I will come back there myself, and I will change everything. But for now, my Princess, I call you to make my ways known, so it can be in that world as it is up here. It is my will that all know our father, for his name to be honored, and for his dream to come true. I want as many of his kids as possible to lift their eyes to him and want to come home. And I am asking you, my Pearl, to be a gate, opening the way for them to come."

The princess knew she had to return. This was only a glimpse of what was to come for her, and what was intended for many. The Prince was asking her to make this place known in her world. The assignment would be a challenge, waking the sleeping below, but she knew she had been entrusted with so much in her journey. Much would now be expected.

"But don't fear, my dear Princess. I remain with you…and as always, I leave you our Jasper!"

"Yes…Jasper!" Pearl smiled, filled with courage at the thought of him. "Anything is possible with him."

"Indeed," the Prince added, "for he, the father and I are one in the same, a mystery you cannot fathom, yet should find great comfort in. We are all One, and all for you! Without us, you can do nothing. With us, you can overcome the world!"

Pearl's heart was stretched to fill up even more. She threw her arms around her Prince and her head into his chest, unable to express her own heart to him. After a long embrace and drink of great love by her soul, the Prince relaxed his firm hold on her to look down into her face. "It's time, my love, my treasured possession, my Pearl. It's time to return and make all of this known. It's time to go…" The princess stared back into those eyes of love, and then, woke up back below.

✳✳✳✳✳

Golden light streamed through the windows of the little stone house in which the Princess stayed. The morning light reminded her of the glory she just traveled from in her sleep. The thick residue of peace remained from the night before, and she inhaled it deeply in her first morning breath. Then she remembered, "I am Sandy no more!"

The Princess rose and got dressed, then opened the door to her room and entered into the open room where all her friends were already seated at the table for breakfast.

"Princess!" Joy cried out, startling her with her cheery presence.

"Joy! You are here! Surprising me once again in the morning," she said.

"I always do, love! I always do!" All laughed along with Joy as she slid over to make room for the princess at the table between herself and little Faithie. Humility and Gentleness were busy about the kitchen making final preparations, and Peace held little Hope in his lap. Faithful, Quietness, and Confidence had come for breakfast too, making it a true feast of fellowship indeed.

The Princess looked around at each treasured face, at each friend she had made on this journey. They had each aided her so much. Each one had played a part in her transforming process. She couldn't wait to tell them about her dream.

When all were seated and thanks had been returned to their King, the Princess spoke up. "I have something to tell you all. Last night…I had a dream." No one spoke. All quietly waited for her to continue. "I saw him. I saw the Prince, and he showed me who

I am. He changed my name." Smiles broke out across every face and tears filled each friend's eyes. Still, they allowed her to go on. "I am no longer Sandy, my friends. He has formed me into his Pearl."

A soft clamor of sighs, cries, and cheers of rejoicing exuded from Pearl's family of friends. Joy threw her hands over her face and cried out, "I knew it! I knew it! I knew all the time you were becoming a gem—*a pearl!* Wait till Ruby finds out! This is just awesome." Joy could not contain her excitement and got up to dance around. Faithie and Hope giggled loudly.

Confidence congratulated her next. "I saw his greatness changing you the whole journey too. I'm so proud to be your friend, Princess Pearl!" They embraced, and Quietness and Faithful joined the huddle, whispering their blessings and praise of his ways as well.

When all settled down and they were seated again, Humility spoke from the head of the table. "Since we are in the mode of celebration, this is the perfect time to share some news. Today I received by post an invitation for us all to come!"

All looked around, excited but puzzled. "Come where, my love?" Gentleness asked on behalf of them all.

"To the Shores, of course! Jasper has invited us all back to the Shores for a gathering of some kind." Humility withdrew the postcard from his shirt pocket and read, 'You are invited, my friends! Pack lightly and come!'" Humility looked up. "And I get the sense he means right now."

Without waiting another moment, the crowd of friends rose and began their happy preparations. Joyous anticipation filled their hearts and thoughts. The Princess knew her season of waiting was over. It had been a beautiful season of learning and growing indeed. But now it was time to return to the Shores and to Jasper, to rejoice over her journey and receive further commissioning. All had come to pass, and now it was time to GO…

25

Deeper Still

*T*he company of friends left the Village of Simplicity as a happy caravan, all excited for their pilgrimage to the Shores. Each knew me in their own special way, uniquely reflecting as much of the King's character as I had helped them develop. They all had journeyed for different lengths of time since their first "yes" to their initial invitations to come. No two travelers were ever the same, nor were their journeys. There were varied obstacles in each one's path to individually overcome with me. But somehow, through all the differences, these devoted ones made up a body of followers that functioned as a beautiful unit, serving their King. They had remained true and loyal, and he loved each one, individually and as a whole. I loved them all too, and was elated whenever we convened all together in one place and time. That was the purpose of this day.

Not only did the villagers from Simplicity come, I summoned others as well. Ruby left the Lodge, bringing along an eager company of kids. Long-Suffering came down from the mountain, needing this retreat with dear friends. Teacher made the trip, bringing her map and cisterns of fresh water to share. And Carry also came with her enthusiastic pack of friends from the River, having much good news to report from their region. Passion, Wisdom, and of course Peace and Joy would never miss an event such as this. And the locals, Kindness and Contentment, helped me host. It was to be a reunion indeed, especially for one girl, who had just been transformed. We all could not wait to see our Princess Pearl.

The old van pulled up along the sandy side of the road beside the beach access. Confidence, Faithful, Faithie, and Hope all piled out first from the side. My Princess stepped out slowly, not wanting to rush or miss a moment of this special return to her Great Sea and to me. She turned to look at the Cottage Café behind her. "Just as I left it," she reflected quietly. Then she faced the beach access, pausing for all of the others to descend onto the shore before her.

Quietness remained with her and squeezed her friend from the side with one arm. "You need a moment, don't you?" The Princess nodded. "I understand. Take your time. We'll be waiting for you on the shore."

Pearl stood alone in her transformed state, breathing deeply of this air that first woke her up. She was giddy with peace, if that was possible. Her life felt surreal, yet she knew it was not. The purpose for existence was clearer than ever. She was different indeed, and far stronger than the last time she stepped in this place. "How sweet to return at such a time," she thought to herself. "His ways are always right. His timing never fails to amaze me. What surprises do you have for me in the sand today, Jasper?" My Princess knew me well.

I answered with the sound of the sea. Its crashes broke through her contemplations. My Pearl came to and smiled. Then she nodded, "Ok. I hear you. Here I come."

The Princess climbed the steps of the access and crossed the familiar planks to the steps leading down to the beach. She paused, taking in the sight of her friends. She gasped, not knowing I had invited them all here. Hope spotted her first and tugged on her sister's shirt.

"Look, everybody! It's Princess Pearl!" Faithie shouted. They all turned to see and, in an instant, erupted in claps and whistles, cheering her to come down.

My Princess was beyond moved. She descended the stairs and

was embraced the moment her feet hit the sand. It was an explosion of love as each friend from her journey gushed over her with sincere affection. How blessed Pearl felt to belong to them all. How grateful she was for each relationship made along that narrow path she followed.

The cluster around Pearl relaxed, allowing her to clearly look around. After surveying each precious face, she furrowed her brow in curiosity and asked, "Where's Jasper?"

Passion was the first to speak up as he turned his body and referred to the sea, "Why, he's out there, Princess—waiting for you!"

She stepped up and squinted, shielding her eyes from the sun with her hand. Out beyond the first break of waves, she saw a small fishing boat. In it, I sat. And I waved.

Pearl laughed, along with our company of friends. "Well, what should I do?" Her eyes searched the crowd, wanting some wisdom. He spoke up.

"I'd say he's motioning for you to come. Looks like he is calling you out into the deep. I'd go, if I were you!"

The others cheered her on as well. Pearl looked to Ruby, her mentor, for the final word. "It's the Great Sea of his love. If you are going to be lost at sea anywhere, that's the right place to be!" Joy chimed in too, "Run, girl! Why are you standing there? He's waiting!"

My princess hesitated no longer. She kicked off her shoes, handed her pouch off to Faithful, and ran for the surf, applauded and cheered by all on the sand. She did not look back but dove right in and swam through the waves, lifting her head only to keep her eyes on the boat.

My Pearl was determined, and made her way right to me without any fear at all. It had all washed away, just as I said it would, in this great ocean of the King's deep love. Pearl lifted her arm to grab hold of the boat. She met my arm instead. I pulled her straight up and lifted her in, setting her before me. She breathed in deeply then looked up and smiled. "I came, Jasper! This time I *really* heeded your call!"

We both laughed, and I took both of her hands in mine. "Indeed you did. And wasn't it fun? It's fun out here in the deep."

"Yes," she said. "It was. More refreshing than I thought it could be...even invigorating, that swim." My princess was still catching her breath, and I took these moments to just stare and enjoy her beauty. How strong and lovely she was. As "Sandy" she so easily crumbled and gave way. As "Pearl" she was resilient and solid. What a lovely work had been done.

"You know," I said, "The Prince would have just walked on that water. He did that one time, you know." I playfully lifted my eyebrow as I smiled.

She laughed. "I don't think I'm quite there yet, but if he should ever call me to do so, I would not refuse him," the Princess returned in confident reply.

"I think you will walk in even more miraculous ways than that. You were made to do wonders!" I now spoke with no hint of humor. My Pearl knew I was not kidding.

Pearl stared into my eyes and we remained silent for a moment. Then my princess looked at the sea. "So this is what it is like out in the deep," she observed.

"No," I answered. "This is only the surface of the deep."

Pearl looked back and tilted her head in wonder, wanting me to explain. "My Princess, I brought you out here to give you more vision. I am always about expanding your view. Just as you stood on that mountain and gained a perspective you could have from no other place, the same can happen out here. I did not bring you out here to float at the surface, but to give you a thirst for the deep."

"The deep?" was all my Pearl could think to ask.

"Yes, the deep. You were not created for surface living. You were made for the heights and the depths. You are meant to *fly*—to *soar*—in the high places, and dive when you are led to the deep. Because of your 'yes's' you have been transformed, and are able to go places others cannot. You will in turn experience perspective and deep beauty that the majority never will. My Pearl, are you ready to see?" I looked on her face, and met only a wide-eyed eager expression, like that of a child.

"Why not? If *you* are going with me, Jasper, let's go!" And without a pause she was up, and inhaled a full portion of the Great Sea's air. I quickly grabbed her hand, and we jumped off the side of the boat.

With love's breath in her lungs, and her hand in mine, my Pearl could go to any depth. I led her to a coral reef where we spied schools of exotic fish. A regal angelfish attracted her focus with its alternating bands of bold, striking colors, and she followed it with her gaze till it darted and disappeared into the cloudy current. We spotted colorful clownfish nestled among an array of sea anemones beneath us. Red sea urchins were in the distance beyond the reef, blanketing a kelp forest where other sea life would feast. My Princess was enchanted by the new world of the deep opened up to her, and was visually arrested by all this mysterious brilliance beneath. Before we came up for air, I pointed to an oyster, and Pearl nodded with a smile, knowing what was being formed in that secret place.

We emerged, and she gasped, then exhaled in a mighty laugh as she threw her whole body back to float on the water. "Jasper, I cannot believe what I saw! Never could I imagine such beauty below—and to think that world exists with so few seeing it."

"I know. But what pleasure is mine when I find those who will come. It is my joy to lead each one in the deep."

After exploring some more, I helped my Princess back into the boat. We talked for quite some time about her journey here and what the Prince had meant at the end of her dream. "Yes, Princess, it is time to go. You now have so much to share, and there is such great need."

Pearl paused and looked at me with a questioning face. I

explained a deeper meaning in what lay beneath us. "Not only is there beauty in the deep, there is an abundance of life represented in all of those fish. You know, the Prince paralleled 'going' to 'fishing' when he walked in this world. He called his friends, who were fishermen-turned-followers, to go after *people* for the Kingdom as they had caught fish. They understood this language. They followed him, and allowed him to change them. In time, he used *them* to change the world."

Pearl desired to be one used to change the world, but dropped her head for just a moment, recalling her failure at her last attempt in the Wastelands. I knew her thoughts and responded to them. "My princess, you are ready now. Your stay in Simplicity and lessons taught by Humility have prepared you for this call. You have been tempered by your study of the map and by the teaching you've allowed trusted others and me to provide. So now, as an ambassador of the Prince, the King desires to make his appeal through you to beckon others back to him. Just as Page once did for you on his behalf, it is your turn to call others out of the Wastelands and into the Kingdom of Love."

"And my mother? Jasper, what about my mother? You called her once and she never responded. Is it possible that I could reach her?"

I stared intensely at my Pearl who wanted so desperately to share her new life with the one who gave her life. I answered her in truth, "There is always free will involved, but I can tell you this: Just as your mother once sang a song over you to put you to sleep, I will give you a song to sing over her life that could wake her up forever."

That was all the encouragement my Princess Pearl needed. Her eyes were wide and determined again and in all confidence she replied, "Ok. Let's go!"

We rowed back to the shore to rejoice with the others in this day. There was much celebrating to do. Passion had started a fire, and all of our friends were gathered in small groups around it, telling stories and encouraging tales of their adventures. When the Princess and I arrived on the shore, each group eventually caught sight of us and clapped to welcome us back. We then converged into a circle around the fire, and praise broke out to our King. Peace had his fiddle and Passion played guitar while Brave and Fearless beat on some makeshift drums from the kitchen of Kindness and Contentment. The rest of us clapped and sang Kingdom songs we all knew from the parts of the journey we shared. Then one by one our friends shared from their maps, highlights from their journeys so far. Teacher began:

"For the word of the King is right and
true; he is faithful in all he does."

Faithful took her cue:

"Let us hold unswervingly to hope, for
he who promised is faithful!"

Long-Suffering continued:

"Therefore we will not lose heart. Though outwardly
we are wasting away, inwardly we are being renewed every
day. For our light and momentary troubles are achieving
for us an eternal glory that far outweighs them all."

Joy jumped in:

"Rejoice in the King always! I will say it again; rejoice!"

Gentleness followed with:

"Let your gentleness be evident to all. The Prince is near."

Carry kept going from this same spot on the map:

> *"Do not be anxious about anything, but*
> *in everything ask and make petition, and with*
> *thanksgiving, present your requests to the King…"*

Peace completed the reading from this section of the map book:

> *"And the peace of the King, which surpasses all*
> *understanding, will guard your hearts and your minds."*

Then Wisdom led them to his call and read aloud:

> *"I love those who love me, and those who seek me*
> *will find me. With me are riches and honor, enduring*
> *wealth and prosperity. I walk in right ways, along the*
> *paths of justice, granting true wealth to those who*
> *love me, making their treasuries full."*

And loving Ruby could wait no longer to bless us by reading from her favorite spot:

> *"I ask that out of the King's glorious riches he may*
> *strengthen you with power through his spirit in your inner*
> *being so that the Prince may dwell in your hearts through faith.*
> *And I ask that you, being rooted and established in love, may*
> *have power together with all the citizens, to grasp how wide*
> *and long and high and deep is the love of the Prince, and to*
> *know this love that surpasses knowledge – that you may be*
> *filled to the measure of all the fullness of the King!"*

Then I stepped up to quote from the map as I looked to all, but focused in on the eyes of my Pearl:

*"See, the former things have taken place and new
things I declare; before they spring into being I announce
them to you...I will lead the blind by ways they have not
known, along unfamiliar paths I will guide them; I will turn
the darkness into light before them and make the rough
places smooth. These are things I will do..."*

I paused, watching the anticipation rise within her eyes, and then proceeded with my word and promise:

*"Forget the former things; do not dwell on the
past. I am about to do something new. Now it springs
up; do you not see it? I am making a way in the
wilderness and rivers in the Wastelands."*

The Princess simply nodded. She knew what I meant and received this promise into her heart, putting past failures behind her.

Then Faithie jumped out front, dragging little Hope with her. She could not contain herself as she shouted,

*"How great is the love the father has
lavished on us, that we should be called the
children of the King! And that is what we are!"*

Brave and Fearless banged on their pot-drums and all the kids repeated in a shout,

"..and that is what we are!"

As if they were cued, all the adults in the circle joined in as well, declaring,

"...AND THAT IS WHAT WE ARE!"

270

Great laughter and a roar of praise swelled from the crowd, then the music started up again. The rejoicing of this group could not be restrained.

Eventually, the songs subsided, and we broke to partake of bread and drink together, remembering all our Great Prince had done to bring us here. After that, the friends talked and encouraged one another in little clusters on the beach. Each heart was being refilled for the next leg of their journeys ahead.

Contentment settled down into the sand with the kids to build sandcastles with them, helping them to "practice" their "Kingdom building." He looked up to see Pearl and me watching. "You'll have to take these young ones out deeper, Princess! I think they are ready to go!"

The kids cheered and hollered, and Pearl laughed while nodding that she would.

As the sun began to set, I led my girl a short distance away from the rest. I wanted one last minute alone with her. I looked on my Pearl, who looked over our sea. She was as lovely as she ever had been. I then leaned in to whisper into her ear, "Are you glad you came, Princess? Are you glad you 'woke up' to come?"

The Princess Pearl moved her head slightly, overwhelmed by thought of it all. Then she looked up to me with those tear-lined eyes I had always so greatly adored. She had come to know me so well on this journey, since that first day on the Shores. But in that moment, all she could utter was the question, "Who are you?"

"I am Jasper. And we will never give up on this pursuit with you."

We both turned our gaze back to the sea, and Pearl squeezed my hand tight. Our *new* dream had now just begun.

IF YOU WANT TO KNOW MORE ABOUT
"JASPER AND HOW YOU CAN JOURNEY WITH HIM,
PLEASE VISIT OUR WEBSITE AT JaspertheStory.com.
LINKS TO FAMILY STUDY QUESTIONS AND TIPS ON HOW
TO START A JASPER BOOK CLUB ARE AVAILABLE THERE.

TO CONTACT THE AUTHOR FOR LIVE READINGS
AND SPEAKING ENGAGEMENTS, OR TO SHARE YOUR
PERSONAL EXPERIENCE WITH "JASPER," PLEASE EMAIL:
dar@dardraper.com.

WE WOULD LOVE TO HEAR HOW THIS
STORY HAS AFFECTED YOU!